**DISCOVER THE REAL NEWMANS—
A STORY OF LOVE, TALENT,
AND DRIVING AMBITION**

**THE DREAMS**
Paul's uncanny ability to move from one blockbuster and starring role to another . . . and Joanne's sacrifices to let him do it.

**THE HIDDEN FAMILY**
Paul's three children by his first wife . . . hurt, rebellious, and ultimately a tragic end for a troubled son.

**THE OSCARS**
Joanne's tearful triumph in *The Three Faces of Eve* and her screaming backstage tantrum when Paul lost for *The Hustler*.

**THE DEFEATS**
Their embarrassing flops when starring together . . . and Joanne's painful disappointment in not getting the Shirley MacLaine role in *The Turning Point*.

**THE DARING**
Paul's addiction to the thrill of car racing despite Joanne's fears . . . and the breakthrough film no one wanted him to direct or her to play—*Rachel, Rachel.*

AND MUCH MORE ABOUT
THEIR NOT-SO-PERFECT MARRIAGE
AND THEIR REMARKABLE COURAGE
ON SCREEN AND OFF!

OTHER BOOKS BY
JOE MORELLA AND EDWARD Z. EPSTEIN:

LORETTA YOUNG: *An Extraordinary Life*
JANE WYMAN: *A Biography*
RITA: *The Life of Rita Hayworth*
THE "IT" GIRL: *The Incredible Story of Clara Bow*
LANA: *The Public and Private Lives of Miss Turner*
BRANDO: *The Unauthorized Biography*
LUCY: *The Bittersweet Life of Lucille Ball*
REBELS: *The Rebel Hero in Films*
GABLE & LOMBARD & POWELL & HARLOW
THOSE GREAT MOVIE ADS
THE FILMS OF WORLD WAR II
THE AMAZING CAREERS OF BOB HOPE
JUDY: *The Films and Career of Judy Garland*
THE INCE AFFAIR (A Novel)

# PAUL
# and
# JOANNE

## A Biography of
## PAUL NEWMAN and JOANNE WOODWARD

JOE MORELLA and EDWARD Z. EPSTEIN

A DELL BOOK

Published by
Dell Publishing
a division of
Bantam Doubleday Dell
Publishing Group, Inc.
666 Fifth Avenue
New York, New York 10103

Unless otherwise indicated, all photos courtesy *Phototeque*.

ISBN: 0-440-20465-8

Reprinted by arrangement with Delacorte Press

Printed in the United States of America

Published simultaneously in Canada

November 1989

10  9  8  7  6  5  4  3  2  1

KRI

To my father, Leonard J. Epstein, whose support and inspiration, generosity of spirit, and devotion to his family and friends will always be lovingly remembered

—E. Z. E.

Thanks to the actors, writers, producers, directors, photographers, publicists, executives, stagehands, and non-industry people who contributed valuable reminiscences for this book. In certain instances names have been withheld at their request. A special thank-you to Chris Kachulis in New York and the people in California and Connecticut who were most helpful in obtaining research material.

# FOREWORD

There is no question that one pays a terrible price for celebrity. Privacy becomes something that exists only in the abstract; even family cannot be trusted to keep secrets. Who are your "friends," and what do they want from you? Attempts at maintaining dignity become acts of hostility. Your life, your every act, and everyone who ever touched you, all are fair game for the gossips, the reporters, and, yes, for the biographers.

Although Paul Newman and Joanne Woodward have fostered the perception of a lifelong pursuit for "privacy," in truth they have done as much as—if not more than—other celebrities to earn publicity. In fairness, much of this has been publicity for "causes," but if one expects to use celebrity to achieve an end, then one must accept the fact that any exposure invites comment and, sometimes, criticism. Through the years, the Newmans have used the media when it suited them, as when they had a movie, a project, or a cause to publicize. Always, however, there have been sentinels guarding the flow of information—the Newmans employ (and have for many years) the very powerful public relations firm of Rogers and Cowan to orchestrate the proceedings, handling not only their professional publicity, but managing the news of their personal lives as well. Rogers and Cowan have done a masterful job. Their most difficult task was "managing" the news concerning the tragic death of Paul's son Scott, revealed to have been an alcoholic and drug addict. Neither Newman nor Woodward will speak much about Scott's death; it is far too painful a subject and whatever guilt there may be is a private matter. However, they have publicly endowed the Scott Newman Foundation and the Scott Newman Center to fight drug abuse. In all publicity about the organizations there has never been any mention of Scott's mother, Jacqueline, and no statement from her. When we began this biography, we made many attempts to locate and interview Jacqueline Witte Newman (the mother of three of Paul's six children). Research indicated that she was still receiving financial support from Newman. We had corresponded with a Jacqueline McDonald, a current administrator of the Scott Newman Center. In a letter to us, Ms. McDonald had referred to Scott as "Paul Newman's son," therefore it did not occur to us—at first—that she might actually be Scott's mother.

Warren Cowan, of Rogers and Cowan, denies that the first Mrs. Newman's involvement with the center is deliberately kept secret, but it appears that it is. Cowan's official response is, "I think she just recently came on board," but she has been involved with the foundation for years. The sentinels are ever vigilant.

There is undoubtedly much information in this book that Paul Newman and Joanne Woodward would rather not share with casual readers, but it is only fair that information they wish to suppress or downplay receive the same consideration as information they wish to broadcast. They are not merely actors working at their craft. They are, after all, stars who have sought celebrity and use it to their advantage.

It is an accepted fact that it takes a tremendous ego, an incredible amount of self-confidence, for public figures to reach the highest level of recognition. When they do so, they are not asking merely for respect for their talents, they are asking for love.

Paul Newman and Joanne Woodward, as individuals and as a

couple, are admired and even loved by many, many people. The public adores them, although they feel they know *him* better than *her*. Many of the people who have worked with them also speak of them with admiration, if not always with affection. On one thing they all agree—Newman and Woodward have "class." They are two highly intelligent people with not only the aptitude but the ability to be successful at whatever they choose, unlike most other celebrities who are equipped only for stardom.

Newman and Woodward. Paul and Joanne. The auto racer and the ballet dancer. The superstar and the character actress. Contradictory, complex personalities: He is serious, bawdy, whimsical, closed in, quiet, controlled, irritating; she is mercurial, quixotic, steadfast, startlingly blunt, the ultimate lady whom her husband has described as a functioning voluptuary.

He claims to abhor the excessive attention and publicity inherent in superstardom, particularly the decades-long emphasis on his blue eyes. Yet, before appearing in public, Newman uses eyedrops to be sure those eyes are at their bluest.

For years she has been adamant in declaring that she is *not* a star—but she *is*, and has been a star for thirty years, ever since she won an Oscar practically her first time out.

Theirs isn't a perfect marriage and it never has been. When Joanne tried to combine career and motherhood, she, like millions of other women, found that it was an incredibly difficult task. There has also been the inevitable tension between stepmother and the stepchildren from Paul's first marriage. Over the years Paul has had, in his own words, "body-bending confrontations" with Joanne. Both are strong-willed and opinionated, and on occasion one or the other reportedly has packed up and moved out. But only for a while.

There have been rumored infidelities, plus lots of insinuation from wishful thinkers. For years Paul Newman's acknowledged alcoholic tendencies were a problem in the marriage. Woodward's tendency to become too involved in her work, and especially in the character she is portraying at a given moment, has frequently put strain on everyone around her. Yes, there have been problems, but the marriage has endured, and obviously so has the love and respect that brought them together in the first place. They are best friends.

This is a true story of two people who wanted to have it all and who have come amazingly close to realizing their goals despite the tragedies, despite the struggles, and, most of all, despite the fame.

# BOOK I

☆ **1** ☆

☆

Where do movie idols and sex symbols come from? Paul Newman was born in Cleveland Heights, a posh suburb of Cleveland, Ohio, on January 26, 1925, the second son of Arthur S.
and Teresa Fetsko Newman. Shortly after Paul's birth the family moved to an eleven-room house in Shaker Heights, where
the Newmans lived alongside other financially comfortable
families.

Paul's parents came from diverse backgrounds. Arthur Newman was born in Cleveland of German Jewish parents. One of
his brothers, Joe, had founded Newman-Stern, a sporting
goods store, in 1915. Arthur joined the venture and helped to
make it one of the most prosperous and well-respected busi-
nesses in Cleveland.

Teresa Fetsko had been born in Hungary but emigrated with
her family to Ohio when she was four. She was raised as a
Catholic. Paul and Arthur junior, however, were brought up
neither as Catholics nor Jews, but as Christian Scientists, since
when the boys were five and six, their mother converted to
Christian Science. However, the precepts of the Christian Science religion were not strictly adhered to. For example, the
boys continued with their regular medical checkups and saw a

doctor whenever medical attention was called for. Arthur junior, and Paul were given information on the Jewish, Catholic, *and* Christian Science beliefs—enough so that in later years Paul Newman would caution people not to parry with him on the subject of religion; he had been through plenty.

Arthur Newman, Sr.'s, business weathered the Depression with relative ease. Discussing those years, Paul once said: "I never came home and found there was no food on the table, but we felt the pinch. Sporting goods are a luxury, and the business always suffers in a depression."

The boys were raised much like other progeny of the Midwest's upper middle class. Newman once described his mother as someone who had grown up in a very poor family and as a result had rather materialistic values. He remembered her also as a marvelous cook, who gave him his love of food. Paul read a great deal and took music lessons. He also spent lots of time outdoors, on fishing trips and in various sporting activities.

Paul was not close to his father, however, and once remarked, "I didn't have any idea of what being close to an older person was." Arthur Newman, Sr., in fact, worked six days a week and insisted that his boys also learn the value of work. Paul had a paper route, and when the boys were older, both worked at the store.

Asked to characterize his relationship with his brother, Arthur junior, Paul has used the word "belligerent."

Teresa Newman gave the young Paul his first exposure to the theater. According to some observers, she was a volatile woman who had wanted to be an actress. Whatever her motivation, she was a frequent theatergoer and often described the plays she saw to her young sons. It was at her urging that Paul joined a children's division of the Cleveland Playhouse.

These excursions into the theatrical world certainly must have been a change from the strictness and discipline of the Newman household where Arthur senior felt it his duty to teach his sons morals, ethics, and the value of hard work. His philosophy was that anything of worth was attained only through hardship.

While at Shaker Heights High School Paul worked in school plays both as an actor and as a stage manager. The boy yearned to be a football player but did not, even in his early teens, excel at athletics. He was too short and too light for football. "I've had to work hard to achieve everything," he noted decades later. "I was a short, scrawny, ninety-nine-pound kid in high school who couldn't qualify to try out for the junior varsity football team. You had to weigh one hundred pounds. I really wanted to be a baseball player most of all, but I wasn't big enough for that, either."

However, Newman also recalls these high school days as being among the best years of his life: "In high school I was a very active kid. I was wandering at that age, but I had a good time as a teen—it wasn't a very difficult period for me."

Although he was still developing, both in physical appearance and as an actor, people who were in school with Paul recall that he made an impact both on the stage and in the hallways of Shaker Heights High. He reportedly had the normal adolescent's interest in girls, but he was not wild—his parents' strict standards on that score had been firmly ingrained. The girls at school were, nonetheless, more than casually aware of him. Even then, according to women who knew him at the time, Paul possessed the intensity that was to one day surface in his screen characterizations.

There is no doubt he was mischievous and fun-loving in school, but he was also articulate and well-spoken. Everyone undoubtedly assumed that Paul would go into the family business, although some contend that he was already interested in acting as a career. Whatever the case, there was certainly some ambivalence on the young man's part about a future career.

The Newman family knew no financial hardships, yet money was never taken for granted. When the boys worked at their father's store, no favoritism was shown, and in fact, they generally had to start work earlier and stay later than other employees, plus they were paid less. Arthur senior wanted his boys to continue their education, with an eye to joining the family business.

After high school, Paul entered Ohio University but stayed

only a year. While there he was cast in the part of a boxer in a
production of *The Milky Way*. This and other early forays into
acting tend to discount his later claims that at this stage in his
life he had expressed no interest in acting.

When Paul joined the navy in June 1943, America had been
at war for over a year. After the Japanese attack on Pearl Harbor, young men like Paul needed little encouragement to enlist,
and the various branches of the service had set up crash pro-
grams at colleges and universities to train pilots and officers,
who were desperately needed in the war effort.

Paul joined one of these programs, the V-12 program of the
Navy Air Corps, and was sent to Yale University for training.
One of the first tests he took revealed that he was color-blind.
Failing this test dashed his aspirations to be a pilot. As he said,
the navy "didn't know what to do with me." Then he was sent
to boot camp, where he was "a pretty good radio man, but a
terrible gunner." (Robert Stack was his instructor.)

Newman saw very limited action during the war but did
serve two years in the Pacific. According to him, most of that
time was spent drinking and reading. He went through as
many as a dozen books a week.

Paul Newman has often referred to "Newman's luck," his
belief that he has been blessed by the gods, and his navy stint
provides perhaps the earliest example of this principle at work:
"I've always been lucky; incredibly lucky. The old 'Newman
luck.' Somehow, it's allowed me to get close to a lot of edges
without falling off. I think I survived World War Two because
of Newman's luck. It's an extraordinary phenomenon. During
the war, I was a back-seat man on a Navy torpedo plane. The
pilot I flew with had an ear problem one day and we were
grounded. The rest of our squad transferred to an aircraft car-
rier. They were seventy-five miles off the coast of Japan that
day when the ship took a direct kamikaze hit and they all died."

Newman, in retrospect, has described himself during this
period as having no idea of what was going on, as being simply
an irresponsible kid. "I came out of the Navy [in 1946]," he has
said, "just as dumb as I went in." Newman at twenty was a
self-described "bourgeois, provincial, emotional Republican."

Newly released from the service, Newman had changed physically. He had put on weight and had grown six inches. He chose not to return to Ohio University, and now entered Kenyon College, an all-male school located about ninety miles from Cleveland.

At Ohio University Newman had been too interested in girls to concentrate on his studies. Both he and his family felt that at Kenyon he would have fewer distractions.

Discussing his college years, which were well in advance of the sexual revolution, Newman has admitted that there wasn't much opportunity to get into trouble. Dating couples went on hayrides, went for walks, or went to the movies. He concedes that everyone was thinking about "it," but nice girls didn't do it, and nice guys didn't try to force them to.

With his new height and increased weight, Newman now qualified for the football team—albeit the second string.

He chose economics as his major that first year, obviously a move calculated to please his family. He subsequently changed to an English major, then later to a drama major. His plan was to pursue a career in teaching, specifically the teaching of drama in college.

Many years later Newman offered a candid appraisal of this period in his academic life: "I started by majoring in economics and business administration. After I flunked all those courses, I switched to an English major. Then I found myself completely disenchanted by lyric poets of the 17th Century."

At Kenyon, when Newman and a group of football buddies caroused a bit too loudly and roughly at a local bar, the guys had to spend a night in jail. Two of the boys in the group were expelled from college, and four, including Paul, were put on probation and kicked off the football team. The incident made the front page of the *Cleveland Plain Dealer*.

The Newman family was not amused, and in later years Paul would say of his years at Kenyon, "It wasn't their fault I hated what I was doing there." He has acknowledged that he was influenced much more by his peers than by his parents. He was involved in many brawls at college and has admitted to being arrested three times for minor offenses.

With football off the agenda, Paul focused all his energies on drama. Over the next couple of years he appeared in a dozen plays, including campus productions of *The Front Page*, *R.U.R.*, and *Charlie's Aunt*. One of his professors at Kenyon has noted that he had trouble *not* casting Paul as the lead in every production.

Newman also wrote, produced, directed, and starred in a musical while at Kenyon—not an insignificant creative contribution at an all-male college in the 1940s. One of Paul's drama teachers at Kenyon was J. G. Mitchell. He thought the young Newman was a good technician, and told the youngster that if he disciplined himself, he would have a career on the stage.

Newman has recalled that in his own opinion he definitely wasn't anything special as an actor in these early tries—his actor's intuition, or lack of it, left a lot to be desired. There was a lot he would have to learn, a lot he would have to overcome; his upbringing hadn't equipped him to exhibit his emotions in public, to reveal his inner self onstage. He was admittedly "terrorized by the emotional requirement of being an actor," for "acting is like letting your pants down. You're exposed."

Paul's business acumen was evident during his college days. He launched a modest laundry facility, offering free beer as a lure for customers. He sold the laundry at a profit, but Arthur Newman, Sr., reportedly was not impressed since the hijinks surrounding the venture smacked of irresponsibility to the elder Newman (a subsequent beer bust put the laundry out of business).

Paul remained undaunted in his ambition to become an actor. In the summer of 1948, Paul worked at the Priscilla Beach Theater in New England. According to one source, he was there with the full cooperation of his parents. Terry Lewis (then Terry Rudd) was a young actress who worked with Paul that summer. "After an initial six-week period during which you had to pay," recalls Mrs. Lewis, "the Trasks [the producers] then picked promising young actors and sent them to their other theaters. Then we were paid around eighteen dollars a week. The rest of us may have struggled to make ends meet, but Paul didn't. He told us that he had made a deal with his family. They would support him for a year while he was trying to be an actor, but after the year he either had to go back and work at the store like his brother, Art, or he was on his own. But I remember he didn't feel a whole lot of pressure about it."

One of the other actors whom Paul became friendly with in Plymouth was Ward Ohrman, and for the next couple of years, Ward, Paul, Terry, and several others kept in touch with one another. Mrs. Lewis also recalls that even back in 1948 Paul had a "propensity for beer."

At Plymouth that summer the troupe performed *Dear Brutus*, *The Doughgirls*, and *All My Sons*. Terry Lewis says, "Even then Paul was unhappy with people who talked about his blue eyes and his handsomeness. He wanted character parts. He was always hardworking, and he never goofed off. He hasn't changed much. Even then he was solid; he knew who he was, and he knew what he wanted." (Newman himself has said, "I was always a character actor. I just looked like Little Red Riding Hood.")

According to Lewis, Paul had already graduated from Kenyon, and after Labor Day, when the summer stock season was over, Paul took a job with a winter stock company on a lake in Massachusetts. "We corresponded for a while and then lost touch." It should be noted that this account varies from Newman's official biography, given out by his public relations people, which says he graduated from Kenyon in June 1949 and went to Williams Bay, Wisconsin, to do summer stock. Terry Lewis distinctly remembers that this was not the case, and wonders why Paul has eliminated that year in stock from his résumé.

In any event, in the summer of 1949 Newman was at Williams Bay, Wisconsin, doing stock; following that he joined a winter stock company, the Woodstock Players, in Woodstock, Illinois, a city near Chicago.

It has been reported that he met his first wife, Jacqueline Witte, in Williams Bay, but some say that it was in Woodstock that they met. She is a native of Wisconsin and attended Lawrence University in Appleton, Wisconsin, so it is more likely that Paul met her in Wisconsin, and that they went to Woodstock together.

Jackie was a tall, pretty, brown-eyed blonde. It certainly must have been love at first sight and a whirlwind courtship, for by December of that year they were married.

During the year Paul appeared in such plays as *John Loves Mary*, *The Glass Menagerie*, *Our Town*, and *Cyrano de Bergerac*. He was developing his craft. In addition to talent he possessed two other significant gifts: remarkable good looks and a rich, full baritone speaking voice. He had a talent, too, for directing, and even put on a play at the nearby Brecksville Little Theater.

Paul and Jackie bought a used car, a 1937 Packard. At the time he was earning forty-five dollars a week, and their rent was ten dollars a month. Although this must have been a heady time for him, inevitably the realities of life began to close in on Paul. He had taken a wife, and soon they were expecting a child. Marriage and fatherhood were major responsibilities, which Paul accepted with great seriousness. He has always prided himself on accepting responsibility for his own actions.

When he found he wasn't earning enough money at acting, and had to supplement his income, he worked as a farmhand. Also, his father was ill, and the family was putting pressure on Paul to return to Cleveland and take up his duties in the family business.

Arthur Newman, Sr., at fifty-seven, died in May 1950. Like many parents, Mr. Newman had viewed show business as an unreliable profession. It offered no security, no future.

*Paul Newman:* "I think he always thought of me as pretty much of a lightweight. He treated me like he was disappointed in me a lot of the time, and he had every right to be. It has been one of the great agonies of my life that he could never know. I wanted desperately to show him that somehow, somewhere along the line, I could cut the mustard. And I never got a chance, never got a chance."

On September 23, four months after Arthur senior's death, Jackie gave birth to a son, Alan Scott. Now Paul had a wife *and* a son to support. At his mother's urging, he returned to the store and proved himself to be adept at running things. According to one uncle, Paul had even bought a house nearby and seemed to be settling into life in suburbia.

Outward appearances aside, he remained a discontented young man. The retailing business held no romance for him, and although he was doing a good job, after eighteen months of agonizing, at his request, his brother took over the sporting goods business.

"It's easy to give something up when you're no good at it," Paul Newman would later note. But he had been *good* at running the business; he was, in effect, giving up a certain future for something uncertain.

With some money to back him up for the first year, Paul took his wife and infant child to Connecticut, where he would enroll in the master's program of Yale's famous drama school. "It seems to me that I was instinctively pursuing the *one* thing I'd ever really done well."

Few people realize that Newman's active interest in social and political issues blossomed at this early stage. In 1952, the still unknown actor "campaigned" for the Democratic presidential candidate Adlai E. Stevenson. It was ground-level participation and involved, to quote Newman, "stuffing envelopes." But like most twenty-seven-year-olds, in the early fifties, Paul Newman was more concerned with a livelihood than with politics.

The Newmans didn't live lavishly in New Haven. At one point Paul sold encyclopedias for extra income and apparently was good at it, reportedly even bringing home almost a thousand dollars in one two-week period.

While at Yale, according to various accounts, Newman concentrated on directing because he intended to stay in the academic arena and would need to master the technical aspects of theater. Other sources, however, claim he was as interested in acting as in directing. In fact, it is likely that Newman was still ambivalent, torn between what he enjoyed doing and what he felt he should be doing to insure his future.

At Yale, Newman was asked to do a part in a student production of *Saint Joan*. He immediately said yes but, after reading the script, found that "the muscles contracted in [his] stom-

ach." He recalls that he was trying to devise ways to play the
scene facing upstage—when it occurred to him that he had
uprooted his family and moved them to Connecticut to pursue
theater, and now he was looking for ways to avoid having to
face the issue of acting!

*Paul Newman:* "I'm not very good at revealing myself. I cover
up for it by telling terrible dirty jokes. That first time, when I
read a stage direction—'Weeping is heard offstage'—I didn't
know what to do. But there I was in drama school. I'd left a
good-paying job and I said, 'Well, kiddo, better do it or go back
home.' So I took the script down to the basement and worked
on the scene, and that performance was probably as full and
rich as anything I've done."

There were many aspiring playwrights at the Yale School of
Drama. One student had written an original piece about the
life of Beethoven, and Paul Newman had been cast in a small
role as Beethoven's nephew, Carl. There were high hopes for
the play. Everyone at the premiere in New Haven was excited
because they knew Audrey Wood was in the audience. Not
only was she Tennessee Williams's agent, but she also handled
William Inge and other successful playwrights. Accompanying
Wood that night was her husband, William Liebling, who was
an actors' agent. The couple weren't particularly responsive to
the play, but both recognized that young Paul Newman might
very well have a future in the theater. Liebling told Newman
to let him know if he ever came to New York; he would see
what he could do for him.

Liebling's and Wood's interest confirmed the opinion of
many others at Yale. Newman, his colleagues advised, should
forget about taking an advanced degree and simply go to New
York, where he was sure to make it.

Newman wasn't so sure, however. This would be a *real* risk.
Although he subsequently told one interviewer that it was lack
of money that finally forced him to leave Yale, professors at the
university have stated that he had obtained employment in
New York even before he left drama school.

The most likely version is that in the summer of 1952,
strongly encouraged by his wife, Newman took the plunge. He

would give himself a year, and if nothing really important happened—by then, he would be twenty-eight, hardly a kid—he would go back to Yale, get his degree, and settle down.

Newman was not expecting miracles in the big city. Liebling *might* be able to help him, but it was more likely, considering the odds, that he would not. Certainly, living in Manhattan was impractical: the rents were too high. Jackie had relatives on Staten Island, so the Newmans found a modest apartment there, so that her family might help out with baby-sitting while Jackie sought work as a model. Scott was almost two and already, by certain accounts, a problem child. A longtime friend of Newman's has recalled: "I remember going to Paul and Jackie's apartment when Scott was two years old and not being able to carry on a conversation because he was yelling and screaming. He was uncontrollable."

Soon the young couple was expecting another child. To make money, Paul again traveled the proven encyclopedia route. Even though the hot and humid summer, with school out of session, was not the ideal time for selling encyclopedias, Newman was again successful. His daily routine during this period, however, was hardly enviable: He'd catch the early morning ferry into Manhattan, go to casting calls, see agents, then travel back to Staten Island to try to sell more encyclopedias.

Certainly, it wasn't easy, but Paul was vitalized by what was going on in New York. These were the early fifties, when theater was at a zenith. Actors not only worked on Broadway but were doubling in live drama on television. Newman later said, "I wanted a piece of that action, and getting into television was the first step, the right kind of break."

Where his experience differs from most others is that within a few weeks there were important signs that Paul Newman was not wasting his time.

# 2

Thomasville is a rather typical small town in southern Georgia, about ten miles from the Florida border. It had withstood the Roaring Twenties and was about to encounter the harsh Depression when Joanne Gignilliat Woodward was born there on February 27, 1930.

Wade Woodward and Elinor Trimmier Woodward already had an older child, Wade junior. Mr. Woodward was an administrator in the school system. Joanne was raised an Episcopalian, and the family lived in very modest circumstances.

There was little culture in Thomasville, but there were movies, and Elinor Woodward was an avid moviegoer. ("I was nearly born in the middle of a Crawford movie, *Our Modern Maidens*," recalled the adult Joanne. "Mother named me after Joan, but my southern relatives made it into Joanne.") Undoubtedly, Elinor took Joanne to movies at a very early age, and movies and acting made a great impression on the girl. In fact, Joanne has said that as far back as she could recall she had wanted to be an actress: "I have been dedicated to acting since I was able to talk."

Whether her parents—her father in particular—encouraged her obsession is questionable. Undoubtedly, they viewed the dreams of a child with some skepticism. Like all little girls across the country, Joanne was star-struck. When she was nine and saw the film *Wuthering Heights*, she fell madly in love with Laurence Olivier in his portrayal of the brooding Heathcliff.

It is not known if it was Joanne who convinced her mother to take her, or if it was Elinor Woodward's idea, but in December 1939 mother and daughter made the trek to Atlanta for the premiere of *Gone With the Wind*. Joanne was in the crowd lining the streets to catch a glimpse of the stars, and she shrieked hysterically when she spotted Laurence Olivier, who was accompanying the love of his life, Vivien Leigh, who was the female lead in *Gone With the Wind*. To this day Olivier claims to remember Joanne Woodward because the nine-year-old leapt into his car and landed smack on him! Obviously Joanne, even at this early age, was a person who went directly for what she wanted.

"When I was twelve," Joanne once recalled, "I kept a list on my bedside table: 'How To Be a Fascinating Woman.' It had items on it like: Pausing in doorways when entering a room. Reading everything so that I'd be really well read. . . . Talking very little. Being a good listener. Speaking in a low voice."

The family, because of Wade Woodward's profession, moved around for several years before settling down in Greenville, South Carolina. By then Joanne was fifteen. Although she later revealed that her lifelong interest in needlepoint began during her childhood, restrained pursuits of this sort were certainly not her main interest. With her mother's encouragement, Joanne was busy entering beauty contests; her goal was to leave the South and to go to New York or Hollywood. Quite simply, she wanted to be an actress, perhaps most like Bette Davis. Southern girls from good families, however, were not supposed to entertain thoughts about professional careers, let alone have dreams of becoming "an actress"!

There is a question as to whether Elinor Woodward's encouragement of her daughter's ambitions was a source of tension in her marriage to Wade Woodward. The couple had been unhappy for a long time, and while others in their circumstances might have kept going—for appearance' sake—this couple did

not. The Woodwards separated and subsequently divorced, but
Mr. Woodward remained an important force in his children's
lives. Wade junior had gone off to college and was pursuing a
career as an architect. Next it was Joanne's turn, and her future
was the topic of heated discussion.

Speaking of those years in Greenville, Elinor Woodward has
described Joanne as "the prettiest girl in town." ("That's what
all mothers say" was the adult Joanne's response.) She was also,
according to Mama, a nonstop talker and reader.

In high school, teenage Joanne greatly impressed her drama
teacher, Robert McClane, who saw thrilling potential in the
girl. She was *so* good, the story goes, that he saw no reason why
she shouldn't go to New York right away. Joanne's father,
needless to say, did not agree. He wanted his daughter to go to
college, and apparently Papa convinced Mama and Joanne, because the girl was enrolled at Louisiana State University. Her
major: "Drama, what else?"

At LSU she tackled the theater classics and played Ophelia—
"southern style," complete with drawl. "It was horrible," she
recalled, "and I vowed never to play Shakespeare again until I
could speak the English language."

College apparently did not fulfill Joanne's yearnings, for after two years at LSU she left. After working as a secretary for a
couple of months, she returned to work with Robert McLane
and appeared in several of his little-theater productions in
South Carolina. Her father saw her in one, Tennessee Williams's *The Glass Menagerie*, and was impressed—so much so that
Joanne was finally able to convince him that she was ready to
go to New York. First, however, she spent a season in summer
stock in Chatham, Massachusetts, playing starring roles in
*Liliom, All My Sons,* and *Ten Little Indians.*

Things happened relatively fast for Joanne Woodward, although it might not have seemed so to her at the time. In New
York she enrolled in the Neighborhood Playhouse where she
studied with Sanford Meisner. "I hated him at first," she recalled, "but he is absolutely the greatest dramatic coach in the
world."

She has also noted, "The first day, when we had to stand up

and give our names and where we came from, the whole class fell on the floor at my accent." She took speech lessons to eliminate her southern accent. "A Georgia drawl is all very well in Georgia," she explained, "but speech is an actress's stock-in-trade and speaking with a regional accent is not only limiting oneself to certain type roles, but shows a lack of businesslike application to one's chosen profession."

Early on, Joanne had to contend with a harsh fact of show business life: "Type" was everything. If you were not "the type" currently considered commercial, you were in trouble. Even lofty temples of learning that catered to the artist were not immune to types, places like the Neighborhood Playhouse. "That's where I acquired the belief that I wasn't attractive," Joanne has said. "The fashion at the Playhouse was for little, dark neurotic girls from the wrong side of the tracks. The boys wouldn't date anybody else. I tried to turn myself into that type, but it didn't work."

Joanne has also recalled: "I remember how my roommate and I used to compete to see who was more neurotic. We *wanted* to be the worst neurotic."

She also found there were no "easy ways" to learn the craft of acting: "For two years I was slapped down, torn apart, and taught to act by Sandy Meisner. One of my ambitions has always been to 'show' Sandy Meisner. I have never been able to figure out why he took me in the first place . . . they turn down a lot of people."

For a few months during this period she worked as a model for the John Robert Powers agency. Home was a cold-water flat. She went job hunting. She did the things struggling young actresses are supposed to do. Unlike most young hopefuls, however, Joanne received an allowance from her father—sixty dollars a month, enough to cover basic expenses, if she was frugal. Joanne later recalled these days: "Another girl and I, Rawn Harding, had this barren apartment at 72nd Street and York Avenue. We had a little gas stove—and roaches. A horrible old man used to peek out at us. Our breakfast was hot dogs, which we bought from those street wagons."

The will to achieve is as important as one's resources, and

fortunately Joanne had both going for her. She loved the theater and, as she put it, was determined "to be a *good* actress whether [she] ever [became] a *star* or not." More than thirty years later this statement would still represent Joanne Woodward's philosophy.

During her second year in New York, an agent from the powerful and prestigious talent agency MCA saw her perform at the Neighborhood Playhouse and placed her under contract. Not quite so dramatic (and so unlikely) as the tale of the teenage Lana Turner's being discovered at a soda fountain, but it actually wasn't that different. Joanne became a working actress very quickly, and from the beginning, she won respect.

John Foreman, a young agent at MCA, was instrumental in bringing Woodward to the renowned actor-producer Robert Montgomery, who was then producing his famous hour-long weekly anthology *Robert Montgomery Presents* on NBC-TV; he had an original teleplay, "Penny," in preparation and Foreman thought Joanne was right for the title role. Everyone apparently agreed; she got the part.

"I had to audition for the *writer*," she later recalled, "which gives you an idea of the difference between New York and Hollywood."

"Penny" was aired on June 9, 1952. A few months later Joanne was cast in a *Studio One* production, "The Kill," which aired on CBS; in short order she appeared in two *Omnibus* episodes, also on CBS. It was obvious that Joanne could have a successful career in live television drama if she wanted one, and live television was exciting, especially in that era, on the threshold of what would later be dubbed the Golden Age of Television.

It was while making the rounds of agents who might get him jobs in television that Paul met Joanne.

*Paul Newman:* "I saw her coming out of the door at MCA, the theatrical agency, and I just thought, jeez, what an extraordinarily pretty girl. I had on my one suit—I had one seersucker suit which I, you know, would wear all week and wash over the weekend. A button-down collar. A knit tie, a black knit tie. I said hello."

According to Woodward, they were introduced by Maynard Morris, a well-known agent at MCA.

*Joanne Woodward:* "He [Morris] had discovered Barbara Bel Geddes and Gregory Peck and he discovered me and he discovered Paul and he introduced us one day. I had been making the rounds and I was hot, sweaty and my hair was all stringy around my neck. He brought out a pretty-looking young man in a seersucker suit, all pretty like an Arrow Collar ad, and said, 'This is Paul Newman,' and I hated him on sight, but he was so funny and pretty and neat."

It was inevitable, of course, that the young actors would encounter each other frequently in the small community of struggling talents trying to make it on Broadway and in television.

Joshua Logan takes credit for advancing the relationship between Paul Newman and Joanne Woodward, for in 1952 he cast them both in his upcoming Broadway production, William Inge's *Picnic*.

Bill Liebling had arranged the audition. Newman read for Inge, badly—or so the young actor felt. To his surprise, though, Liebling told him that he had set up another audition, this time with Joshua Logan, who would be directing the play. This was the big time—Logan was at his peak, having won enormous acclaim for *South Pacific* and *Mr. Roberts*.

"I first met Paul when we were casting *Picnic*," recalls Logan. "He was Bill Liebling's favorite client—Bill always had somebody he was pushing." Logan liked Paul immediately. "We had a character called Jockser in the third act," relates Logan. "Jockser was just a boy who came along after the play was practically over—only had three or four lines. And Paul was cast in that part. Everybody made a joke about the fact that finally Bill Liebling got his client a job. But," states Logan, "Paul was very good. He didn't brag, he was modest, and yet he was this handsome, spectacularly beautiful man—or boy, he was in those days."

Paul would be earning over a hundred dollars a week—a very respectable salary in 1952 dollars. There was no question that wife Jackie and son Scott would have plenty to eat and a roof over their heads.

"On the day I signed for *Picnic,*" Paul recalled, "I had less than two hundred and fifty dollars in the bank and a wife about to give birth to our second child. If *Picnic* hadn't been a good play, if it had folded after only a week or two, I don't know where I would have gone."

Joanne was signed to *Picnic* as understudy for two parts, Madge and Madge's younger sister, Millie.

Logan makes the point that Madge had to be played by a girl whose beauty would make the audience gasp, and Janice Rule filled the bill. He also notes that Kim Stanley, cast as Millie, was so consummate an acting genius that she could transform herself from a woman who looked thirty years old into a seventeen-year-old adolescent. Joanne didn't have the perfect qualifications for either role, but as Logan humorously notes today, "She saved us a lot of money by being able to play both parts." (During the play's 477-performance run, Joanne was called in fifty times.)

Logan's memories of Woodward are vivid. "I don't know her anywhere near as well as Paul because we didn't work together so closely," he says. "But she was a brilliant girl in her own way and she *made* you notice her somehow—her great talent made you notice; her personality and her drive."

There were other great talents involved in this venture: Eileen Heckart was playing the old-maid schoolteacher; Arthur O'Connell, her suitor. The leading man was Ralph Meeker in the role of Hal.

Typically, the production was to have its share of crises. Once the show was mounted and playing out of town, major problems surfaced. One was to greatly benefit Paul Newman.

Logan recalls: "The actor who was playing Alan Benson, the older boy who was Hal's roommate-friend in college, was a boy who was not as attractive as Paul by any means—he was a nice actor, but he was kind of dull. I mean we realized that every time he came onstage the audience started to yawn. I felt terrible because we had spent so much time and been so careful casting.

"It occurred to me, 'Why do we have to have Alan older than Hal, why can't we have him younger than Hal? He can look up to Hal. Why couldn't we have the boy who was 'Bill Liebling's client,' as we still called Paul jokingly, for that part?' And Bill Inge, who liked young boys very much, said, 'Oh sure, we can make the character younger.' So he just changed a few lines, and Paul changed character from Jockser to Alan Benson, who was one of the chief people in the show. And right away we could tell that the audience loved that character and loved Paul as that character."

In fact, it wasn't quite "right away." According to Newman's memory of events, they gave him the part, but after a few days of rehearsal they said it wasn't working out, so they made the character older again and hired another actor. A week later Newman was back in the role, but only temporarily. Joshua Logan told him some people would be coming to a rehearsal and if they liked Paul, the part was his. The "people" were Tennessee Williams, Dorothy McGuire, and Elia Kazan. Newman felt trapped, and later recalled how his knees shook when he went on stage. All went well, however, and the role was his.

The show went on the road, where rewrites continued. One such change added a scene between Newman and actress Peggy Conklin, one that gave a different interpretation to another character and that earned the play the reaction everyone had hoped for.

*Picnic* opened in New York at the Music Box Theater on February 19, 1953, and was the enormous hit all felt it would be. Newman was hardly the star, but the critics praised him, and audience response to him was visible, electric. The word was out: Catch the hot "new kid" in *Picnic*.

Newman had also been cast as the understudy to Ralph Meeker, in the role of Hal. And it was in this capacity that his relationship with Woodward began in earnest.

Logan relates: "Ralph Meeker and Janice Rule did a dance in the second act, the famous *Picnic* dance, and they could both dance, they were both wonderful dancers, had wonderful rhythm. Now, Paul, of course, playing Alan, didn't have a chance to do anything like that. But I could tell that Newman had a good build and was as strong-looking in his way, when he was stripped down, as Ralph Meeker was. So I made him the understudy for Meeker. And he went into the understudy rehearsal every day and danced with Joanne Woodward, who was Madge's understudy.

"Paul was rehearsing every day, doing the dance, with Joanne. And, of course, he was such a clean-cut, well-put-together boy that I said, 'Now, you've got to learn how to be a little "dirtier" to play the part of Hal.' And he said, 'How do you mean?' I said, 'Well, wiggle your ass a little bit when you're dancing.' And he said, 'Do you think I really should?' And I said, 'Sure, go ahead.' And he did, and was just as physical, quickly, as Meeker. He changed from all of his nice-boy upbringing in order to aim for this kind of a dirty Hal, and I think it did Paul a lot of good, and I *know* it did Joanne Woodward good. Joanne and he, I guess, got to know each other very well."

According to an actress who was in the cast of *Picnic*, Joanne picked Paul out and said, " 'I'm going to get that one.' And she did everything she had to in order to hook him and she got him."

Logan recalls a story that circulated to the effect that Paul's first wife, Jacqueline, by encouraging his theatrical ambitions, "lost him." Logan also recalls Joanne was usually in the background when Paul was around— "She was carefully working on her life, I'm sure!"

Logan was impressed by Joanne's acting ability. "She was *very* good as Madge, and as Millie too. And I didn't think anybody could play those roles as well as Janice and Kim—but Joanne made me listen to her. She was a talented girl."

He was also impressed by Paul's acting ability. "I saw him at the understudy rehearsals—he was excellent. I knew he was pretending, because he wasn't that way at all—he had the looks, and he had the body, and he had the freedom of movement for Hal. Meeker was made by God for Hal—he was well built, he could dance, he was free and had been a rough kid who became an actor. Paul was a well-bred kid with plenty of money, I guess, who had been to the best schools, the best colleges—he just wasn't Hal, that's all. He wasn't 'low-down,' as they'd say today. He wasn't a *crotch* actor."

Through the years Newman has recalled his experiences somewhat differently. According to him, Logan told him that if he wanted to understudy Hal, he had to get in shape. "The way I translated that was six hours in the gym every day." Certainly, Paul's life until now had not given him the necessary experience for such a role. It was too great a stretch, one that could be mastered only with hard work.

*Joshua Logan:* "Paul was such a bright man—he was such a brilliant person that he was able to conquer that upbringing of his and go back to the raw self that he could show—and he's gotten more and more so as the years have gone by. I can't *believe* that the Paul Newman that I knew is the Paul Newman of today—it's unbelievable that he could have gone that far back into his ego, his realities; I can't give you the reason for it, except that he's an extraordinary man because of that. To be able to bury all of that strict upbringing—all that money, all that ease of life—and become a rough-hewn person, which he was in many of the pictures I've seen him in, it's just a miracle to me, and it's one of his greatest assets, one of his greatest achievements."

Logan agrees that both Newman's and Woodward's personal backgrounds stood them in good stead in the business of managing and maintaining their careers. "Definitely. I think Paul and Joanne had a certain discipline about their lives that has made them into the great people they are, as well as great talents. I'm talking about outside of talent; I'm talking about intelligence."

On a few occasions during the out-of-town tryouts, Woodward filled in for Rule or Stanley. Director Logan missed all of Joanne's performances: "Something happened, I can't remember what it was. . . . But we were in such trouble with other parts of the play, I was spending a lot of time with Bill Inge, and we were having problems."

Logan recalls meeting Newman and Woodward years later, when both had achieved stardom: "Joanne said to me, 'Why didn't you come to see me when I played Madge?' I said, 'I was in trouble, I couldn't come.' She finally said she forgave me, but I don't think she ever has. She's a very tough lady."

John Foreman received a call from Paul back in 1953, alerting him that both he and Joanne were playing the leads in the Saturday matinee. The MCA agent went to the theater that afternoon, and seeing their electric performances, he knew they were in love.

During the run of *Picnic* both Paul and Joanne continued to pursue careers in live television. Foreman was now handling Newman. "He looked like a Greek god," Foreman has said. "I sent him over to read for a part in a television series, *The Web*, and he got the part. Paul was cast for nearly every part he tried out for."

Paul liked television: "It was the best thrill in town, a totally new experience. I was able to play all kinds of roles. I hadn't been categorized." Already Newman was more interested in playing character parts than in being cast as the romantic lead.

Now Newman had the security of a Broadway run and the money to pursue his interest in the Actors Studio. He said of this period, "I could study." And it must have been a welcome relief to finally admit that being an actor was what he really wanted to be.

Newman has given his version of how he got accepted at the Actors Studio: "You got two auditions. One before a large group, and then if you passed that one, you would go on to another with just Kazan and Cheryl Crawford. Well, one day some girl asked me if I would work with her for the second test. She passed her first audition, but the actor she'd worked with was out of town. She asked me if I'd take the male role during her second audition, so I did."

According to Newman, "Somebody must have got things mixed up, because about four days later I got a card saying I'd been admitted, and I hadn't even had a first audition." What Newman does not mention is that Kazan, Crawford, and others at the Actors Studio were already familiar with his work.

At the Studio his classmates included James Dean, Marlon Brando, Kim Stanley, Julie Harris, Eli Wallach, Anne Jackson,

Geraldine Page, Eva Marie Saint, Rod Steiger, and Karl Malden. "It was monkey see, monkey do," Newman has said. "Man, I just sat back there and watched how people did things and had enough sense not to open my big mouth."

But Newman has also said, "The Actors Studio, whether they like it or not, has either credit or blame for what I've become as an actor. I certainly came out of a very academic background, which was not very helpful, and I learned everything I've learned about acting at the Actors Studio."

Martin Ritt was there too: "It was an extraordinary experience, and it was a marvelous period of work, because nobody made any money. We somehow got enough money—or [Elia] Kazan did—the rooms were rented, we had dancing teachers, voice teachers—it was a very exciting time in the American theater because all the people were working for something they believed in, which happens very rarely. It was probably the most important period in the history of the American theater as evidenced by the lifeblood of the theater, which is playwrights."

Most of the people from the Actors Studio were also heavily involved in live television. To Martin Ritt this was "very exciting." As he explains, "There were a lot of technical problems at the time, but the audience understood that, and we did some terrific work."

Jack Garfein was a young director at the Actors Studio in the early fifties, having already had a success on Broadway. Today Garfein recalls that he liked Newman immediately: "There was a sweetness about him and yet an ambition. Even then I sensed that he was ambitious, yet he was nice about it, without stepping on anybody's toes. . . . But yet with one eye, I always felt, he was looking out to see how truthful people were—what their integrity was; and it's interesting because that quality's still there."

Garfein elaborates: "Even then I had a sense that here is a guy that if he saw something that you did to another person that was dishonest or cruel, you were written off and that was it. You were finished. I think a person would have a hard time struggling to get back into his graces."

Garfein recalls the few occasions when Paul replaced
Meeker: "[Paul] was *desperate* to get people over there to see
him, and to see . . . that he could play romantic parts, because
he wasn't cast in a romantic part [at the Actors Studio]. So he
was very anxious and he went around begging people, because
the play had already been running, people had seen it, and he
was a young actor who was after all doing a little character part
in it; and I remember he came to me and he said, 'Jack, it's very
important to me; *please*, you've gotta come and see me do the
part,' and I said, 'Paul, you're a leading man to me anyway, this
is nonsense,' and he said, 'No, no, that's talk; if you're serious,
come and see me do the performance.' And I did. I went to the
matinee and he was wonderful. But I didn't have any doubt
about that anyway."

During the run of *Picnic* many people became aware of Joanne's and Paul's attraction for each other, and it was apparent
that a difficult—and potentially painful—situation was developing. Not only was Newman a married man, but his wife,
Jackie, had just given birth to their second child, Susan. Paul
had moved the brood into an apartment in Queens, from which
he commuted every day in his newly purchased Volkswagen.

The up-and-coming young actor living in suburban Queens
had another life in the city, and although Newman and Woodward may well have been fighting their attraction for each
other at this time—as they later claimed—it could not have
been easy. They were together at the theater every night for a
year, as well as all day Wednesdays and Saturdays (matinee
days). In addition, they were taking classes, and both were pursuing careers in live television.

Life for Joanne during these months in New York City was
hectic and exhilarating. She had moved to an apartment on
Fifty-sixth Street and Madison Avenue, "a five flight walkup—
one large room and a tiny kitchen." Years later she recalled it
fondly: "Every year, lovingly, I painted the place. I'd come
home from the theater and stand on a ladder stark naked, except for a shower cap, and paint the ceiling and walls. The lack
of costume, you understand, was to preclude ruining clothes
with spilled paint. I remember I did my laundry, including

sheets, in a bathtub, and then hung it over the shower rod. I'm so grateful for having been poor. The experience taught me never to take money for granted."

Joanne, too, had become a member of the Actors Studio. It was Jack Garfein who was the judge at Woodward's audition there: "She came in while understudying in *Picnic* and auditioned. I didn't know about how good she was. I knew her and saw her around, but then when I saw the audition, I was *very* impressed."

Garfein says that Joanne in civilian life "seemed like a very quiet, inward person." When he saw her name on the audition sheet, he naturally assumed she was going to do a scene where she played a sensitive, inward girl. But Garfein was in for a stunning surprise: "Suddenly this girl's on the stage with a *sharp edge*. The opposite of what you see when you see her in person."

The Studio had strict rules for auditions: Audition scenes could not exceed five minutes and actors could not be told whether they had passed or not. "Joanne's scene went to seven minutes," recalls Garfein, "and I was so excited that I couldn't resist. I told her, 'Gee, you were good!' I told her that night."

Joanne was accepted at the Studio. Garfein, however, doesn't remember her doing any scenes there. He points out that it was terribly important for actors of that day to be accepted by the Studio, to win the approval of Lee Strasberg, but that actors seldom performed scenes for Strasberg. They didn't want to expose themselves to the master's brutal critiquing. Garfein recalls, "James Dean did a scene, and Strasberg absolutely slashed him, and he never did a scene again! But Kazan was different. He set up the atmosphere of 'the artist.' 'Let's all work together, what's your idea? What can we do?' "

While Paul and Joanne may not have been doing scenes for the class in these early years, they were certainly getting experience in live television. During the year Joanne did "The Young and the Fair," an original production for *Goodyear Playhouse*. Paul had been cast by his new pal, the director Sidney Lumet, in several episodes of the *You Are There* series on CBS; he played such diverse parts as Nathan Hale and Julius Caesar.

Newman was also a favorite of the producers of *The Web*, a popular CBS series; in July 1953 he appeared in an episode called "The Bells of Damon," and in September, in "One for the Road."

His performance in *Picnic* had earned him an entry in the *Theater World* anthology that year; he was said to be "one of the most promising personalities."

He was indeed the fair-haired boy of Broadway, and his agents were busily submitting him for every available part both on Broadway and in Hollywood. Patrick O'Neal, who met Newman around this time, recalls: "We all knew Paul was headed for the movies, whether he wanted it or not. It was so obvious, we would have been surprised if it *hadn't* happened!"

The film director Robert Wise recalls meeting Newman in New York at this time. He was casting a role for the movie epic *Helen of Troy*. "I was looking for someone to play Paris," Wise says, "and Paul was one of the rising young people. I met him at some costume house; I think it was Berle's. He might have been in a TV show that he was being costumed for. At any rate, I had to go to the costume house to meet him because of his schedule. It turned out that he didn't do the part."

Another director was interested in helping Paul to the big screen: Elia Kazan. Kazan tested Newman and another Actors Studio student, James Dean, for the roles of the Trask brothers in his upcoming Warner Bros. film version of John Steinbeck's *East of Eden*. Newman and Dean did the screen test together, interchanging roles. It was filmed in New York.

Paul's powerful talent agency, MCA, was also interested in getting the actor a screen test—Columbia Pictures had bought the rights to *Picnic* and was testing unknowns. Paul wanted to audition in a scene with Carroll Baker, another MCA client and fellow Actors Studio student. Baker at the time was dating Paul's pal, Jack Garfein.

Garfein says, "Instead of just calling Carroll direct, as most young actors would have done, . . . Paul phoned me and said, 'I know you're going out with this girl, her name is Carroll Baker, and she's very attractive, and Jack, is it all right for me to call her and ask her to work with me on a scene? Is it all right for me to call her?' "

Garfein emphasizes, "Now that's something that happened thirty-five years ago, and I've never forgotten it. It's rare. It's very touching, very moving, that this young man would do that. He said, 'I don't want any misunderstanding here. I want to be sure.' And I said, 'By all means, go and call her. It's perfectly all right.' "

Garfein then told Baker: "Look, this young actor who's in *Picnic* is going to call you. He wants to do a test for MCA." Carroll, of course, was interested in getting a part as well; she and Newman got together, rehearsed, and did the test. "After the test," recalls Garfein, laughing, "Columbia wasn't interested in Paul, they were only interested in Carroll!"

Columbia may not have wanted him, but Newman's career in television continued in high gear, as did Joanne's. In early 1954, in quick succession, Joanne appeared in *Danger*, *Philco Television Playhouse*, *Studio One*, and *Kraft Television Theater*. That spring Paul did an episode of *The Mask* on ABC.

When the national tour of *Picnic* was being planned, Paul wanted very much to play Hal on the road. According to Newman, when he asked Logan if he could take over the role in the touring production, Logan told him, "I don't think so, because you don't carry any sexual threat." (Newman has said, "I've been chewing on that one for twenty years.")

Had Paul gone on the road for an extended run, the separation from Joanne might have altered both the way in which their relationship developed, and the speed with which it did so. As it was, Woodward has said they spent the time "running away from each other." She has also made the point that ever since they did *Picnic*, Newman has been her "closest friend."

There were other men in Joanne's life, and over the next several years she would become engaged three times. "All southern girls like to get engaged even when they aren't ready to get married," she wryly noted.

One of those men was Gore Vidal, the brilliant, handsome young novelist with a blue-blood background and a life-style that (especially for the fifties) was avant-garde. To Joanne

Woodward's father, who had become a publishing executive
with Charles Scribner's Sons, Vidal certainly must have appeared a spectacular choice for a possible son-in-law, and Joanne's mother could proudly brag to her friends about "the
divine young man Joanne is engaged to." Woodward often
noted that her mother's greatest fear was that her daughter
would be a spinster.

A man of unusual knowledge, Vidal had a cunning, cutting
humor and held controversial opinions on all subjects, including sex and politics. He and the girl who was interested in
learning must have had many lively discussions, for Joanne was
a person with interests other than herself and acting. She was
the antithesis of most "dedicated actresses." Vidal was later to
point out that most really *good* actresses were not particularly
intelligent; Joanne was a rare exception, and Vidal and Woodward have remained lifelong friends. ("Gore is still teaching
me words," she stated years later.)

Apparently Joanne enjoyed the company of writers. Another
of the men she was "engaged" to in these early years was the
playwright James Costigan.

She was in no rush, however, to get married. Woodward had
observed on many occasions that her parents' marital discord
and divorce made her less than starry-eyed about romance and
marriage.

# ☆ 3

In 1954 the average income in the United States was perhaps fifty dollars a week. Certainly by the standards of most working people, a thousand dollars a week was an incredible sum; such was the offer Warner Bros. now made to Paul Newman—the man who less than two years before had arrived in New York almost broke, with no clear prospects. It was a deal he found impossible to refuse, regardless of the pitfalls. He sent his wife and two children back to her family in Wisconsin, and Newman headed for Hollywood, hopeful but full of misgivings. "The moment I walked into that studio I had a feeling of personal disaster," Newman would later recall.

By now the story of Paul Newman's unhappiness with his first film, *The Silver Chalice*, has become legend. He said it has "the distinction of being the worst film made in the 1950s." In *Chalice* Newman played a Greek slave who sculpts the silver cup used at the Last Supper, and indeed the film did have lines like "Oh, Helena, is it really you? What a joy."

In retrospect it's simple to sneer at the stupidity of Warners, to wonder how any company could be so off base as to cast the very modern Paul Newman in a period piece. To understand the rationale involved, one must consider what was selling in

the cinema marketplace at the time. The previous summer
Marlon Brando had starred in a film version of *Julius Caesar* for
MGM, and in the fall *The Robe*, starring another highly regarded young stage actor, Richard Burton, was a blockbuster.
Obviously Warners was hoping for a similar success with *The
Silver Chalice*. Like *The Robe*, *Chalice* was based on a best seller
with a religious theme. Newman's chiseled features were perfect for the role. All the other elements, however, were out of
sync—the script was ludicrous, the director was wrong, and
the film was given a most peculiar production design. Even the
beautiful leading lady, the Hollywood veteran Virginia Mayo,
then only in her mid-thirties, was sadly miscast as an evil
femme fatale. (A teenage Natalie Wood, with hair dyed blond,
played Mayo as a youngster.)

The popular young ingenue Pier Angeli was on loan, from
MGM, as the love interest. On a neighboring set on the Warn-
ers lot, Elia Kazan was shooting *East of Eden* with James Dean.
Dean often went to the *Chalice* set to visit his New York buddy,
Newman. It was Paul who introduced Dean to Pier Angeli,
with whom the doomed rebel had a brief but intense affair.

Of course, in Hollywood Newman ran into many old pals
from New York. One he encountered was Jack Garfein, who
was there directing for Columbia. "We would run into each
other every once in a while and we'd always kid about his
career," Garfein recalls. "Paul had a very good sense about how
to make that artificial part—that superficial part of Hollywood
—work and at the same time be able to keep one foot in integrity and in a vision of what life can be like."

Garfein was impressed that Paul was always "himself": he
"saw all the bullshit going on around him," yet he was never a
part of it. Garfein also knew James Dean from the Actors Studio days. Dean, he says, did things that Newman would *"never"*
do. Garfein explains: "I loved Jimmy and we were very close to
each other, but if I was in a restaurant with him and Hedda
Hopper walked in, he would get up and walk over and say
hello. . . . He would stay there with her for forty-five minutes
and you're sitting at the table. That's something that Paul
would never do."

On the soundstages Newman found himself in an alien medium, one that did not understand how the new breed of actors functioned. At the Actors Studio Newman had worked with supremely knowledgeable directors, such as Kazan and his assistant Martin Ritt. There actors were encouraged to build performances from within. That wasn't the case with Paul's first film—*The Silver Chalice* was old-fashioned moviemaking. Here they were concerned not with motivation or character development but with good looks and lighting. Newman was appalled, but there was nothing he could do as the wheels of production ground heavily on.

Paul later recalled how rotten he always felt after a day's work, especially since there was no choice but to continue. Traveling to Hollywood and signing a lucrative, long-term studio contract had been *essential* to his becoming a success, he argued defensively years later. What he hadn't bargained on was landing in such a bad film. Desperate to get away from the negative pull of Hollywood, he invoked a clause in his contract which permitted him to appear in plays in New York. His agents alerted him to the role of the psychopath in *The Desperate Hours,* and even before production had been completed on *The Silver Chalice* he had signed for the Broadway role.

Newman's contempt for the "old" Hollywood system was firmly entrenched by the time *Chalice* was finished. And although in an early stage of his film career, Newman wasn't shy about expressing his discontent. Even Jack Warner, who had survived many years of dealing with what he regarded as "difficult" actors whose ideas of what was in their own best interests often conflicted with Warner's, recognized in Paul Newman a whole new breed.

Meanwhile Joanne, too, was in Hollywood. She appeared in her first filmed television show, starring with Dick Powell in an episode of *Four Star Playhouse.* In "Interlude" Woodward, twenty-four, played an adolescent who thinks she is in love with an older man. Powell was so impressed by Woodward's enormous talent that he sent a print of the show to Buddy Adler, a key production executive at 20th Century-Fox.

"If Joanne had a discoverer, it was probably Dick Powell,"

recalled the screenwriter-director Nunnally Johnson. Johnson, who was at 20th Century-Fox at the time, also recalled that Buddy Adler was being groomed to succeed Darryl F. Zanuck as head of production. "He was going through a kind of training period," Johnson said. Adler wanted to sign Woodward, but Zanuck didn't think the girl had possibilities. There were discussions, and Zanuck finally told Adler, "All right, go on and sign her. Like everybody else in this job, you're going to make mistakes. So go ahead and make your first one."

Joanne had MCA to negotiate her deal, and she landed one of the first seven-year contracts that permitted an actress to appear on television (no more than six shows per year). Since Fox had nothing for her right away, she availed herself of this clause immediately, commuting back and forth between New York and Hollywood for the remainder of the year. She did a slew of television dramas, including *Ford Theater*, *The Elgin Hour*, *Lux Video Theatre*, *Robert Montgomery Presents*, and *Armstrong Circle Theater*.

Buddy Adler may have been quick to sign Joanne, but the studio was slow in finding something for her to do on the big screen. One assumes Newman commiserated with Joanne, and that she now fully understood what *he* was going through. It's hard to say how much the pair actually saw of each other during this year, since they were both moving back and forth across the country. Both Joanne and Paul had an important goal, however, one that was a vital common ground between them: They were determined to do *quality* work; they would not simply climb the ladder to stardom.

Paul's contract also permitted him to do television, an option that he would exercise as well. He returned to New York, and in short order his agents had lined up several dramatic parts in live television, including one in a script by a young writer, Stewart Stern, who had also recently returned to New York from Hollywood.

Stern's script, "Thundering Silence," was being presented on *Philco Television Playhouse*, on the eve of Thanksgiving. During the rehearsals and production of this teleplay Paul Newman and Stewart Stern developed what would become a lifelong friendship, one that would result in several collaborations of high artistic merit. (Stern, of course, would also become a close pal of Joanne's.)

Paul also appeared in an episode of *Danger*. He did all of this television work while in rehearsal for *The Desperate Hours*. Robert Montgomery was directing Joseph Hayes's adaptation of his best seller. The project had *hit* written all over it. The story concerns a group of escaped convicts who hold a typical American family hostage in their own home. The central character is a killer—and that's the role Newman was playing. Karl Malden had been cast as the other lead. A major role was played by James Gregory, who had worked with both Paul and Joanne in live television. Gregory recalls his immediate reaction (a typical one) on meeting Paul: "There's a guy with a really classical puss."

Gregory also remembers: "We went to Hartford, Boston, and Philadelphia for pre-Broadway tryouts for *Desperate Hours*. In Philadelphia *The Silver Chalice* was playing at a nearby movie house, and Paul was going around saying he hated it and wanted to buy back the print. One night after the show, about six of us—myself, George Grizzard, my wife, a few others, and Paul—got about three or four six-packs and went up in the balcony of this all-night grind house to watch *Silver Chalice*. Paul was sitting there slouched over, hating every minute of it. It was not that bad a picture, but he thought it was awful."

Gregory had a nickname for Paul: "I used to call him 'grabby-fist,' because every time you'd see him after the show, he had a beer in his mitt."

During rehearsals, Gregory says, "Montgomery and Paul used to go at it from time to time over the interpretation of his role. But they settled it out of court."

On February 18, 1955, *The Desperate Hours* opened on Broadway to terrific notices and big box office. Paul Newman was singled out for his brilliant performance.

Paul's mother had come in from Cleveland for the opening, and she stayed on for a while, spending time with her grandchildren, Scott, now four, and Susan, almost two. Jackie was pregnant again. Family life seemed to be smooth. Paul's professional life had apparently fallen into place—he could now bounce back and forth between Broadway and Hollywood, earn a substantial living, and support a large family.

Joshua Logan saw *The Desperate Hours*. Newman, he recalls, "was not *quite* convincing, but he was such a bright guy that he knew how to play it so it was believable. He wasn't the right type for it. He grew into that part."

Logan was directing the film version of *Picnic*. Paul was already "too big" for the supporting role he had played onstage (Cliff Robertson would be "introduced" in that part), and William Holden wanted the role of Hal. Columbia had a commitment with Holden, so that was that. (None of the principal actors in the stage production, except for Arthur O'Connell, appeared in the film.)

As for *Desperate Hours*, the noted director William Wyler was to bring it to the screen almost immediately. Certainly, Paul was perfect to repeat his role; The only problem was, the studio wanted a *big* name, and Humphrey Bogart wanted the part, even though he was decades too old for the role. He got it.

Joanne Woodward, meanwhile, had been called back to Hollywood. Buddy Adler had instructed the casting people at Fox to "get her work," and so they did, loaning her out for a "small" movie to be made by Columbia Pictures. The film was *Count Three and Pray*, a Civil War drama. In it Woodward would play—what else?—a teenager, and an orphan, to boot. Her costume was to be baggy pants and a shirt.

"I was recommended for the role by a man I'd never met, Richard Quine," recalled Joanne. "I was in New York when producer Ted Richmond sent me the script on Mr. Quine's recommendation. I read one paragraph and decided this was the role for me. My first line of dialogue was 'Git up, stranger, I ain't hurt you a bit.'"

Joanne thought: "What better part can you have? I get to wear funny clothes, cut my hair, and smoke a cigar. At twenty-four, I didn't think in terms of what was the significance of this film—it was a helluva good part. I worked with a man I adored, Van Heflin, with a director I adored, and a part that I absolutely worshipped." For his part, Heflin was pleasantly surprised at the ability and honesty of the young newcomer, who seemed remarkably free of pretensions and nonsense.

With the filming completed, Joanne returned to New York where she did extensive work in live television. Soon, however, she was called back to the Coast, this time for a role in what would turn out to be *her* "worst picture." In fact, she later described *A Kiss Before Dying* as "the worst picture ever made in Hollywood."

She may be right. While the ingredients of the 20th Century-Fox package, sold to United Artists, were first-class, the finished picture was a ludicrous melodrama complete with a musical score, à la *Dragnet*, that constantly underscored the obvious. The cast was talented; Robert Wagner, Jeffrey Hunter, Mary Astor, and Woodward were top-lined, with Woodward billed over Astor. The picture was adapted from a best-selling novel by Ira Levin, and the production values included CinemaScope and color. Unfortunately, director Gerd Oswald was totally unable to pull it all together.

Joanne played a whining, nagging, very *dumb* girl—and one almost can't blame Robert Wagner's character for wanting to kill her! Woodward was miles ahead of her fellow actors in the business of approaching a role; she tried to give a certain depth and texture to her ridiculous character, and in the process she made absolutely no attempt to glamorize herself.

Joanne hated the whole project, and besides, she was unhappy in Hollywood. She wanted to *work*. One picture every few months was "not enough activity to keep me interested," she observed. "In New York I could have done a dozen or more TV shows."

Meanwhile Paul was ensconced in the long run of *The Desperate Hours* and had once again become involved with his family. Jackie had given birth to their third child, Stephanie.

Whenever he was working in New York, Newman would return to the Actors Studio to take classes. "Even when you're in a show, you become stagnant in a part after the first six or seven months," he has explained. "The important thing is to keep acting. That's the only way you can grow."

Whether it was to stretch himself as an actor, or to supplement his income, Paul continued to work steadily in television. The best live television shows were still emanating from New York, and like Joanne, Paul was anxious to appear in as many as possible. That spring he appeared in two episodes of CBS's *Appointment with Adventure*. Newman next played the title role in "The Death of Billy the Kid," a teleplay written by Gore Vidal for *The Philco Playhouse*. Arthur Penn was the director.

"Paul and I had worked together in live TV on *Philco*, around '53," recalls Penn. "Many actors appearing in Broadway shows did *Philco*—it was an opportunity for them to get away from the roles they were playing eight times a week, and *Philco* was done live on Sunday nights. We had Janice Rule, Kim Stanley, many others."

In these early years of televised drama a fascinating phenomenon was known to occur: If a teleplay was a huge success, it might then be made into a movie—as happened with *Marty*, *Requiem for a Heavyweight*, and *The Catered Affair*, but typically the actors who originated the roles for television did not get to repeat them in the film version.

After "The Death of Billy the Kid" aired, there was talk that the movies might be interested, but it seemed likely that Paul would lose out to a big star, as he had lost to Bogart in the casting of the film version of *The Desperate Hours*.

In any event, Paul's career in television continued unabated. He was signed to play the teenager George (Paul was then thirty) in the *Producers Showcase* presentation of *Our Town*. Frank Sinatra starred as the Narrator, and Eva Marie Saint co-starred with Paul, in the role of Emily. The adaptation had added music, with an original score by Sammy Cahn. "Love and Marriage" was written for Sinatra to sing in the show, and it became an instant standard. The production is regarded today as a great example of the Golden Age of Television.

Newman's next undertaking was even more dramatic. He was signed for a major role in a TV version of Ernest Hemingway's "The Battler." Written by A. E. Hotchner, and directed by Arthur Penn for NBC's new series *Playwrights '56*, the show was to star James Dean in the title role. "The Battler" was scheduled to be broadcast live from New York on October 18.

On September 30 Dean was killed in an automobile accident. The producer and director decided against scrapping the project. Their idea: to offer Newman the role intended for Dean. Newman recalled: "They asked me to play his part. I said, 'I can't do that emotionally.' But I did it." Newman wore complicated makeup to create the punch-drunk prizefighter with a swollen eye and cauliflower ear, and proved once and for all that even with his looks concealed, he could deliver a powerful performance.

Penn remembers, "We got a fantastic result. I think it's because of that performance that Paul got *Somebody Up There Likes Me.* You have to understand that he suffered a little bit from being so handsome—people doubted just how well he could act. 'Battler' proved he could."

Through the years there has been much speculation about how and when Paul got to play Rocky Graziano in *Somebody Up There Likes Me,* the work that really launched his superstar film career. One source relates a colorful, if probably apocryphal story: after "The Battler" was broadcast, the producer, Fred Coe, took the cast out for drinks. Newman, discontented with his personal life and his disintegrating marriage, was drinking a great deal, and on this particular night he became drunk and belligerent. A man in the bar, who had supposedly just seen Newman as the prizefighter in "The Battler," challenged him, and they brawled. Newman wound up with a black eye, a swollen face, and many bruises.

The tale continues: Newman's agents had already arranged an interview for the actor with the producer Charles Schnee, who was in town casting for the Graziano story. When Schnee saw Newman, the day after the bar brawl, the actor convinced the producer that he had gotten the black eye and bruises as part of the previous night's "Battler" telecast—that's how realistic the fight scenes were. Schnee was so impressed, the story concludes, that he signed Newman for the role on the spot.

Another, and much more plausible, account is told by the director of *Somebody Up There Likes Me,* Robert Wise: "James

Dean had agreed verbally to do the part on the basis of the book. He wanted to do the film. I had never met Dean. All this was done through the studio and Charlie Schnee. I was off doing *Tribute to a Bad Man* when I was told that Dean liked the project and was waiting to read a script. But he didn't live long enough to read the script.

"Paul had already made *The Rack* at MGM. As a matter of fact, I recall seeing *The Rack* because *The Silver Chalice* wasn't anything to look at to see what one thought of Newman. So I remember seeing *The Rack* and liking it very much."

*The Rack* had originally been a teleplay. Rod Serling had written the script, and MGM was scheduled to do a motion-picture version starring Glenn Ford. Ford, however, withdrew unexpectedly, and Newman quickly accepted the role. It was a challenging assignment—a role he could sink his teeth into, the kind his twice-weekly classes at the Actors Studio had made him eager to portray. He would play a man accused of collaborating with the enemy during the Korean War. Arthur M. Loew, Jr., was the producer, and Arnold Laven, the director. Cloris Leachman (who was to become one of Joanne's best friends) was in the cast, along with Wendell Corey, Walter Pidgeon, Edmond O'Brien, and Anne Francis.

Ultimately, it was, no doubt, a combination of factors that got Newman the Rocky Graziano role in Schnee's production: one, his performance in "The Battler"; two, his screen presence in *The Rack;* three, that MGM had bought part of his contract from Warner Bros.

Robert Wise went to New York to meet with Newman: "Paul and I spent a lot of time together in New York. We wanted to make this right, as close to the actual Rocky as we could. So we spent quite some time with Rocky himself, long before we started to shoot. . . . We studied him, and studied his walk and his talk, and Paul studied and noticed that his heels were kind of round and produced that special kind of bouncy walk. . . . We both decided that we wanted to do only what Paul could make honest for himself, not just a mimicking of Rocky. I think he did a very good version of Rocky, his walk, his mannerisms."

Newman later noted: "Characters have a tendency to wipe off on the actor. For instance, I spit in the street. Now, I never spat in the street until I played Graziano. Graziano spits in the street." He also wryly noted: "I catch myself walking up Fifth Avenue and doing it. That's not Paul Newman of Shaker Heights, Ohio, and Yale University."

There had been talk that Brando had initially been sought for the role. When Brando was appearing on Broadway a few years earlier, he met and spent time with Rocky Graziano. "That's how Marlon picked up a lot of his walk and talk," Newman told the writer Peter Maas. "Now I've got to play Graziano, and they'll say I'm just like Brando."

Apparently the initial concept for the picture did not offer an ideal opportunity for a powerful characterization of the title role. As Newman recalled: "There had to be some character progression, or else the whole thing didn't make sense. They wanted it played for comedy, and you can't make anything threatening out of a buffoon. Rocky had to be more than a poor, misunderstood kid. He had to be brutal because his only business was survival." Newman did not play for comedy. And his sensitivity and underlying anger worked perfectly in his characterization of the boxer.

Appearing in the film with Paul were Pier Angeli, Everett Sloane, Robert Loggia, and Sal Mineo. A young actor, Steven McQueen, had a bit part.

While Newman was on the Coast filming *Somebody*, Joanne was in New York continuing with her television career. She did *Kraft Television Theatre*, *The U.S. Steel Hour*, *Alfred Hitchcock Presents*, and *General Electric Theater*.

Woodward felt her future was in television and on Broadway, not in films, even though she had received excellent reviews for *Count Three and Pray* in the all-important motion picture industry trade papers and had been singled out as a hot "new find."

Twenty years later Woodward would reminisce: "Yes, it was my first movie and also the only movie I really liked—that I really, really enjoyed. I never see it without total enjoyment and thinking, 'Oh, God, aren't you darling!' It's not a film I could be objective about. I'm not objective about any of my films, period. They're all like babies I've had. You know, I either like 'em or I hate 'em. In this case, I love that movie—I'm sure it's not great, but I love it."

But she, like Newman, complained about the studio system. She had been under contract for a year when she declared: "20th has failed to find what they consider a suitable role for me. Perhaps because I'm definitely not the glamour type." She might had added that she didn't *want* to be the glamour type, and any serious attempts by the studio to mold her into a femme fatale were met by a sincere "Forget it."

Joanne had continued to work in television to the maximum that her film contract would permit, and now she was willing to break that contract rather than pass up an opportunity to return to the stage in a new play. The studio relented, and Woodward took a part in the Leslie Stevens play *The Lovers*, which was set to open on Broadway in May 1956. The show's publicists claimed this was Joanne's "Broadway debut," which was stretching the truth, since she had gone on for both Janice Rule and Kim Stanley during the Broadway run of *Picnic*.

*The Lovers* was a somber drama in which Woodward portrayed a medieval peasant bride. There were problems getting the play in shape, and at one point Arthur Penn was brought in to take over the direction. He remembers that the play "almost made it." Also starring were Darren McGavin and Hurd Hatfield, and the play featured newcomers Robert Lansing and Pernell Roberts. (Many years later *The Lovers* was filmed as *The War Lord*, with Charlton Heston and Rosemary Forsyth in leading roles. The film was a critical and box-office disaster.)

In June, Woodward's new movie, *A Kiss Before Dying*, was released, and the event aroused unusual controversy: The dialogue contained the word "pregnant"—a very big deal at the height of the Eisenhower years. The Breen Office, the motion picture industry's self-censorship organization, would not allow United Artists to use the word in ads for the film, and at a preview of the picture in Chicago, the word was actually excised from the soundtrack!

Something interesting and more than a little odd happened

at this time. Although Joanne had vehemently declared herself *not* the glamour type, when she arrived in New York to publicize *A Kiss Before Dying*, she posed for photographers at the airport, wearing a sexy tight-fitting sleeveless dress, and sitting on top of her luggage, her legs crossed in quintessential pin-up style. Furthermore, the studio distributed photo art on Joanne that pictured her in very typical Hollywood-style layouts.

Whatever the cause for her uncharacteristic behavior, Woodward really hadn't changed. Earl Wilson, the Broadway-Hollywood columnist who thought, with good reason, that he had seen it all, was both amused and impressed by Joanne when they met at the Russian Tea Room. "The Jimmy Deans and Joanne Woodwards amaze me," he wrote. "They're so absurdly worldly at their age."

When he asked Woodward about James Dean, who had been dead less than a year, she said, "I feel he's sitting somewhere in hysterics over this whole excitement about him. He didn't talk much, except about the bongo drums. He'd find it funny thinking back to the Cromwell Pharmacy at NBC. When they raised the minimum to fifty cents, most actors couldn't go in anymore. We hated anybody that had a job."

She admitted her cold-water-flat days were behind her: "I've gone one step up now. I have a heated apartment—but you have to walk up five flights. I don't know why actors go through this. Maybe it's because they're crazy."

Joanne was in town not only to publicize her film, but to do more television. She was booked for *Kraft* and *The Alcoa Hour*; she was willing to tackle any role as long as it was good.

She did not warm up to compliments that compared her with other actresses, even when they were great actresses. When, after a television performance, a top Hollywood director told her that she was "another Bette Davis," she was puzzled. "I'd rather be the *first* Joanne Woodward than a *second* Bette Davis," she said. "And I'm sure Miss Davis felt the same way when she was getting started."

Another director said of Joanne: "All she delivers is talent. No particular glamour, not publicity—just talent."

Woodward, however, had no illusions about one thing: that

is, despite her dedication, ambition, and drive, another factor was operating, namely, luck. For as she has readily admitted: "I have been incredibly lucky."

In the spring of 1956, however, Newman's own luck encountered a stumbling block. MGM had released *The Rack* in April in selected cities; when it performed poorly, the studio pulled it from release. Robert Wise recalls: "They felt that *Somebody* was a stronger piece for Paul, and maybe *The Rack* would benefit by coming out after his appearance in *Somebody*." Surely it was a tense period for Newman; *The Rack* was not standing on its own and could be another box-office disaster like *Chalice*.

While *Somebody Up There Likes Me* was in post-production, Paul continued with his breakneck work pace. That summer he appeared on *The Kaiser Aluminum Hour* on NBC, and he was set for two *U. S. Steel Hours* and another *Kaiser* drama later that year. (The two *Steel Hour* appearances were so powerful they're still remembered today—the kinescopes are often shown as examples of television's golden age. Newman played an Italian immigrant in "The Five Fathers of Pepe," and starred in "Bang the Drum Slowly," about a baseball player who is dying of cancer.)

*Somebody* opened in New York on July 5 to excellent reviews. Hopes were high and Newman should have been a very happy man. Personal problems, however, were overshadowing his professional successes. They came to public attention a few days later when police in Mineola, Long Island, arrested Newman and charged him with leaving the scene of an accident and going through a red light. Although no other cars were involved, and no one was hurt, apparently Paul had resisted arrest. The police had handcuffed him and taken him in.

Newman, through the years, has freely discussed his drinking problems. "Sure, I drank whiskey a lot," he has said. "For a while, it really screwed me up. There are periods of my life in which I don't take any particular pride."

A severe bout with the bottle occurred during this period. The immediate cause is unknown. Some sources state he had already left his wife for Joanne but then, guilt-ridden, had left Woodward and returned to his family.

One of Paul's long-time friends from Studio days remembers this period well: "Paul was miserable then. I was commiserating with him one day. He kept asking, 'What should I do? What should I do?' And I finally said, 'Look, do you love the girl?' "

" 'Yes.' "

" 'Then marry her.' "

Although it is hard, today, to think of Paul Newman asking advice on such a personal matter, one must recall that this was a period of great emotional upheaval for him, and his pals at the Studio knew that his judgment, at this time, was often impaired by his problems with liquor.

Paul Newman later admitted: "In those days, there was, at times, a serious problem of moderation. Sure, there was a monkey on my back, and its name was booze. If things were going well, I would drink to celebrate. If I was in the doldrums, I'd drink to get out of them." Newman was hardly exceptional in this regard; he had run with a horde of hard drinkers and held his own with the best of them. He has told of a contest he and his pals indulged in: filling glasses with ice cubes, then with gin, the object being to gulp down the liquor before the ice cubes melted, then start all over. As Newman noted, it was quite a way to go.

Newman's arrest was in 1956, so not a word about his drinking problems appeared in the press. Substance abuse had yet to become an issue of public concern, and if someone was arrested for drunken and disorderly behavior, especially a celebrity, it was considered an acceptable part of the world they lived in. In fact, whether it was the doings of the still-powerful studio, MGM, or of private public relations agencies, Newman's arrest was reported almost as though it were promotion for the film. In resisting arrest, the accounts implied, Newman was acting "in character," that is, Rocky Graziano's character.

Fortunately, Newman realized the implications of his compulsive behavior and began seeing an analyst. Years later, when he discussed this process, he revealed that he learned a great deal about himself and that his problems were those that faced everyone in analysis: liking himself more; recognizing his achievements for what they were; not placing too great a bur-

den on himself in terms of striving to reach unrealistic goals. In
the eighties he admitted that he still had not conquered these
problems but has continued to work on them.

Eventually Paul Newman made the wrenching decision necessary to overcome the problem that was causing his *angst*. He
asked Jackie for a divorce. But she refused. Her reaction put
Joanne in a precarious position—she was seriously involved
with a married man with three children and no prospects for a
divorce. Nonetheless, when both Newman and Woodward returned to Hollywood, they took a house in Malibu with Joanne's pal Gore Vidal. Vidal has said: "It was a marvelous time.
Like a delayed adolescence for Paul and me."

If, as has been reported, up to this time Newman and Woodward were careful to avoid being seen together in public, from
this point on all pretense was over.

# 4

Now they were in Hollywood. Newman, his star on the rise, was in great demand and was immediately cast in two films that would be shot back-to-back. No small part of the excitement was the expected Academy Award nomination for his performance in *Somebody Up There Likes Me*.

Joanne's studio had also found a property for her, albeit by default. Judy Garland had been the writer-producer-director Nunnally Johnson's first choice for the role Woodward was assigned. Johnson felt that Garland was the actress to create one of the most complex characters to be presented to date on the screen—a young woman with a split personality, indeed several personalities. Nothing like it had ever been attempted in films before—*Spellbound* (1945) and *The Snake Pit* (1948) had been Hollywood groundbreakers in dealing with mental illness, but no film had as yet explored multiple personalities.

Johnson had gone so far as to meet with Garland and show her a sixteen-millimeter film of the actual patient, whose story it was, being interviewed by her doctors. Judy reportedly was very excited about the part and was anxious to play it. Nunnally Johnson, however, knew the problems in getting Judy to commit to, and actually complete, a film, so when he did not

hear from her, he dropped the idea of casting her in the role
and took a different tack. Both he and Buddy Adler now decided that, instead of going for a name, they should give the
part to a newcomer. Johnson had been impressed by Joanne
Woodward when he saw her in Dick Powell's TV drama and,
in fact, later said: "I never forgot her. And when I finished the
script for *Three Faces of Eve*, I still had her in the back of my
mind."

Although Joanne had both the director and the head of production in her corner, the studio's New York office reaction
was: "Who? Are you crazy? We've just read the script. This
part calls for a star. What about Susan Hayward?" Hayward,
under contract to Fox, was famous for playing troubled, highly
emotional women. Her portrayal of Lillian Roth's struggle
with alcoholism in *I'll Cry Tomorrow* had almost won her an
Oscar the previous year. Other stars the Fox front office
wanted to consider included Doris Day, Jennifer Jones, and
June Allyson.

Joanne Woodward later admitted that she had wondered why
she had gotten the choice role. "Then I learned they couldn't
get any of the people they wanted, so they decided to use me,"
she said.

Nunnally Johnson contradicted this. His version is that once
he and Adler had decided on Woodward, they battled the New
York office: "Finally we had our way."

Once cast, there was a big change in the studio's attitude
toward Woodward: "The thing that amused me was they met
me this time with a limousine when I arrived by train. The first
time no one even knew I arrived." She also said, in retrospect:
"Curiously, if I hadn't needed something big right then, I
never would have played it. I didn't read the script 'til I got on
the train. I came close to telling them I wouldn't do it." She
added, with typical candor, "You can be awfully wrong."

Johnson recalled that when Woodward arrived at the Fox lot,
she came in to see him, and they talked about the part for a
while. According to Joanne, "I was afraid I couldn't make the
part believable . . . three completely different women all in
one woman." There were other problems.

"Do you want me to use a southern accent?" she asked.

"Over my dead body," answered Johnson. "I've heard some pretty phony southern accents in *Baby Doll*, and I don't want any part of that kind of acting."

"Mine wouldn't be phony," Woodward told him. "I'd just have to slip back into it."

According to Johnson, "Joanne then made a few remarks to me in pot-likker talk, and I recognized it for the real thing." It hadn't occurred to Johnson, who was from the South himself, that Woodward was also from the South. "She had no accent of any kind in the television show. . . . I was delighted by the fact that she was a southerner. To be able to use this dialect properly was a great asset, both to the character and to the picture. As fellow crackers [Georgians], I think we hit it off very well from the first."

If Joanne hadn't recognized a great script, others had. Orson Welles was on the Fox lot at the time. He told his pal Johnson that he had never read a part "more likely to lead the girl to an Academy Award."

*The Three Faces of Eve* was to be a relatively small, artistic movie in black and white, and in CinemaScope. The script had a documentarylike structure; there was even a prologue narrated by Alistair Cooke. It also had a strong supporting cast, including Lee J. Cobb as one of the psychiatrists and David Wayne as Eve's husband.

Internalizing the complex characterization of Eve was surely a grueling and agonizing experience for Woodward. Her years of training, like Paul's, emphasized tapping what was painful in her own background to make believable and texturally rich what the character was experiencing.

Woodward has recalled: "I started on the characterization by exploring how each [of her personalities] moved and used her body—Eve White, the miserable, withdrawn woman—Eve Black, the loose, wicked woman—and Jane, the upright, straight-forward girl. . . . It was frightening, but it was a great opportunity for any actress."

Paul meanwhile was making another film for Robert Wise, *Until They Sail*, once again at MGM. The script, a good one by the award-winning playwright Robert Anderson, was based on a story in James Michener's *Return to Paradise*. Today Wise says: "For *Until They Sail* I had to, as I recall, sell Paul on the idea of doing the picture. He didn't respond one hundred percent overly enthusiastic. I think he thought the part was a little mild, a little soft. It wasn't like *Somebody*, which he was all out for."

In *Until They Sail* Newman plays a marine captain stationed in New Zealand during World War II. Basically a "woman's story," the movie is about four sisters (played by Joan Fontaine, Jean Simmons, Sandra Dee, and Piper Laurie) and how each one, in a different way, deals with sexual development and romance with soldiers who are about to go off to battle and possibly die. For Newman, unfortunately, the role was window dressing.

Another disappointment came in January 1957 when the Oscar nominations were announced and Newman was not recognized for his tour-de-force portrayal of Rocky Graziano in *Somebody Up There Likes Me*. Even Robert Wise says today, "I was surprised and disappointed when he didn't get a nomination, and I very seldom make statements like that about actors in my films." Wise also remembers, however, that that spring, on the night of the Oscar ceremonies, Paul and Joanne had a small party down at the beach. A friend of Wise's made a little mock statue which the group dubbed "Noscar." As Wise remembers, "We presented Paul with a Noscar that night."

Both Paul and Joanne were used to the fast-paced production of live television and the more leisurely building of character through rehearsals for the stage, so for them the grind of moviemaking was frustrating. Woodward described what it was like for her in these early days: "You get up at 5:30 A.M. to be at the studio at 6:30. Get your hair washed at 6:30 when you can hardly see, get makeup slapped on your face, be on the set at 8:30 ready to act. Ready to act? I'm not even awake. Then you're supposed to give a level performance of four pages of dialogue you just learned the night before and aren't sure you know, and do it with an actor you never met before. The rehearsal is interrupted by the cameraman saying you can't stand there because the light won't hit you there, and you trip over the cables, and people drop things on your head. Nothing did, but I had some awfully narrow misses, and I'm in constant terror of all those lights overhead."

As the Fox executives viewed daily rushes, however, it was apparent that a unique performance was emerging. Joanne may not have been the studio's first choice for Eve, but she was on their minds now.

Producer Jerry Wald was preparing a film of the best-selling novel *No Down Payment*, which would feature several of the studio's "rising stars." Wald, supposedly the prototype for the ambitious producer in Budd Schulberg's classic novel *What Makes Sammy Run?*, had been instrumental in furthering the careers of many of Hollywood's top actresses. He immediately cast Joanne in *No Down Payment*, and she started production as soon as she finished *Eve*. Martin Ritt, in Hollywood now under a long-term contract with Fox, directed the film.

Today Ritt says that he can't honestly pinpoint when he first met Paul and Joanne. "It could well have been on *Danger*, the live TV series that I was doing with Lumet and Yul Brynner." According to Ritt, "Joanne was really more of an accomplished actor than Paul was in the early days."

While the film was in production, Woodward noted, "Marty is a doll. Going to be an important director. As far as I'm concerned, he could direct me in every picture."

Also in the cast of *No Down Payment* were two highly attractive young stars who were favorites with young audiences, Barbara Rush and Jeffrey Hunter (the couple had recently divorced), and the young character actors Cameron Mitchell and Pat Hingle.

While Joanne toiled at Fox, Paul, after completing *Until They Sail*, reported to Warner Bros. to make his first film there since *Silver Chalice*. It seemed that he was again to be window dressing, this time in *The Helen Morgan Story*, a film biography of the famous torch singer. Ann Blyth was cast in the title role, even though her operatic singing voice was unsuitable. The vocals were to be dubbed by Gogi Grant. Judy Garland reportedly had wanted this part; Jane Wyman had also been considered.

The project, which had been knocking around Warners for over a dozen years, had—on paper—the makings of a hit. Michael Curtiz, the director of *Casablanca* and many other Warner Bros. classics, was directing, and Martin Rackin was producing. The story of Helen Morgan had mass appeal, as evidenced by the fact that Polly Bergen had recently scored a huge hit in a live television version of the late singer's life.

But from Newman's point of view, the film had a major and ultimately unsolvable problem: his character was neither hero nor heel. The actor was unhappy with the final result and with the way the studio was handling him. He refused to play the gigolo-acting teacher–camp counselor in *Marjorie Morningstar* and risked suspension of his Warners contract.

There was a role he *wanted* to play on the big screen, however—he wanted to re-create the character Billy the Kid—and he had been trying to sell Warners on the idea for months. "But," he noted at the time, "they think it ought to end happily. That's like filming the life of Lincoln and having it end happily; like having his wife come in and say, 'Abe, dear, I forgot the tickets for the theater tonight. We'll have to stay home.' "

Arthur Penn recalls: "I was doing *Playhouse 90* at the time— *The Miracle Worker* and scripts by Rod Serling. Fred Coe asked me to direct *Left-Handed Gun*. We worked with Leslie Stevens on the script." It would be Penn's first feature, but Paul would be re-creating the role he had originated on television.

As production progressed, the rushes indicated the director was developing a striking visual style for the film. Says Penn today: "I didn't know I was doing anything special. When I did TV, I would hand in a blueprint of every shot to the technical director. I worked the same way on *Left-Handed Gun*—I told the cameraman exactly what I wanted—flat, black-and-white, hard edge. I wasn't paying any special attention to 'the look.' The studio cameramen in those days were used to being little kings —they weren't too thrilled by us young whippersnappers."

Penn notes there wasn't excessive interference by the front office. "Warners was preoccupied at the time with big-budget pictures like *Spirit of St. Louis*, *The Old Man and the Sea*, and

*Lafayette Escadrille.* We were the Young Turks, the snot-nosed kids on the block."

The production took shape under the supervision of an executive who was sensitive to the creative people. "Fred Coe was a great producer," recalls Penn. "Whatever positive feedback we needed came from him. We all had deep affection for him. We were all family. We'd rehearse at my house even before we started shooting. We weren't supposed to do that, but we did. I brought in Hurd Hatfield. It was all very pleasant. I didn't overshoot at all—I shot what I needed, kind of like live TV technique."

Penn enjoyed working with Newman. "Paul is a hellion on a movie. Loves to have fun. We were all quite broke then. My wife and I had just married. She was pregnant. I was driving this old heap of a car. It used to embarrass the guards who parked the cars at Warner Bros. They'd steer me way into the back of the directors' parking lot. Paul knew what I was driving. One day after work I got into the car, and it sounded like it was falling apart. Terrible racket. What was going on? Then, way over at the side of one of the studio buildings, I spotted Paul. He was doubled over with laughter. He had put pebbles into the hubcaps. I pried the caps off, and we went out and had drinks."

Years later Newman reflected on *The Left-Handed Gun:* "I still don't like the film. It's artificial. It was taken from a television show which had no straight line to it." The film "was to be very basically the idea of a guy who fights his way up, and who realized that he's going to become a legend. Then someone says, 'Get out.' He's got a choice. Either he can get out as he's been advised, or he can sustain that promise of becoming a legend, but in order to do so, he must face the obvious prospect of his own death. He could have run away from it very simply. That's what I thought the picture should be about. But somewhere between the time when I shoved the idea of that down Warner Brothers' throat, and the time when the script was finished, something happened to the material. It didn't turn out that way at all."

Newman recognized the ability of Penn: "I knew he was good . . . it was evident that he'd really make it."

Joanne had finished *No Down Payment*, and studio publicity said she was going to appear next in *The Young Lions*, starring with Marlon Brando, Montgomery Clift, and Dean Martin. Suddenly she was becoming known, getting a "star" buildup, and already, inaccurate information was being disseminated about her. Articles implied that she had graduated from college. They also said that when in New York, she had experienced "the heartbreak that accompanies the business of twiddling one's thumbs"—this about one of the busiest young actresses in the city.

Such misinformation may have been part of the business, especially in those days when studios still had publicity departments that specialized in creating myths about their stars, but certainly Woodward disapproved of this approach—as did Newman. Both became wary of the press as they saw more and more distortion of fact reach print. Both had two films waiting for release, however, and the studio publicity departments were in existence to garner press coverage, not avoid it, so there was little either actor could do—for now, anyway.

At this point Newman was still not divorced, and all concerned wanted to be discreet. It was, however, no easy task, for, as Joanne learned, Hollywood was a small town, like the one where she was born. She later observed: "I spent all my life trying to get away from it. Everything in Hollywood is small town. Everyone knows everyone's business. If you date a boy, people whisper and ask, 'Are they going to marry?'"

And, of course, a major topic among the whisperers throughout 1957 was, "Are Joanne Woodward and Paul Newman going to make it legal?"

Although Paul had left his wife, he had not, of course, abandoned his three children, who were still living in New York. (The adult Susan Newman recalled that she did not know what the story was involving her mother, her father, and Joanne, until years later. "That had been quite a scandal while it was going on, and no one ever mentioned it. I'm very ignorant about my family history.")

Newman spent visitation time with his children the way most separated and divorced fathers do. He took them for rides, bought them toys; while he was visiting, he was the generous, benevolent prince. Then, after he left, the kids had to return to their mother and the "real" world. Apparently young Scott's temper tantrums (the child was then seven) had intensified in reaction to the growing conflict between his parents. The two girls, however, were still too young to feel the full impact of what was happening. Later, Jacqueline would move with the three children to the San Fernando Valley district of Los Angeles.

*The Three Faces of Eve* was previewed in August 1957 at Grauman's Chinese Theater, the movie palace famous for the handprints and footprints of stars impressed in cement in the forecourt. The Hollywood preview, especially then, was an all-important ritual, and word spread quickly as to whether a picture was a hot one or a dud. Many in town were more anxious to spread the word of a disaster—as Jack Benny once observed, "The only thing that depresses Hollywood people more than their own failures is one of their friends' successes!"

Fortunately, *Three Faces* played well, and Woodward's performance garnered strong applause. The feeling of hit was palpable.

Paul Newman was with Joanne at the theater that evening when the Hollywood columnist Sidney Skolsky approached them. Skolsky was blunt: "I thought you were great," he told Joanne. "You're certain to get an Oscar nomination. And you could win it."

"Aren't you sweet," replied Woodward. "I sure wish I could agree with you. And I'm not being coy. You know me—I'm not the coy type."

Paul could agree with Skolsky's prediction—but added a conditional clause: "If it's done strictly on merit."

Skolsky observed that perhaps Newman was recalling how he had been, to quote Skolsky, "unjustly overlooked." Skolsky bet Joanne then and there that she would *win* the Oscar.

"I don't want to take advantage of you," she said. "Winning

the Oscar is too much. I'll bet you three dollars that I don't get a nomination. I've never won a bet of any kind. Wouldn't it be awful if I spoil my record?"

Paul and Joanne were anxious to work together in a film, and now there was a suitable property at Fox, a Jerry Wald–Martin Ritt project—*The Long, Hot Summer*. There were reports that the studio's first choice for the male lead had been Marlon Brando, and Joanne noted that Wald had said, "Everyone says Newman is a road company Brando. It's like the Mark of Zorro on him."

Newman himself has said: "I've signed as many Brando autographs as he has. Sure, it bugs me. You're only in this business to have a sense of special identity."

Martin Ritt points out that Newman "admired Brando and was probably intimidated by him."

In actuality, the media of the day compared all actors with Brando, but a comparison between Newman and Brando was inevitable because, for one thing, physically they resembled each other, and, for another, it was widely publicized that all the actors involved in the Actors Studio—notably Brando, Newman, and Dean—made a point of researching their roles. Martin Ritt confirms that for *The Long, Hot Summer* Newman did go to Clinton, Mississippi, before shooting started, to research his role. "He always does that. It really is a mark of many of the serious actors from the Actors Studio. They all have a tendency to do that sometimes—make it overly important. But it certainly never hurts."

Joanne, like Paul, had very definite opinions on her craft: "For me, acting has very little to do with the intellectual process as such. Some of the groundwork may be intellectual, perhaps, but the only general rule you can make is that whatever works is good for you."

The screenplay for *The Long, Hot Summer* was by the talented husband-and-wife team of Irving Ravetch and Harriet Frank, Jr. The writing couple, it would seem, had a lot in common with the acting couple, but oddly enough, even though Ravetch-and-Frank scripts would figure prominently in the futures of Newman and Woodward, the couples never became close friends. Today, queried about Paul and Joanne, Irving Ravetch states: "We don't really know them. A close personal friendship never took hold . . . they were very reserved."

Furthermore, the script was not tailored to either Newman or Joanne. "We don't write that way for people," says Ravetch. He also recalls, "There was never a bad moment with either Paul or Joanne."

Martin Ritt did, however, get to know the Newmans quite well. He has noted what he feels is the secret of Paul Newman's great success as an actor: "Paul always had that cool sexuality, what I call a great fuckability quotient, which, let's face it, is part of what makes a star. Men and women are sexually drawn to stars."

Among the other actors appearing in *The Long, Hot Summer* were Orson Welles, Angela Lansbury, Anthony Franciosa, and Lee Remick.

Welles would make a particular impression on Woodward: "I think one of the most fun people I've ever worked with, once I caught on how to work with him, was Orson Welles. I loved him because he was so *there*—everything was just coming at you."

Joanne was pleased with her own part in the film. Her character, Quentin, is plain, introverted—the exact opposite of the flashy trollop Lee Remick had been cast to play, and Joanne tackled the role with gusto. As she explained: "I think I play best the parts that are far away from myself. . . . Quentin, who is closer to me than most, was hard to feel sure about. Marty [Ritt] said one thing that helped. I think it was practically the only thing he did say. He said, 'She has a tremendous appetite for any experience. When she cries, she really cries. When she laughs, she really laughs. There's no halfway measure for her.' "

Woodward insisted that she did not find the character until she had her hair cut: "After that, I knew just what to do." She could now easily relate to the role: "I knew what it means in the South to be twenty-three and not even engaged."

In the fall of 1957 both *The Helen Morgan Story* and *Until They*

*Sail* reached neighborhood theaters, and neither film was commercially successful. Joanne, however, was on the big screen in two hits—*The Three Faces of Eve* and *No Down Payment.* It was definitely Woodward's year. In a *Film Daily* poll she and Andy Griffith (who had starred in the critically acclaimed *A Face in the Crowd*) were rated the two top star finds of the year. Critics and television and radio commentators across the country voted Woodward and Griffith "the actress and actor giving the best star performances of 1957."

Joanne told the press at the time that she was living with a girlfriend—the director Victor Saville's secretary—in the San Fernando Valley. She was also quoted as saying that she was too busy to move into town, but that she and another Fox contract player, Joan Collins, were looking for an apartment to share.

While Woodward was loath to discuss her personal life, she was specific about her career direction: "I'd rather have a small role that I feel would be good for me than star in a part unsuited for me. I think I'd even risk studio suspension to turn down a role I felt wasn't right. I believe in what James Dean said, 'You can turn down a picture morally, if not legally.'"

Fox was touting her for an Oscar nomination, and she was reluctantly making the publicity rounds, answering quote-seeking reporters' questions on various subjects. She may have tried to play the game, but her answers were not always the most orthodox. When asked if she dieted, she did not settle for a simple no. She added, "I have digestive problems, nervous indigestion. I only have it in Hollywood, where you have to play politics. You have to be nice to the right people, and I've never been able to do that."

Joanne typified the new breed of actor. She noted, "Young actors have different goals today; we're no longer stereotyped. We want to play roles we like . . . we have an artistic drive, rather than a commercial drive."

She also preferred New York to Hollywood, and openly declared she had come to Tinseltown strictly for practical reasons: "I had to face the fact that the only way to make a name for myself was in pictures." She didn't even like California's legendary weather: "I love horrible weather," said Joanne. "I was raised on *Wuthering Heights.*"

There was one major problem with her New York–Los Angeles commute: she was doing it by train. "I never fly now. I hate flying," she said late in 1957. "One day after a bad flight I decided my number was up, and I haven't flown since. I love trains. I sit there for three days going to New York, reading science fiction and knitting." She also noted that she preferred the television done in New York rather than that done in Hollywood.

The wily columnist Sheilah Graham was not interested in this kind of information. She asked bluntly, "When will you and Paul be getting married?"

"I don't know," Woodward told her. "I'm about the only girl I know who isn't married. But I'm in no hurry. Too many divorces among my friends." Joanne also pointed out that because of her parents' divorce, she was being "more than careful about getting married."

She said to others around this time, "Either marriage happens or it doesn't. I guess I'm afraid of marriage. I tell myself, 'If it doesn't work out I can get a divorce,' but it seems to me that would be like scouring your skin off." It was apparent that Joanne was obliquely referring to Paul's agonizing situation.

What Joanne did not discuss, and what the press did not learn at the time, was that after filming had wrapped on *The Long, Hot Summer*, Paul apparently made a trip to Mexico. Parties involved would not discuss it then, and will not discuss it today, but by the end of the year Newman had obtained his divorce.

Over the years there has been much speculation on what went on behind the scenes. The story that most people like to believe is that Jacqueline saw the torment Paul was going through, and finally set him free. One fact is certain: The parting was not friendly, although fortunately for all concerned, the dirty linen was not aired in public. There was no acrimonious, irrational behavior that reached the press. Naturally, the absence of negative publicity was in the best interests of the children, but one must also assume that, emotional wounds notwithstanding, Jacqueline Witte received a lifelong financial settlement that satisfied her, since it produced a "No comment" attitude about the divorce that has continued to this day.

Fact: By January of 1958 Paul Newman was free to marry again.

5

Despite his love for and commitment to Joanne Woodward, Paul Newman was only human and not impervious to the charms of another beautiful woman. Sometime before his marriage to Woodward, Paul made the acquaintance of a spectacularly beautiful six-foot-tall blonde with a soft Texas drawl, a magnetic personality, and an adventurous spirit. Today, reflecting back on the interlude, the woman speaks of Newman as being "darling, sweet," "the most beautiful man I'd ever met." At the time Newman made it crystal clear to the glamorous sophisticate that he was already in love with another woman and was planning to marry her. He explained there was no possibility for any other relationship in his life. The woman accepted the ground rules and relates the two enjoyed a very brief but decidedly intense liaison.

The public, of course, had been reading more and more about Newman and Woodward and would soon have a chance to see them act together on television. Paul and Joanne had signed for the leads in an upcoming episode of *Playhouse 90, The 80-Yard Run.* It would be the first time since *Picnic* that Paul and Joanne worked together "live," and it would be the first time they worked together on television and were seen by the general public as a team (*The Long, Hot Summer* was not yet in release).

Mickey Rooney—at thirty-eight, only five years older than Paul Newman, but, as far as the public was concerned, a member of the *old* generation—was host for this particular *Playhouse 90* presentation. A fair amount of anticipation surrounded the show, since it was a television event to have stars who had established themselves in the movies doing live television.

Woodward was portraying an aggressive, ambitious rich girl who falls in love with a college football hero (Paul), pursues him, and marries him. The hero, however, cannot adjust to the business world and, when his father-in-law's business fails, finds he cannot earn a living. In despair, he turns to the bottle but later redeems himself and returns to his alma mater where he gets a modest job as a football coach. In the end, Joanne's overachiever character gives up her own successful career to join the man she loves.

Although the drama received acceptable reviews, the newspapers made much of the fact that the outspoken Woodward had commented that the ninety-minute script would have been a perfect thirty-minute vehicle.

Woodward told the press she would soon be going to Europe with her mother. The truth was, she would be traveling to Europe, but it wouldn't be with her mother.

A week and a half after the broadcast of *The 80-Yard Run*, Joanne was tracked down by a leading Hollywood columnist and asked, "When are you and Paul getting married?"

"Tomorrow."

"Don't kid me," said the reporter.

The following day Newman and Woodward flew to Las Vegas and were married. Paul had just turned thirty-three, Joanne was a month shy of twenty-eight. They had been waiting almost a year and a half for Paul's divorce, but studio publicists told newspapers, "They decided to get married while both were making a TV show several weeks ago."

Surprisingly, their wedding was typically Hollywood, not Shaker Heights or Georgia. Just like the relatively recent unions of Rita Hayworth and Dick Haymes, Joan Crawford and Alfred Steele, and other show business luminaries, the marriage of Joanne Woodward and Paul Newman took place in a glitzy Las Vegas hostelry (in this case the El Rancho Hotel and Casino), in the presence of a Nevada judge. Singer Eydie Gorme, entertainer Sophie Tucker, and comedian Joe E. Lewis were in attendance. One can only assume that the event was arranged for the Newmans by their various agents. Since it was certainly uncharacteristic of Newman, even this early in the game, to share an important private event in his life with the public, one must assume that the availability of the couple for publicity was in concert with Joanne's wishes.

Accounts of the event noted that this was "the second try" for Newman and "the first marriage" for Joanne. In general, the coverage they received at the time of their wedding was purely puff material, concentrating not on their relationship but on such details as the bride's wardrobe. "For her honeymoon trip, she permitted herself a special luxury," went one account. "My first fur coat," Joanne was quoted as saying. "I got black Alaskan seal instead of mink, just to be different. . . . I wouldn't have bought a fur coat, but everyone who had been to London in the winter said I had to have one, not especially to wear outside. To put on my bed at night to keep warm in those conservatively heated, airy London hotels."

Before embarking for London, the newlyweds quietly checked into a small Greenwich Village hotel for several days. (They liked New York's Greenwich Village in the fifties and would live there for a while— "but we're not Village characters," Joanne later candidly declared.)

In London Paul and Joanne stayed at the elegant Connaught Hotel in Mayfair. Again, in very uncharacteristic fashion for Newman, the couple not only gave interviews but permitted photographers into their honeymoon suite, where they were photographed (fully clothed, of course) in the bedroom. The British liked the two refreshingly candid Americans. Joanne said she was delighted that she and Paul had had an intimate wedding, unlike Jayne Mansfield's, which had had so many guests it was like a circus.

Newman's marriage to Warner Bros., however, was on the

rocks. "Warners was so tactful," he has said of the studio's actions when he and Joanne were on their honeymoon. "The studios I did pictures for on loanout—Fox and MGM—sent flowers, arranged a car for us, took care of theater tickets, but Warners left us completely alone, ignored us."

After their marriage newspapers ran follow-up stories on their "romance," stating how Paul and Joanne had tried desperately to fight their attraction to each other through the years, since "both were determined to keep their careers free of emotional involvement."

Almost all accounts ignored the fact that the feelings of people other than Paul and Joanne were involved. Jacqueline must have been hurt when she read accounts that stated: "The truth of the affair was and is this: Joanne and Paul started to date when his marriage was definitely down the river"; and "his wife and children were ensconced in a separate apartment, but the wife was being a bit on the bitter side." Of course, only insiders knew just how wrenching the divorce had been for all concerned.

To the outside world, the newlyweds were leading a fantasy existence, one that became even more like a fairy tale when the Academy of Motion Pictures Arts and Sciences announced that Joanne had been nominated in the best actress category for *The Three Faces of Eve*. The other nominees were Anna Magnani for *Wild Is the Wind*, Elizabeth Taylor for *Raintree County*, Deborah Kerr for *Heaven Knows, Mr. Allison*, and Lana Turner for *Peyton Place*.

Not only was an Oscar the most prestigious prize of them all, it also meant, in most cases, far more money for the actor on future projects, and—even more significantly—it meant power, the freedom to pick and choose not only scripts but the other people involved in a project. That is why, when Joanne Woodward told more than one journalist, "I don't feel the performance was my best," even Joanne's strongest supporters winced.

Studios spend hundreds of thousands of dollars campaigning for their pictures to win Academy Awards, and the awards can translate into millions of dollars at the box office.

"I'm not trying to wipe out any possibility of getting an award," she told Joe Hyams, "but if I get it, I hope it will be for my acting ability and not for the things I say or don't say on interviews."

Fox had two other pictures, and actresses, in the Oscar race that year, so Joanne was far from a shoo-in. There would be a divided vote as far as the studio's Academy members were concerned. Deborah Kerr was the favorite, and Lana Turner was a surprise nominee. Joanne needed all the favorable public relations she could get.

Joanne knew who she would vote for: "I think I will vote for Deborah Kerr. The Oscar for best performance should not be given for a single role; continued excellence should be the basis." Today this philosophy makes perfect sense, but in the Hollywood of 1958 statements like this were suicidal. People wondered why Woodward seemed to have a compulsion to "destroy herself."

In the all-important weeks between the announcement of the nominations and the close of voting, most nominees often become suddenly humble, kind, considerate, friendly, and thoughtful of their peers. Not Joanne Woodward: "If I had an infinite amount of respect for the people who think I gave the greatest performance, then it would matter to me" was a typical comment from the actress.

Joanne Woodward's colorful statements certainly stood out. They were a wonderful topic of conversation—that is, if you weren't in the employ of 20th Century-Fox. Of course, saying the "wrong" thing, especially at that critical time, only made Woodward more desirable and quotable to the press. They knew by now that Woodward was the exact opposite of the studio-produced stars—Woodward *didn't* say anything unless she *believed* it.

"I don't like getting myself in hot water," Joanne observed. "But suddenly I find that every minute I have to stop and think about what I'm saying. I can see what's going to happen. I'm going to have to stop giving interviews, because I'm always saying the wrong thing. I don't want that to happen."

At this point there was of course no question that she intended to pursue her career. "I am not the domestic type," declared Joanne. "There will be babies, but I couldn't sit home and just be a mother."

Her husband's career was about to take a forward leap. Newman was going to star with Elizabeth Taylor. MGM had bought Tennessee Williams's controversial play *Cat on a Hot Tin Roof*, and the role of Brick was being given to Newman. And in addition to the fact that it was a prize role, there was the prestige of being Taylor's leading man. She was one of the top young film stars in the world, already a legend at twenty-six and more in the public eye than ever because of her current marriage to the flamboyant Mike Todd. Todd was campaigning vigorously to get his glamorous wife the coveted Oscar, a prize that Joanne seemed to be doing her best to avoid.

Hollywood observers noted that Joanne was managing to offend the entire movie colony *and* her studio, "which had spent hundreds of thousands of dollars for an Academy Award campaign." But the truth was the truth, as far as Joanne was concerned, and she had no intention of changing. She applied that principle to her acting as well: "It's *not* telling the truth that would destroy me as a person and destroy my integrity as an actress."

She pointed out that she had worked for twenty-eight years to be as truthful as she could be, both as a person and as an actress. "Now I'm finding out that honesty doesn't always pay —at least, in good public relations."

She spoke to the New York reporter-critic Wanda Hale about winning the Oscar: "I don't care one way or the other." She was pleased, however, when the National Board of Review voted her best actress for *The Three Faces of Eve*. She said she felt this award "mattered" because from what she knew about the organization, she *respected* them: "They vote for who they really believe is the best actress." She was obviously referring to all the other considerations, besides the performance, that supposedly influenced the voting of Academy members.

Reportage on Woodward bounced back and forth between pithy, truthful quotes from interviews, to flowery, nonsensical tales from publicity handouts. There were fanciful accounts of her youth: "Joanne has been earning money since she was five, when she swiped the jonquils out of her own back yard and sold them for five cents a bunch." Another example: "She modeled when she was in high school and college for a dollar an hour, and in between classes held rummage sales on the street corner, and used the pin money to buy chocolate sodas. She also conducted variety shows on her front porch (playing all the leading roles herself) and charged customers a nickel apiece."

But this year she had received one interesting offer that she said she was tempted to accept. She wanted to continue to work in the theater, and John Houseman had invited her to perform Shakespeare in Connecticut. "Can you imagine Mr. Houseman asking me to do Shakespeare?" she exclaimed. "I only wish I could, but the studio won't let me off."

As Oscar time approached, Joanne said Deborah Kerr would win for sure.

There was always enormous interest in what the stars were planning to wear to the Oscars. Drop-dead glamour was always the byword. Elizabeth Taylor was going to wear a spectacular Helen Rose original, accented by the highly publicized diamond-and-ruby *parure* (matching tiara, necklace, bracelet, and earrings) Todd had given her.

Joanne Woodward had other plans. "I'll be the only Oscar nominee to show up in a homemade dress," she declared. Her outfit, a green satin-and-velvet creation, certainly looked Paris-couture, but apparently the actress was serious about having made the gown: "I am the most parsimonious soul in the world," she explained. "But I never throw anything away, and I know more ways of using leftovers than anybody else I know, and I rarely buy clothes."

Over at MGM *Cat on a Hot Tin Roof* had begun production. Certainly, Newman and Taylor were physically well matched. Elizabeth was at her sexiest, and in the film her costumes consisted of tight-fitting skirts, blouses, and dresses. In one sequence she wore a satin slip that, it seemed, she could only have been poured into.

"Paul and Elizabeth looked so gorgeous together I thought

I'd die," one MGM designer recalled with a laugh. "The director, Richard Brooks, had worked with her before, you know,
and knew how to get the best from her. But Elizabeth was not,
like Paul, from the Actors Studio school of training. She was a
product of MGM, and to say there was a difference in approach
is the understatement of the century."

Elizabeth was, however, a master at working the camera, and
while often it appeared to the other actors that she was doing
little in a scene, in the rushes they discovered her performance
was remarkably intense and on target.

Her husband, Mike Todd, was continuing his all-out campaign for his wife to win the Oscar. The man himself was so
dynamic, and his flair for showmanship, so dazzling, that his
excesses did not offend people; rather, they were amused. He
spent money on a life-style so ostentatious that nothing seemed
impossible for him to achieve. He seemed indestructible.

That is why the world was stunned when Todd's private
plane crashed on March 24, 1958, killing the irrepressible show-
man. Only a bad cold had kept Taylor from accompanying her
husband on the flight. The accident occurred on the weekend
before the Academy Award ceremonies. Production on *Cat* was
shut down. But the Oscar show would be broadcast Monday
night.

Paul and Joanne, for the first and probably the last time ever,
were part of the nationally televised Oscar ceremonies that
year. They presented the Academy Award for film editing and
bantered with each other in an affectionate and seemingly
spontaneous way.

The award for best film editing went to Peter Taylor for *The
Bridge on the River Kwai*. That blockbuster film was the favorite
in many categories. The *Daily Variety* poll (an annual survey
that canvassed people in the industry) had predicted *Bridge*
would be voted best picture, Alec Guinness (of *Bridge*) would
be voted best actor, Joanne Woodward would be voted best
actress, and Red Buttons (*Sayonara*) and Elsa Lanchester (*Wit-
ness for the Prosecution*) would win in the best supporting actor
and actress categories. The poll was not always correct.

After their stint onstage the Newmans returned to their

seats in the audience of Hollywood's Pantages Theater. People wondered if the little boy sitting next to Paul was his son, Scott. Joanne sat on the other side of Paul, in the aisle seat, of course. Toward the end of the evening John Wayne took the podium to read off the nominees for the best actress award. The tension was palpable. Joanne looked beautiful and anxious. Wayne announced the winner: "Joanne Woodward."

Joanne and Paul appeared shocked, then jubilant. All her statements about how it didn't matter, and how she thought someone else deserved the award, seemed to vanish as she ran down the aisle to claim her prize.

"I've been waiting for this moment since I was nine years old!" she exclaimed into the microphones. "I'd like to thank my parents for having more faith in me than anyone could."

Backstage after the program a grinning Newman embraced his wife as she held her Oscar. She looked relieved and happy, and he looked very, very proud.

At the postceremony party at the Beverly Hilton Hotel, congratulatory telegrams poured in. Orchids arrived for Joanne, with a note from Elizabeth Taylor. A telegram arrived from Deborah Kerr: "Congratulations, Joanne. Here I go again. Always the bridesmaid, never the bride."

Joanne's dress at the Oscar ceremonies had created a stir. Joan Crawford complained, "Joanne Woodward is setting the cause of Hollywood glamour back twenty years by making her own clothes." But Woodward's fans loved it—here was a real actress, not a studio-manufactured star.

When a museum in Georgia subsequently suggested it would like to have the dress, Woodward said; "I spent $100 on material, designed it, and worked on it for two weeks. I'm almost as proud of that dress as I am of my Oscar."

The morning after the Oscar telecast the TV critic and columnist Harriet Van Horne wrote that the show had been dull: "Only Joanne Woodward, clutching the gold-plated token of her excellence in *Three Faces*, conformed to Oscar tradition by crying copiously." Van Horne added, "One liked her the better for it."

Many years later Joanne said the exhilaration had actually

lasted only about "nine minutes." In its wake came an is-that-all-there-is? feeling, which lasted much longer.

Patrick O'Neal relates how Joanne's New York pals from her Neighborhood Playhouse days reacted. "The morning after she'd won the Academy Award, everybody was, like, stunned. The whole class was on the phone checking in with each other. 'Joanne! Do you believe *that*?' "

It wasn't Joanne's acting ability that had been the surprise, O'Neal explains: "It was that she was not the likely movie star type; she was a very pretty, young, talented girl, but my God! Look at who was out there in those days—you think of Vivien Leigh, Montgomery Clift, Doris Day—*movie star*, I'm talking about. Joanne's acting ability and talent are unique. But *movie star* is different. Paul, you know *movie star*. But Joanne was a surprise that way. She did it on acting ability, because that part was incredibly challenging. It just never occurred to anybody that you could win an Academy Award just by being good."

Her old classmates must have been equally stunned when the network TV documentary news show *Wide Wide World* devoted most of its ninety minutes to the new winner of the Oscar for best actress. The program interviewed other actresses at the Studio Club in Hollywood, all of them aspiring stars. These young women invariably stated they wanted to become stars because they felt they had something special to offer the world. However, when Joanne was asked the question "Why do you want to be a star?" her reply ignored the cliché and hit the bull's-eye: "Because it's exciting." Critics found her candor refreshing.

Soon after winning the Oscar, Joanne did her first sitting for the famed Hollywood photographer John Engstead. Engstead had photographed all the legendary actresses and glamour girls —from Clara Bow to Carole Lombard, Bette Davis, Ingrid Bergman, Marlene Dietrich, Lauren Bacall, and many others. He had done the actors as well, from Gable to Bogart, from John Garfield to Brando.

"Joanne hadn't mastered posing techniques for stills when she came in for her first sitting," recalled Engstead. "A nonegotistical, intelligent lady, Joanne hadn't spent hours in front of mirrors studying her face. I explained that each star has her own particular aura, which is what I wanted to photograph. I remember her asking, 'What is Joanne Woodward?' " The stills turned out beautifully. Woodward (and Newman) posed for Engstead many times over the next few years. Because of the unwieldy camera equipment, these sessions were time consuming. Joanne adapted. "The reverse was true of Newman," noted Engstead.

*The Long, Hot Summer* opened successfully in New York. Few careers had progressed so far, so fast, as both Woodward's and Newman's. They were eager to work with each other again, and as soon as possible, but for the time being Paul had to return to MGM and complete *Cat on a Hot Tin Roof*. The picture was an exceptional opportunity for Newman and he knew it; it offered a role that would show to advantage both his Actors Studio training and his movie star persona.

Elizabeth Taylor, needless to say, was still in a very bad state. There were many delays in filming and, in addition, there were problems with the script. In the play, Paul's character, Brick, is a latent homosexual, a plot point that had to be changed for the screen. The diffusing of the character's motivation meant that Newman's performance would be that much more difficult to get across.

Newman's sense of humor did not abandon him on the set. Everyone knew he had studied the famous (or infamous) Method at the Actors Studio. One day he decided to treat the director, Richard Brooks, and the others to what he thought was a funny prank. There is an emotional scene in the script involving a heated discussion about Skipper, Brick's dead, allegedly homosexual friend. At the climax of the scene Brick, wearing pajamas, storms out of his wife's bedroom. As he does so, he "inadvertently"—and symbolically—touches her negligee, which is hanging on the inside of the door. Rehearsing the scene, Newman, without warning, ripped off his pajama tops and began to climb into his wife's nightgown, crying, "Skipper, Skipper!"

No one on the set—not a single member of the cast or crew

—even smiled. They took Newman's prank *seriously*. Method actors were not known for practical joking during working hours.

One cannot blame Californians for not understanding the humor exhibited by certain "serious" actors and actresses, because usually there isn't a laugh to be had in dealing with them. The late actor Robert Preston once observed: "I know that gang that got started in the fifties. They're all guarded and withdrawn. They're a little suspicious. They don't believe anybody outside their group is really sincere."

Shortly after their marriage Paul and Joanne moved into a house in Laurel Canyon. "We live quietly," Joanne noted. "Paul reads scripts every night. I think he's going to wind up a director." She was right in predicting his future but wrong in predicting her own: "I'll never be anything but an actress, I'm afraid."

There was—and is—no question that marriage is a *serious* commitment for Joanne Woodward. "As a child of divorce, you don't go into marriage lightly. I had to learn more about myself. The only real teacher for an actress—or for anyone—is herself. Analysis teaches you to really look at yourself *honestly* —that's the toughest part."

Certainly the queen of the Old Guard, Hedda Hopper, did not approve of the outspoken Newmans. She criticized their life-style in typical Hedda fashion: "They bought no property, lived in a simple home without swimming pool, on a month-to-month basis, and drove rented cars."

Unlike stars from the old days, who would under no circumstances reveal that they were undergoing psychoanalysis, Woodward and Newman were totally open about it. Joanne said analysis had enabled her to be more accepting of herself. It's fascinating that she still didn't consider herself really attractive: "That's one reason why I'm in analysis. I know I'm not unattractive, but I still can't believe it deep down inside."

And she still wasn't, in her mind, a "movie star," despite her Oscar. A statement Woodward made at the time is no less relevant today: "Winning the Oscar tells you that you've made it, that you're a star. But nothing is really different . . . you never really make it once and for all. Every new part, every picture, you have to make it all over again."

And Joanne's definition of "star" definitely did not apply to herself: "I think a movie star is someone people recognize on the street. They go to see her movies whether the reviews are good or not. . . . I just don't feel like a movie star. I think you have to feel like it before you are one. I still hope I never feel like one."

When reminded that she once said that she hoped to marry an actor better than herself, she quipped, "I think I made good on that."

Following the Oscar, Joanne was anxious to get back to work. She rejected the lead female role in *Some Came Running,* however (a part eventually played by Shirley MacLaine). "I didn't want to work with Sinatra," declared Joanne. "He has a reputation for coming in late, shooting a scene just once, then running out, and I don't work that way."

And so she waited: "I'm the hottest unemployed actress in town," Woodward remarked.

Paul and Joanne, as co-stars, had been commercial in drama, and so that was the formula the studio wanted to repeat. The couple would have none of it. Eventually Paul managed to persuade the studio to use him and Joanne in a comedy they wanted to do. "Paul really had to *sell* them on me," recalled Woodward. "It's funny. The same people who gave me the award are afraid to use me, because they're not sure people really know my name. So no one quite knows how to handle me. . . . Except Paul, that is."

The comedy was *Rally 'Round the Flag, Boys!,* co-starring Joan Collins, Jack Carson, Tuesday Weld, Dwayne Hickman, and Gale Gordon. The film, based on Max Schulman's recent best seller, a spoof of suburbia, was Paul's and Joanne's first try at all-out comedy. Their parts were the type Cary Grant and Irene Dunne had performed so brilliantly in the Leo McCarey films of the thirties and forties. McCarey was directing this film, and the ingredients for a winner certainly seemed abundant. McCarey even liked his actors to improvise, and encouraged them to do so.

It was soon apparent, however, that the chemistry between Leo McCarey and his two stars, Paul and Joanne, was not producing the kind of results the director had achieved in past endeavors. The characters in a comedy have to play the material absolutely straight for it to work. They must be believable at all times, never heavy-handed—a light touch is essential. Cary Grant and James Stewart were masters at this type of acting, as were Irene Dunne, Carole Lombard, Jean Arthur, Claudette Colbert, and Doris Day. A knack for light comedy, however, would not prove to be the Newmans' forte.

According to Joanne, she made some wrong choices in playing her role in *Rally:* "When I wasn't playing small, I was busy making faces. I loathed myself in it."

In the picture she and Paul play a nineteen-fifties version of what today would be termed a Yuppie couple, with kids et al. Joanne's character is very cause-oriented, "the most public-spirited citizen in town." But the voice-over narration was a disaster, and the fantasy sequences, involving Paul and Joanne as a Sheik and his Dancing Girl, were forced and unfunny. Their best scenes together were their love scenes. Not unexpectedly, there was intensity, intimacy, and believability there. These moments, however, were all too few and far between.

Upon completion of the picture, Paul immediately returned to Warners to do a drama, *The Young Philadelphians.* He had gotten his chance to do "art" with *Left-Handed Gun,* now it was back to soap opera. Based on a popular novel, the film was directed by Vincent Sherman, who was adept at melodrama; *The Damned Don't Cry, Mr. Skeffington,* and *Affair in Trinidad* were Sherman *oeuvres.*

*Philadelphians* had a top-notch, old-line cast, including Alexis Smith, Billie Burke, Otto Kruger, and John Williams, along with a set of striking contemporary players, Barbara Rush, Robert Vaughan, Paul Picerni, Adam West. (Rush voiced the reaction women and men had when they met Paul: "He reminds me of a sculpted Roman statue.")

Fox cast Joanne in another William Faulkner story, *The Sound and the Fury*, with Martin Ritt set to direct. Her leading men were the Oscar winner Yul Brynner and Stuart Whitman. It was once again a tale of the decaying modern South, shot in CinemaScope and glorious color. The producer Jerry Wald had sought Lana Turner for the role of Joanne's mother—a once glamorous, but now timeworn figure—but Turner would have none of it; Margaret Leighton got the role. Joanne's part did not really offer her any challenges; it seemed she was the current first choice for southern belle roles.

That year at the Cannes Film Festival Paul was named best actor for his performance in *The Long, Hot Summer. The Left-Handed Gun* opened in the spring to decidedly uneven reviews. Critics either hailed it or hated it, but all recognized it as something interesting and different. Eventually it would become a cult film. "The picture was really discovered in Europe," states Arthur Penn today. "Belgian film critics named it the best first picture by a director."

Newman was by now intent on getting out of his Warners contract. For years he had been grousing about his relationship with Warners, and it had finally reached rock bottom. Never before had an actor discussed his animosity toward his employer in such a specific, and public, fashion.

With sarcastic humor Newman observed: "Major studios have a way of taking care of their contract players in even the most minute respects. For example, Warners has done everything possible to keep me from getting into a high income tax bracket."

But then he got more specific: "[It's] wonderful to know that I can go to see the head of the studio any time. Like last year [1957], when I went to see him when he did me out of five thousand dollars. He couldn't have been nicer. Of course, I never got the money, and I did get ushered out of the office, but he smiled all the time."

Even Bette Davis, at the height of her feud with Jack Warner in the late thirties, had not gone so far in publicly denouncing the studio or its boss. Newman had much more to say: "It's a wonderful thing for an actor's confidence to be under contract. For example, Warners had such confidence in me that, immediately after I was signed, they gave me to MGM on loan-out for four pictures.

"When I got back on my home lot, I was offered the pick of properties, which I refused. It was only because of my basic immaturity that I disputed the fatherly advice of the studio head. The fact that the pictures were dogs was only a trick of fate."

Newman wouldn't have gotten away with this years earlier; he would have been blacklisted by the moguls. But Newman was a star on the rise, and he was getting hotter all the time. *Cat on a Hot Tin Roof* was released in the fall of 1958 and was a huge success, becoming the top-grossing film of the year. *The Long, Hot Summer* was a substantial hit as well. It was obvious that Paul Newman no longer needed studio backing, but the problem was buying himself out of his contract. Warners, too, realized his enormous value. Negotiations began.

For an artist, the business side of show business is usually far more draining than are the daily creative skirmishes that are part and parcel of being a successful actor. For the Newmans themselves, trips back to the East Coast were like deep breaths of life-saving oxygen.

"I remember one time we came back over the Fifty-ninth Street Bridge," recalled Newman, "and it was as though someone had dropped the flag or something. We both were quietly weeping into our beer, at just the joy of coming back to where the action was."

The couple had taken an apartment in Greenwich Village. The big news was that Joanne was pregnant with their first child, so she would rest, while Paul exercised the clause in his Warners contract and signed to do a Broadway show.

**6**

Elia Kazan and Tennessee Williams wanted Newman to create the role of Chance Wayne in Williams's new play, *Sweet Bird of Youth*, opposite his Actors Studio pal Geraldine Page. For Newman, it was an exciting challenge.

While in rehearsal for *Sweet Bird*, Paul learned that he had been nominated for an Oscar for his performance in *Cat on a Hot Tin Roof*. Also in the running were Spencer Tracy for *The Old Man and the Sea*, Sidney Poitier and Tony Curtis for *The Defiant Ones*, and David Niven for *Separate Tables*. It certainly seemed Newman had a good chance of joining his wife as an Oscar winner, although, according to Joanne, winning an Oscar was hardly an answer to anything: "It's funny. Getting an Oscar makes you more secure, and, at the same time, more frightened," she remarked.

Newman, at this point, may have been *too* secure. His Actors Studio buddies and *Sweet Bird of Youth* would soon change that, however. As he later admitted: "I was getting successful and very confident, and that's exactly the quality that Kazan didn't want. And the thing that I give him points for in terms of the play is the way he handled me. I learned a great deal from that. Whenever he would give me a piece of direction or whenever I would come over with an idea, he would say, 'Paul, try this.' And I'd say, 'Okay.' Or he'd come over to Geraldine and say, 'Ah, right on!' I'd say, 'God, I thought she was really off a little bit, that's not what I expected her to do.' Then he would walk over to me and say, 'Ah, try it again.' He was chopping me down. By opening night, it was marvelous. I didn't have any security in the part at all. And that's precisely what he wanted."

Reports are that, for characterization, Newman's hair was tinted red, and his hairline was shaved. Kazan wanted the character to have a receding hairline and look a bit over-the-hill.

Chance Wayne, the character Newman was portraying, is a past-his-prime gigolo who has latched onto an alcoholic, drug-ridden, fading movie queen, played by Page. The characters are traveling through Chance's southern hometown where there is a political boss who has a young daughter whom Chance had left pregnant and with venereal disease. The girl had to have a hysterectomy, and the girl's father and brother want revenge. The climax of the play occurs when the movie queen abandons Chance, and instead of fleeing, he awaits his fate, which is castration at the hands of his enemies.

With Kazan directing, and a cast that included a number of actors trained at the Studio, rehearsals were, not unexpectedly, intense.

Meanwhile the pregnant Joanne was being totally domestic: "I sit around and read cookbooks and sew and wait for Paul to come home. And I love it." She was surprised at how she felt, and remarked: "I guess one's childhood conditioning really does stick."

The Newmans had an enormous brass bed that they had brought back from New Orleans. An antiques dealer had told them it had been used in a bordello. "Tennessee Williams considers it the perfect example of southern decadence, and is hoping that sooner or later I'll sell it to him," Paul told friends.

The couple often spent their evenings alone together, generally reading. Their fans' interest in their personal lives was keen, but Paul and Joanne were not Tony Curtis and Janet Leigh, and were seldom featured in magazine articles. Newman was quick to point out, "What we do together in the evening and during weekends is nobody's fucking business."

Newman and Woodward also did not frequent places like the "21" Club or Sardi's, establishments that still had a dress code; Newman refused to wear a tie. Instead they would go to a place like Jim Downey's, another landmark bar-restaurant in the theater district.

Paul bought a motor scooter for his commute to the theater, and later graduated to a motorcycle. His style and actions earned him the label of rebel, but, according to him, he was neither conformist, nonconformist, nor rebel: "I hate the word conformity, because it's mediocre. I think nonconformity is mediocre, too. I've gotten all this jazz about being a rebel. I hate anyone whose answers are made up in advance. I guess I'm trying to be an individual."

Newman bristled when advisers cautioned him to "stay out of politics," and really got ticked off when presented with the old saw that actors' lives belong to the people who support them, which to him was tantamount to saying "the public's entitled to know all the facts about your underwear."

When people subsequently dubbed Newman an egghead and an intellectual, he retorted, "I don't want to pose as an egghead, I want to *be* one."

*Sweet Bird of Youth* opened in New York on March 10, 1959. It was an evening to remember, the kind most actors never get to experience. *The New York Times* reported, "The acting is magnificent . . . and Paul Newman's young man is the perfect centerpiece." *The New York Post* said, "The acting is nothing short of superb."

Although the acting received virtually unanimous praise, the play itself received mixed reviews, but with movie star Paul Newman and Broadway star Geraldine Page in the leads, there was no problem with box office. In fact, even after Newman left and Rip Torn took over the role, the play continued to do well.

Nineteen fifty-nine had indeed begun as a great year for Newman. His return to the stage had been a triumph, and he also seemed a good bet to win the Oscar for his portrayal of another Tennessee Williams character. It was not to be, however—the veteran actor David Niven won.

On April 8, 1959, Paul and Joanne celebrated a far more meaningful event—Joanne gave birth to their first child, Elinor Teresa. (The infant was named after her two grandmothers.) The Newmans hired a full-time nursemaid, Tressie.

Newman resumed classes at the Actors Studio during his run with *Sweet Bird of Youth*. When, years later, he was asked if some Studio director or acting coach had inspired him, his answer was surprising: "I never had a good teacher. My debt is to the community of actors I saw working at the Actors Studio whom I tried to learn from—people like Kim Stanley, Karl Malden, Anne Jackson, Eli Wallach, Geraldine Page, Maureen Stapleton, and Darren McGavin."

Jack Garfein recalls Paul Newman during this period: "I felt that Kazan had had a great influence on him. Not just on his work as an actor. But I felt that Kazan had affected him regarding a kind of simplicity and directness. I still feel, even now, that that influence is there. I saw a change after *Sweet Bird* in the sense that I saw somebody very abrupt—like Kazan's manner—direct—sharp—three sentences, two sentences; the romantic idealistic young man had changed."

At the Actors Studio during 1959 Paul saw Michael Strong perform Chekhov's comic monologue *On the Harmfulness of Tobacco*. Newman was quite impressed, and felt the actor should receive a wider audience, so he personally produced and directed a short film of Strong's performance. The movie was shot in five days in the auditorium of the Orpheum Theater on Second Avenue in New York.

Newman later explained: "I did that as an exercise for myself, really. I did it mostly to see whether I could handle a camera and direct actors. It didn't turn out as successfully as I would have liked it to, although it got a very good review in *The New York Times*. The audiences were divided pretty evenly between those who loved it and those who hated it. There wasn't much middle ground."

"Paul wants to become a producer and produce the films he believes in," said his wife. "I'd like to go on acting and do the parts I really believe in. Fortunately, today, you can be a star *and* a character actor, which I am." This was a theme Woodward would emphasize over and over through the years.

Newman had a clear picture of where *he* wanted to be in the business. "I always felt I had a greater talent as an administrator than as a creator," he said. "I think I'm better equipped to be a producer or director. I don't get much fun out of acting." Acting was *work* to him—"Painful!"

New mother Joanne was feeling the urge to go back to work. *The Sound and the Fury* had opened to some good reviews, with Joanne, Yul Brynner, director Martin Ritt, and the writers Ravetch and Frank singled out for praise. Joanne was attempting to mend some fences with her studio, admitting they might well view her as difficult.

Paul was still appearing in *Sweet Bird* when *The Young Philadelphians* opened in the spring. By the summer his agents had worked out a deal with Warner Bros. It would cost the actor a reported half million dollars to buy himself out of his contract, but, his representatives assured him, they could get him upward of $250,000 per picture from this point on.

Paul later told an interviewer, "I had to find out just how far I could go as an actor without commitments to any one particular company." He said of the buy-out: "[It] kept me poor for several years. But I was free, at last, to make my own decisions. If I failed in anything, it would be my failure, no one else's. All things considered, it was the best financial transaction I ever made."

As it turned out, Joanne did not have to return to Hollywood to work. She and the baby would remain with Paul in New York where she would star in a very important and challenging film. Paramount was going to film Tennessee Williams's *Orpheus Descending* (retitled *The Fugitive Kind*) in Milton, a small town about eighty miles north of New York City. Sidney Lumet was directing, and Marlon Brando and Anna Magnani had been signed for the roles the playwright had hoped they would play on Broadway.

For this epic Magnani, who had scored so dramatically in the film of Williams's *The Rose Tattoo*, was again cast as a doomed heroine. Brando's character is an ex-gigolo trying to go straight, and Woodward plays an aggressive, rebellious southern belle who likes booze, fast cars, and men—even if she has to buy them. Hers is a low-down character—she knows that Brando is an ex-hustler, and she is *hot* for him. After a joyride in her beat-up sports car, they stop at a cemetery, where, in a highly dramatic scene, she falls on her knees and attempts to unbuckle his belt. It was a shocking scene for its day.

Filming this picture was, for Woodward, a bleak experience. She later confessed: "I hated working with Marlon Brando, because he was *not* there, he was somewhere else. There was nothing to reach out to." When she made this comment, she also noted that she wasn't saying anything behind his back, because after the picture she had let one thing be known: "The only way I'd work with Marlon Brando is if he were in rear projection."

But she felt differently about her other co-star. "I loved Anna Magnani. That beautiful woman. She was very kind to me, very gentle in her own strange way. Brando was mean to her, and I hated him for that. . . . Anna was very ambivalent about her looks. She'd tell the cameraman she wanted every line in her face to show on film. Yet she was very vain, and it was touching—she hid her neck with scarves and was constantly pushing them closer to her chinline. As you get older, and the wrinkles come, you realize the tragedy of the worship of the young in films."

At the time Joanne was ambivalent about her performance in this film: "I don't know whether I'm any good or not. All I could see was the insecurity in my eyes."

Filming over, Woodward returned to domestic life. "Tennessee Williams calls me 'just plain old Mary Cook from across the street,'" mused Woodward. Gore Vidal described her as "that clever girl who has everything under control," a description that irritated Joanne. "He's one of my four closest friends, and he thinks *that*?" she exclaimed. "Actually, I'm impatient, overly emotional, and almost hysterical. I have tantrums and throw things. My ambition to be the best actress in the world, as well as best wife and mother, exhausts and exasperates Paul."

It also undoubtedly exhausted and exasperated her. Years later Woodward admitted to a painful self-revelation—she said she had had a baby because that's what people did. She didn't know anything about having babies, and she was scared to death. She even said she didn't like children.

In the late fifties, in addition to her own recent motherhood, Joanne was contending with stepmotherhood. "I became [a] stepmother with that smug attitude that almost all stepmothers have: 'Well, of course, if *I* had raised them,' and—when *I* raise them, it will be different." As she admitted in retrospect: "[This attitude] is a lot of bull. Raising children is very, very difficult, and, certainly, I don't know more than anybody else and a lot less than most."

Although Paul and Joanne loathed being stereotyped as a husband-and-wife team, they did want to continue working together. Fox cast them in *From the Terrace*, a film based on the steamy John O'Hara best seller. Paul and Joanne would be portraying husband and wife, but there was the unexpected twist that Newman's true love interest in the story would be Ina Balin. Myrna Loy was signed to play Paul's alcoholic mother, and Leon Ames, his father. Mark Robson (*Peyton Place*) would direct.

In the film Newman is a stockbroker who marries a wealthy heiress (Joanne), then begins neglecting her. Woodward's character, who is highly charged sexually, starts having an affair with her former lover. Then Newman's character falls in love with someone else (Balin). And though they fight their love for each other, and he is in agony about leaving his wife, he eventually does leave her to marry his new love.

Paul and Joanne were instrumental in having Patrick O'Neal cast as Joanne's lover. O'Neal was a fellow student from their Neighborhood Playhouse and Actors Studio days. He recalls: "I was performing a Dorothy Parker short story at the Studio. Afterwards Paul and Joanne came over and told me how much they liked it. They were about to cast *From the Terrace*. Mark Robson hadn't heard of me, nor had anybody. Paul and Joanne never said they did it, but all I know is, the phone rang the next day telling me to meet Mark Robson, and I was in the picture later that day. I'm sure they had a lot to do with it—in fact, *everything* to do with it."

After completing *From the Terrace*, the bicoastal Newmans were about to become the international Newmans. Now that he was free of his long-term contract with Warner Bros., Paul's agents were close to finalizing the deal for him to star in one of the biggest and most prestigious productions of recent years.

A novel of enormous significance and popularity had hit the best-seller lists. Among the Jewish community in particular, the proposed film version of the book was eagerly awaited. Leon Uris's *Exodus* dealt with the founding of the modern state of Israel. It was an epic tale, and amidst great publicity Otto Preminger bought the film rights.

When Paul Newman was signed for the lead in *Exodus*, it was another prestigious and, at the same time, ultracommercial step up for the thirty-five-year-old actor. Newman was rapidly becoming first choice for every role in Hollywood.

During the negotiations few debated whether or not this combination of actor and director was actually a good one. Newman had recently said of his approach to a role: "I start intellectually. What clogs me up in my acting is my black-and-white attitude. I condemn myself because I think I work too intellectually." The legendary Preminger, on his part, was from the "just perform the script, don't ask questions or offer suggestions" school. He may have been a godsend to actors with no knowledge of their craft, but if a performer was interested in delving into the motivations of his and other characters, then Otto was most definitely not the man to have as director.

In February 1960 Paul, Joanne, and baby Elinor (dubbed Nell) went to Israel for the filming, and remained there for three and a half months. Joanne, for the first time in her marriage, had put her career second to family, and as events would prove, it would not be the last. For Paul, the project was an unhappy experience—one he will not talk about to the present day.

Preminger, on the other hand, said in later years that he had liked and "approved" of Newman, both personally and professionally. He found him genuinely sincere and concerned about the film, but early on Preminger had set him straight about making changes in his role. Shortly after his arrival on location Newman had approached Preminger with rewrites—Preminger wouldn't even read them. He told the actor that his refusal to read the suggested new pages had nothing whatever to do with the quality of the changes proposed; if they *were* good, Preminger reasoned, and he used some of the ideas, Newman would be back "with more changes." Newman studied Preminger for a few seconds, and then said, "Okay, I think you're right." Preminger found that during production Newman was not reluctant to help other actors—the better all performed, the better the final result. That was fine with Otto.

Jack Garfein discussed how someone like Paul could get along with Otto Preminger: "If anyone could deal with Preminger, Paul could. He's got a great sense of humor and is able to do whatever he has to do, and somehow manages to shut off this other part.

"I always admired that about Paul. He's able to say, 'Okay, this is the guy, that's what he does, all right, we've gotta make the movie.' Also, he'll never insult you. Preminger probably never even knew what Paul thought. That's his rare ability. It's sustained him over the years."

In his many years on the Hollywood scene Preminger had virtually seen and done it all. Nothing anyone said or did could surprise him, he thought. But Paul Newman surprised him. Here was a sex symbol who was off limits to that special breed of Hollywood woman who, to quote Preminger, "circles young men like Newman like sharks ready for the kill." To one attractive woman, a writer on location to do a piece on the film, Preminger said: "Try seducing him; I would wager no woman would be successful. He's an oddity in this business. He really loves his wife."

During production Paul, Joanne, and little Nell did a great deal of sight-seeing throughout Israel. They acknowledged, then and today, that film stardom certainly provided them an extraordinary opportunity to see the world. However, the

Newmans were faced with the realization that international stardom was going to infringe drastically on their ability to enjoy any kind of private life. A minor incident occurred in Israel. The family was breakfasting in a hotel dining room when they became aware that more than a hundred people were staring at them through a window. Woodward noted, "I'll never be able to go to the zoo again."

Back in the States, *The Fugitive Kind* opened in the spring. "And now the screen is struck by lightning!" proclaimed a key ad line for the picture. Paramount bought the huge sign overlooking Times Square and Broadway to advertise the movie, but it was all to no avail. The picture did not sustain its promise of big box office, and reviews were decidedly mixed.

*From the Terrace* was released in the summer and became a commercial, if not a critical, success. Fans of Paul's and Joanne's were undoubtedly dismayed that the duo played characters who did not like each other. Joanne later said she had taken the part in *Terrace* because it gave her a chance to wear glamorous clothes.

After the filming of *Exodus* had been completed, the Newmans left Israel directly for Paris and another picture they were scheduled to make together, to be directed by their friend Martin Ritt. The film was called *Paris Blues*, and Sidney Poitier and Diahann Carroll would be their co-stars, and Louis Armstrong had been cast in a featured role.

The film was based on a novel by Harold Flanders that told the love story of a black jazz musician who lives in Paris and a black schoolteacher who is there on vacation. In the movie adaptation two buddies—a black musician and a white musician—who live in Paris meet two tourists, one black, one white. These were the last days of the Eisenhower years, and the civil rights movement had not caught fire yet. Nonetheless there were elements of social consciousness inherent in the story, which was no doubt the reason all concerned had selected the project.

In real life Diahann Carroll was in the midst of a passionate love affair with Poitier, but she was still highly career-oriented. She knew Poitier, Paul, and Joanne were far more experienced actors than she was, and she studied them carefully. She was particularly impressed by Joanne, and noted how impressed Marty Ritt was while watching Woodward in the rushes.

The picture was a happy experience for the Newmans. "The first time we were in Paris, making *Paris Blues,* we lived in Montmartre and had a garden," recalled Joanne. "Paul would stand out in the dead of winter with all the neighbors looking over the gates, grilling steaks in the yard."

Back home in America, the country was becoming charged with a political enthusiasm that it had not known in decades. The year 1960 marked John F. Kennedy's rise to national prominence, and the Newmans were among his staunchest supporters. When Kennedy won the presidential election, many liberal show business people for the first time became visibly involved in national politics. Among them was Paul Newman, the man who had often described himself as an "emotional Republican."

After *Paris Blues* the Newmans returned to New York City. Paul's earnings from *Exodus, From the Terrace,* and *Paris Blues* had paid off the $500,000 debt to Warners. The next vehicle he chose was a small black-and-white film to be shot in New York. Robert Rossen, who had co-written the screenplay, was directing *The Hustler* for 20th Century-Fox. The film, based on a relatively obscure novel by Walter Tevis, was about losers. And the Rossens of the business liked actors who were willing and eager to attempt creative, offbeat projects. Newman was one such actor.

In *The Hustler* he would be playing Eddie Felsen, the pool hustler of the title. "I had a good feeling about this one right from the start," recalled Newman. "When I was preparing for the part, most of the furniture was removed from our dining room to make way for a billiard table. I then spent many happy hours at home playing with Mosconi [pool expert Willie Mosconi]—what I call a perfect way to rehearse a part."

Piper Laurie, who was cast as Eddie's slightly crippled girl-friend, had not seen Newman for four or five years. "I saw him again at a rehearsal in New York," she recalls. "We had two weeks of real rehearsal, not just costume fittings, et cetera. We sat around the table that first day, and I remember I went through this thing that a lot of us have with Paul—it's hard to look at him." But, she continued, once she got past that, and was able to see him as a real person, she found it extremely easy to be with him and to work with him.

Portraying a character with a physical deformity is a delicate undertaking. "We did various experiments," recalls Laurie. "I walked around with pebbles in my shoes. Finally, I just did it without anything, because Rossen didn't want an obvious limp; he didn't want it consistent, because he felt he wanted the audience to be aware of it sometimes and not other times."

When shooting began, Laurie and the Newmans became friendly. She recalls: "Paul and Joanne invited me to a benefit for the Actors Studio, and they arranged for my date, Gore Vidal. The four of us went to the benefit. It was held at Roseland. It was the first and only time I saw Marilyn Monroe. We were sitting around a big table, and I remember Pat Neal came by. And there was such love towards Paul from everybody. He was sitting next to me, and we talked a little bit. I found it hard to believe that he was as modest, as unassuming, and as straight as he said he was, but he was! He really didn't believe in himself as an actor at all. He thought he had great limitations, and owed everything to other people—the Actors Studio, Joanne— he seemed not to take credit for himself. I've never seen an actor develop like he has. I don't know of another actor that's grown as he's grown. I mean I've known a lot who were gifted and stayed right where they were, and twisted that gift around, but haven't matured—certainly not in a graceful way. They somehow become a caricature of themselves. They get into the habit of using the safe things that they know work. Paul's really courageous. He was always very serious, slightly apart from the so-called movie actors. Acting with him, I never felt intimidated or afraid to try things myself."

Laurie makes an interesting observation on *The Hustler*: "Rossen expected it to be the critical and commercial hit that it was. . . . I think he said something about we were all going to win Academy Awards. I thought that was sort of crazy, but sweet.

"I knew it was a good script. I knew it by page forty, that

there was something special about it, but I really didn't think beyond that. I made my decision to do it on page forty, even before you got into my character. I didn't even finish reading the script, as a matter of fact."

Making the film was not a joyous experience. "It was just a working set," recalls Laurie, "just intense work—not particularly fun at all. I never met Gleason, although I visited the poolroom. It was fun to meet George C. Scott. It was really just a working set—some fun, some anger."

Newman and Jackie Gleason, cast as Minnesota Fats, established a camaraderie. At one point, Gleason recalled, Newman got cocky about his pool playing and challenged Gleason to a game. They bet fifty bucks, and after Newman broke the balls, Gleason knocked all fifteen of them in before Newman got another turn. Gleason laughingly recalled that the next day Paul paid him off with five thousand pennies.

The real-life pool ace, Minnesota Fats, noted years later that "Jackie Gleason's skill with a billiard cue made him a natural for *The Hustler*, but Paul Newman could have used a few tips on the game."

Joanne was pregnant again, so the Newmans moved into a large apartment on New York's East Side. People who knew the couple at this time remember that the abode became "a sort of salon for the 'radical chic,'" where people from the political world mingled with people from the show business and literary worlds.

While Paul completed *The Hustler*, *Exodus* opened. It was a reserved-seat attraction in its initial engagements, and the success of the film sent Newman's stock soaring. Although reviews were mixed, it was a box-office smash, not only one of the highest-grossing films of the year, but easily Paul's biggest money-maker up to that time.

Through the years Newman's Actors Studio pal Jack Garfein had approached Paul with various scripts. Newman's criterion was not, "Is it commercial?"; rather, it was, "Is it *good*?" He did not look for the easy deals, not even after *Exodus*. Garfein recalls: "I sent Paul a script that David Merrick was interested in doing, and Paul got in touch with me and said, 'If you had a script like *Something Wild* [Garfein's critically acclaimed but commercially unsuccessful film, which had starred his wife, Carroll Baker], that's something I would do, but not this.' It's like he was saying to me, you stick to what *you* do—don't try now to be commercial, so to speak; just do your thing and I'll be happy to do it."

Garfein wanted to do a film version of *The Wall*, John Hersey's novel about the Warsaw Ghetto uprising. He was rebuffed by the Hollywood moneymen, however, some of whose reactions he found appalling. "One producer told me, 'Who wants to see a bunch of Jews fighting?' And this to a man who had been at Auschwitz—this is the way they talked."

Garfein had even talked to David O. Selznick, who had acquired the rights to the book on an option. But Selznick insisted that Jennifer Jones play the female lead. "We'll put a Jewish nose on Jennifer Jones," he told Garfein.

Eventually Garfein phoned Paul and the men met for lunch to discuss the project. *Garfein:* "I said, 'Paul, I want to do this film. If you say yes, there's a chance of my doing it.' He said, 'Jack, at this point in my career I see a script—gimme a script.' I said, 'Paul, there's no way I can get the money on this for a script, for anything, unless you say yes—if you say yes, I'll develop a script and we'll go from there.'

"At lunch at the Beverly Hills Hotel he said, 'Yes. The story is important. I know your background and relation to it. Okay, you got a yes. Go. Call my agent, then call my lawyer, I'll say fine, that I'm committed, they can put up the money, I trust you and go ahead and develop it.' "

Even with Paul Newman as part of the package, however, Garfein could not get any of the studios to put up the seed money to do a script. "All those nice Jewish producers and guys gave me some of the most vulgar replies you can possibly imagine."

Meanwhile, Newman was filming *Sweet Bird of Youth* for MGM. Richard Brooks, the director of *Cat on a Hot Tin Roof*, had adapted Williams's play for the screen. Because of censorship codes, and Hollywood being Hollywood, the plot had been altered considerably. At the climax Chance Wayne would not be castrated; he would merely be beaten up, and, even more ludicrous, instead of being kept from the political boss's daughter (now played by Shirley Knight), Chance and the girl would drive off into the sunset.

Industry trade papers had been speculating on the casting of the lead female character, Alexandra del Lago, indicating that it was the perfect vehicle for Ava Gardner, Lana Turner, or Rita Hayworth. But theater fans breathed a sigh of relief when Geraldine Page was signed to re-create her mesmerizing performance as the self-destructive over-the-hill love goddess.

Visitors to the set noted that, ironically, the MGM wizard of coiffure, Sydney Guilaroff, along with the studio's costume and makeup experts, had turned Ms. Page's character from the blowsy harpy of her stage Alexandra into a glamorous movie queen. Screen audiences would not accept the tawdriness of the stage character, claimed the front office.

Not only was Page too youthful-looking and well-groomed to be an over-the-hill star, but Newman, as they insisted on photographing him, was much too good-looking and youthful to be an over-the-hill gigolo in this Technicolor version of the story.

Joanne has revealed: "Paul thought it would be a breeze. Because he had played it on the stage so much, he knows it backwards, but the movie version is so different. It's almost like another story."

During the filming the Newmans were living in a Hollywood house that they had rented from Linda Christian. Joanne was very pregnant by now and was trying to cope with Nell, who was going through "the terrible two's." Woodward had engaged a southern woman, who was nanny for Nell and would help with the baby that was on the way. Joanne felt that the new baby would be the best thing that could happen to Nell, their only daughter, and she admitted that she and Paul were "sort of hoping for a boy this time."

Jacqueline and Paul's three children had moved to California on a more permanent basis. When Paul was working there, the children spent most weekends with their father, stepmother,

and half-sister, Nell. Scott was then ten, Susan eight, and Stephanie six, and especially while they were still young, Paul
Newman was intent on keeping his children out of public
view. The adult Scott Newman recalled, "As a child, my parents hid me from the theater, the press, and all those other
chaotic elements."

Joanne denied that there was any jealousy between her child
and Paul's older children. In fact, she said, the older children
spoiled Nell; the girls treated her like a little doll, and even
Scott was wonderful with her.

Paul and Joanne's second daughter, Melissa, was born on
September 27, 1961. That same day, *The Hustler* opened in New
York, and with this significant film Paul's prestige as an actor
climbed yet another notch. Via *The Hustler* Newman left the
arena of traditional leading men and proved he could easily
play rebel heroes, anti-heroes, and, if he wanted to, even vil-
lains. American audiences were ready to accept an American
leading man as a hero with the characteristics of a heel, one
who did not have to die or be reformed at the film's end. *The
Hustler* paved the way for the screen's rebel anti-heroes of the
decade, since not only was it a critical smash, but the public
responded as well. It seemed certain, once again, that Newman
would get an Oscar nomination. Jackie Gleason was also being
touted as a contender for an Oscar in his supporting role.

Generally in the career of an actor for every high point there
is a low. On the heels of *The Hustler*'s success, *Paris Blues* opened
and bombed—commercially and critically. Its failure went virtually unnoticed, however, and Newman's price-per-picture
spiraled upward. He had been paid $350,000 for *Sweet Bird of
Youth,* so no one, especially his agents, could understand why he
accepted a mere cameo role in his next film.

Newman's pal A. E. Hotchner had turned several of Ernest
Hemingway's Nick Adams stories into a full-length screenplay
for Fox, *Hemingway's Adventures of a Young Man.* Another Newman pal, Marty Ritt, had agreed to direct, and Jerry Wald was
producing. Newman eagerly joined his friends as a small part
of the package, once again portraying the battler. With heavy
character makeup, he would be almost unrecognizable. Fox's

up-and-coming young star Richard Beymer had been cast as Nick Adams.

Newman's advisers were horrified when the actor took this role. He later noted: "They screamed at me out there. I was cheapening myself by playing a bit part, they said. I was a star. I couldn't play a bit. You know why I did it? It was the part of a forty-five-year-old, punch-drunk fighter. It was a good part, and I wanted to play it for that reason alone. But I had another reason. It was the part I'd played before on TV . . . I wanted to do it again for myself. I wanted to sit down and look at the kinescope of the TV show, and then look at the movie and see what I've learned about acting over the years." As things turned out, Newman's "bit" was the most interesting thing in the picture.

Early in the new year Oscar nominations were announced and Newman was, as expected, up for best actor for *The Hustler*. As always, competition was formidable: Spencer Tracy and Maximilian Schell were both nominated for *Judgment at Nuremburg*, Charles Boyer for *Fanny*, and Stuart Whitman for *The Mark*.

*The Hustler* was nominated in eight other categories: best picture, best direction, best actress (Laurie), best supporting actor (Jackie Gleason and George C. Scott—although Scott refused his nomination), best screenplay, best art direction, and best cinematography. The powers-that-be predicted that Paul was the man who would cop the prize: "He deserves it—he should have gotten it for *Somebody Up There Likes Me*."

Joanne accompanied her husband to the ceremonies. When Maximilian Schell won, the usually controlled Woodward was livid. She later said that she was ashamed to admit it, but she was "wild . . . furious and upset and in tears." She added: "Backstage, I made a terrible spectacle of myself. I wouldn't even speak to Max, and it certainly wasn't *his* fault."

Joanne felt Paul had been cheated. "I was so sure he was going to win," she said. Joanne also said she was sure Paul was "bitterly hurt and disappointed," although it was not evident in his actions.

The Newmans had bought a house in Connecticut and were determined to make their permanent home in the East, primarily because they felt a "normal" life was easier to achieve there. Their Connecticut neighbors were A. E. Hotchner and his wife, Ursula. Paul and Hotch had bought a boat they would share, naming it the *Ca Ca de Toro* (translation: bullshit). Hotchner, known primarily as Ernest Hemingway's buddy and biographer, was a man's man and the kind of guy Paul liked to spend time with. They would often go fishing on the boat, but, in reality, it was just a great excuse to get away from the world, and, in Hotchner's words, "consume great quantities of beer."

Making the East Coast their home base did not endear the Newmans to many of their Hollywood peers. In reality, of course, since filmmaking was still mainly in Hollywood and on location—and the Newmans were not abandoning film work—their household became bicoastal.

In the summer of 1962, for example, all packed up and moved to California where Joanne would be working again. Richard Beymer, who had co-starred with Paul a few months back, would now be Joanne's co-star on the Fox lot, and the two would be re-creating roles that Kim Stanley and the newcomer Warren Beatty had originated on Broadway. The film, tentatively titled *A Woman in July*, was an adaptation of William Inge's *A Loss of Roses*, which had flopped on Broadway.

After the birth of Melissa it had taken Woodward three months to get herself back in shape. She had been very disciplined with her first child, and within five weeks had been before the cameras in *The Fugitive Kind*. But this time, since she hadn't been signed to work right away, she had let herself go. "There was no activity to occupy me," she observed, "so I got lazy and didn't exercise, and I ate too much. I think not having enough to do causes overweight more than anything else. If your mind is on other things, you don't have time to contemplate food. I gained thirty-five pounds, and I kept telling myself that I'd lose it when the baby was born. But, to my horror, I found myself faced with twenty pounds that had to be taken off. I'll never do that again."

In *A Woman in July* Woodward was portraying Lila, a down-on-her-luck showgirl—a pathetic and poignant character—a woman who takes refuge with an old friend in a small midwestern town. The recently deceased Marilyn Monroe, who had, like Joanne, been under contract to 20th Century-Fox, would have seemed the obvious choice for this kind of part. Woodward admitted, "I had a visual image of Lila as Monroe. But," she hastened to point out while working on the film, "I'm not imitating Marilyn. Lila is."

The screen story was reminiscent of Monroe's life: Lila has been brought up in a foster home, suffers mental breakdowns, and attempts suicide. Eventually she has no place to go—and no career. She becomes a stripper. Gypsy Rose Lee, cast in a small part in the film, gave Woodward pointers on the art.

The picture, in rough assembly, left much to be desired, and so, months later, Joanne was back on the lot for retakes. The film version had not jelled any better than the stage version had. The studio pushed back a release date.

Newman's *Sweet Bird of Youth* and *Adventures of a Young Man* sailed into—and quickly out of—theaters that year, neither one a commercial hit. His next project, however, was to be an entirely different matter. *Hud* was to be a landmark in Paul Newman's career, as it was for the director Marty Ritt.

Today Ritt discusses the *Hud* deal: "Paul and I went into business together. I made a deal at Columbia and at Paramount with Paul, in which I was to direct two pictures, and he was to act in two, and the third was free." (While Newman and Ritt would produce the third film, Newman would not act in it, nor would Ritt direct.) The first film under this deal was *Hud*, which Ritt co-produced with Irving Ravetch.

The genesis of the film is fascinating and in fact owes a debt to the work of the legendary star Clark Gable. According to Ritt: "We had seen Gable in a lot of pictures where for the first half of the picture he's a prick, and then some lady, or Spencer Tracy, or God, converts him in the second half. And we thought it would be interesting to make a picture about a man, the character of a man Gable often played, but then follow it through to its logical conclusion—that was *Hud*. Actually, in Larry McMurtry's novel *Horsemen Pass By* the character of Hud was tiny. He was just a member of the bunkhouse. It was a lyrical novel, and lyric films don't have a history of making a lot of money."

Discussing the script that screenwriters Irving Ravetch and Harriet Frank, Jr., wrote, Ritt continues: "As a matter of fact, we thought we added something, and we felt we sacrificed nothing . . . by making that character a heel—the kind of American heel that had not yet existed in American films."

The three other pivotal roles in the picture were portrayed by Melvyn Douglas, Patricia Neal, and Brandon De Wilde. The behind-the-scenes people were equally top-notch, including James Wong Howe who was director of photography.

On location in Texas Newman lived like the other cowhands, sharing meals, living in the bunkhouses, and working on the ranch so that his hands would be callused, and he would look as authentic as possible in the part. As was his practice, Newman studied real-life examples of the character he was to portray, and absorbed and utilized their walks and mannerisms.

"The first time I remember women reacting to me was when we were filming *Hud* in Texas," Newman later recalled with embarrassment. "Women were literally trying to climb through the transoms at the motel where I stayed. At first, it's flattering to the ego. At first. Then you realize that they're mixing me up with the roles I play—characters created by writers who have nothing to do with who *I* am. As for Joanne's reaction—sure, things like that have an effect on her; they've *got* to."

The couple spent Christmas that year in Hollywood, and as an indication of their increasing social awareness and involvement in social causes, that year the family decided that instead of spending money on Christmas presents, they would send money to C.A.R.E.

Now the Newmans had three homes—New York, Connecticut, and Hollywood—and the household included the kids, two dogs, two cats, and a nurse for the younger children. Rather than taking clothes back and forth across the country, Joanne had three wardrobes—one in each house. For the time being, the Newmans would have to remain in California, where Paul was set for a number of film projects, one of which was MGM's *The Prize*. He wanted to wear a beard in that film, but studio executives decreed that was out of the question. While Paul Newman may have exercised control over many aspects of his career, he did not always have approval over how he looked on-screen. The MGM front office felt the beard made him look older. He countered, "I should look older, playing this part" (he was portraying an antiestablishment Nobel Prize winner, a la Norman Mailer), but the studio wasn't buying his argument. They were paying hundreds of thousands of dollars for *Paul Newman*—the *familiar* Paul Newman that fans would pay to see. Although Newman fought to keep the beard, he had to shave it off.

Paul often grew beards between pictures, however, and around this time he and a half dozen other top leading men played cameo roles in a Shirley MacLaine vehicle, *What a Way to Go!* Newman portrayed a bohemian artist—with beard—and it would be the first time the public saw him that way.

Joanne had found a script she wanted to do, with a role she thought perfect for Paul—a comedy that was scheduled to be produced and directed by Mel Shavelson for Paramount. Newman, however, didn't like the material: "I looked at the script and said, 'Geez, this is yechh,'" he recalled. "And she said, 'I think it's rather cute.' And I said, 'That's because your part is cute. I've just got a bunch of one-liners.' She said, 'You son-of-a-bitch, I've followed you all over the world, to Israel, France—carrying the family, and you won't . . . ?' I said, 'It's marvelous material. When do we start?'"

So, with *A New Kind of Love*, the Newmans were taking another crack at territory they had attacked before, and had failed to conquer: light comedy.

Meanwhile *Hud* opened, launched by a provocative and memorable advertising campaign that spotlighted Newman. The poster for *Hud* became an instant classic—a suggestive, full-length pose of blue-jeaned Paul, which epitomized male sexuality for millions. The ad line was provocative: *Paul Newman Is Hud . . . The Man with the Barbed-Wire Soul*. The award-winning ad campaign featured another key line, *Why Hud?*, which referred to the moment when De Wilde asks, "Why pick on Hud, Grandpa? Nearly everybody around town is like him."

In *Hud* Brandon De Wilde (Lon), a youngster on the brink of manhood, must choose between the values of his upright grandfather (Melvyn Douglas) and those of his low-down uncle, Hud. Patricia Neal portrays the hardened, yet tender, housekeeper, a woman with a warm heart for the boy but with a knowingness about Hud. She tells him, "I've done my time with one cold-blooded bastard. I'm not looking for another." However, she also realizes her attraction to him.

The reviews were unanimous raves. The critic Judith Crist described the film as a story "about the disintegration of a household through the total amorality of one of its members." Crist also noted, "Hud is a soulless man. . . . His characterization leaves us with a knowledge of depravity and, worse yet, that this man is of our day and of our society."

Throughout the film the character Hud is a heel, with no thought of reformation; the young De Wilde watches him with a growing awareness of evil. The perceptive critic Arthur Knight noted in *The Saturday Review:* "[Ritt] uses Newman's considerable personal magnetism first to cover, then reveal, the shallow, egocentric, callous nature of Hud. . . . In this age of heel-heroes and beasts that walk like men, the screenwriters have pulled a switch that is both commercial and commendable. They have created in Hud a charming, raffish monster who demonstrates by inversion that such old-fashioned virtues as honesty, loyalty, and filial duty are still highly cherishable."

But was this assessment true? Such may have been Newman's, Ritt's, and the Ravetches' intention, but the general reaction to the character did not turn out to be what they had anticipated. It was not De Wilde's character that the audience identified with—but Hud's.

Through the years *Hud* has proved to be a classic film, and Newman has found himself in the peculiar position of having to explain that the part has been interpreted differently than he, the writers, and director had intended. He has often voiced disappointment with the movie's impact. "I think it was misunderstood, especially by the kids. They rather lionized that character. But the whole purpose was to present someone who had all of the graces on which there is such a big premium in the U.S.—some kind of external attractiveness, a guy who is great with the girls, a good boozer—but, nevertheless, a man with one tragic flaw. He doesn't give a shit about anything except himself. I must say that most reviewers actually glossed over that. It's related to Tennessee's idea to some extent—that premium which Americans place on external beauty."

Newman has pointed to this as an instance where sometimes one is wrong in his judgment about a particular project. In retrospect he thinks they made a terrible mistake.

Martin Ritt disagrees: "We didn't make a terrible mistake, I don't agree with him. What happened was, when the picture opened, and it was a big hit, I kept getting mail telling me what a great guy Hud was and what a schmuck the old man was, and the kid was gay. What nobody realized was that Haight-Ashbury was just around the corner, and there's no way of topping history. What nobody realized was that kids were that cynical. The people who made the film were highly involved people—the Ravetches, myself, and Paul. We understood that any man committed to his appetite finally is a prick. But the kids—their appetite was so enormous—the whole drug syndrome is somehow a reflection of that."

Joanne's film *A Woman in July*, retitled *The Stripper*, opened a month after *Hud*. It, too, had a provocative advertising campaign, one in which Joanne's sexy likeness dominated the artwork. In it her white-blond hair was styled in a bubble hairdo, and there were balloons covering key parts of her anatomy. The studio was making an obvious attempt to sell the picture in ads and publicity stills as a Monroe–*Bus Stop*–like vehicle, which unfortunately it was not.

Joanne, however, did not want the picture to die. The success of *The Three Faces of Eve* was fading fast from people's memories, but in doing publicity for *The Stripper*, Woodward once again expressed no regrets over the fact that she hadn't zoomed into orbit as a Hollywood personality. It was a choice she had made. "I wanted to be a kook or something," she has admitted, "and then I realized I didn't have the kind of personality that hits people in the eye right away. It just isn't important for me to have an image. What kind of image do Alec Guinness and Laurence Olivier or Geraldine Page have? If you have an identifiable personality, you end up playing the same role all the time."

Behind the scenes her friend Shirley MacLaine was telling Woodward she *had* to come up with a specific image, but in her quest for this image, Joanne became, in her words, "a different person at every interview." Consequently, no specific image emerged, and apparently Woodward abandoned the quest.

Two decades later the marketplace would be such that a Meryl Streep could pick and choose among character roles that were written for leading ladies, but in the early sixties, talents like Joanne's were hard for the industry to deal with because there simply were no leading roles for character actresses.

Although *The Stripper* had flopped, hopes were high for *A New Kind of Love*, Joanne's comedy with Paul, which was due for release later in the year. The couple said they were dead set against becoming a permanent "team"—"We do that bit at home," noted Paul; but they announced they would be doing a Broadway play together the following season.

Meanwhile Newman and Martin Ritt collaborated on another film, *The Outrage* (originally titled *The Rape*), which, fascinatingly, was an adaptation of the *Rashomon* stories. In the classic Japanese tales a violent incident is viewed from the differing perspectives of the participants. *Rashomon* was initially made into a film by Akira Kurosawa, and was later produced on Broadway in an adaptation by Michael and Fay Kanin starring Rod Steiger and Claire Bloom. For the Newman-Ritt film version Michael Kanin rewrote the play, changing the setting from Japan of the Middle Ages to the old American West.

Originally Ronald Lubin, an independent producer, had sent Paul a script of *The Outrage*. Newman did not like it, according to Lubin, and "felt it wasn't right for him." In fact, he suggested that the producer give it to Marlon Brando, which Lubin did. Brando, who supposedly loved the script, would not commit himself to the project. According to Lubin, "When Paul heard how much Brando liked the script, his whole attitude changed, and he accepted the role."

According to Ritt, it was just business; both he and Newman had commitments to MGM, and this project was the result. In the picture Newman would be portraying a Mexican bandit, so he went to Mexico to absorb background for his characterization before tackling the role. To change his appearance, he wore brown contact lenses, a black wig, a mustache, and a stubbly beard. He also spoke with a Mexican accent. Claire Bloom was the leading lady, and Laurence Harvey, Edward G. Robinson, and William Shatner co-starred.

It was during production of this film that Paul Newman learned something about himself as an actor and as a man: "I never really thought about concentration one way or another until someone showed me a take from *The Outrage*. . . . It was a long shot, 500 millimeters, a head shot, just me walking around saying the lines. Finally, when the take was over, the camera drew back, the film still running, and you could see that there had been guys driving trucks through there and pulling lamps and yelling, and what had looked like an isolated moment wasn't that at all. It really amazed me when I realized that I could block out stuff like that."

Their work schedules aside, 1963 was a busy year for Paul and Joanne, especially politically. Gore Vidal has confirmed this: "After Jack Kennedy was elected president, Paul became more active politically, as did many actors." Newman had worked for Kennedy's election in 1960, and now, along with Marlon Brando and a handful of others from the film colony, Paul began donating more than just his money to political and social causes he believed in. He began appearing in their behalf. Woodward heartily approved: "You can't just sit around and be hysterical. You might not be able to change anything, but at least you can try."

Brando phoned Newman to tell him that Martin Luther King, Jr., had been trying to get through to him. King wanted Newman, Brando, and others to come to Alabama to try to reason with the people there for a peaceful settlement of a current racial problem. Newman, Brando, Anthony Franciosa, Virgil Fry, and others went to Gadsden, Alabama, but as Newman later related, "We were wasting our time." He said that if he and Brando and the others had thought they could put pressure on people, they were soon disillusioned. Nonetheless, he appeared with Brando at a sit-in in Sacramento, California, and he also participated in the historic March on Washington, D.C., in August of 1963. "I think there's too much fear of *not* speaking out," said Newman. "If one has strong opinions, why not? . . . I'm proud I was there. There has never been anything like it. We should all be proud to take part in the great events of our time."

In November 1963 Joanne Woodward was shooting *Signpost to Murder*, a movie that wasn't working *at all*. "We had an awful director, and . . . the last scene was so bad we decided to throw it out and improvise on camera," recalled Joanne. "I think the [finished] movie ran forty-five minutes. But I liked the way I looked in the mad opening shot. I wore a bathing suit, a large hat and high heels."

*A New Kind of Love* had opened, and once again the Newmans in light comedy bombed with the critics and the public. Paul had obviously been right about this script, but this was not to be their last attempt at comedy.

For Joanne *Signpost to Murder* was almost a totally unmemorable experience; what she can never forget, though, is that she was working on that film the day John F. Kennedy was assassinated. The Newmans, like the rest of the country, were devastated by the violent death of the president. Paul was becoming more committed to politics than ever.

## 7

*Geraldine Page:* "Lee Strasberg was so happy that Paul, the big star, wanted to do something. Lee said, 'Paul has a play he wants to do. If we do it, he'll bring in some money.' I thought it was a good idea to balance our offerings with a light comedy, but this wasn't it. I suggested *Any Wednesday*, but nobody was interested."

Page was referring to the fact that the Actors Studio had ventured into production, calling their new group the Actors Studio Theater. Up to this point they had done three shows, *Strange Interlude, Marathon 33*, and *Dynamite Tonight*, all of which had failed financially. For their fourth show they chose a comedy by James Costigan, *Baby Want a Kiss?* (which they were opening almost simultaneously with their fifth show, James Baldwin's *Blues for Mr. Charlie*).

Several people at the Studio, Miss Page recalls, "kept saying about *Marathon 33* and *Blues for Mr. Charlie*, 'It isn't a play, it isn't a play.' " She adds, "Did they think *Baby Want a Kiss?* was a play? I hated it!"

*Baby Want a Kiss?* was a play about a married couple who are flamboyant movie stars and their friend who is a writer. Newman's and Woodward's characters were described as "an aging juvenile" and "a fading ingenue."

As far as the Newmans were concerned, this was a play that satisfied actors' needs. Costigan was to co-star with Paul and Joanne, and all had agreed to work for the Equity minimum, which was then $117.50 per week. Their understudies and the assistant stage manager were actually paid more. Costigan, of course, also made more than the Newmans, since he also got a royalty for the play. (Working for scale was a gesture on the Newmans' part. Other prominent players who had worked in Studio Theater productions had opted for the $1,000-per-week top fee the group had decided on.)

It was quite a time for Paul Newman to be appearing "in person" on Broadway. *Hud* was a huge popular success in New York. *The Prize*, a thriller in the Hitchcock mode that mixed adventure and comedy, opened in the spring and was one of MGM's biggest grossers. Newman had, as expected, been nominated for an Oscar for his performance in *Hud*, and most of the other principals had received nominations as well: Ritt for best director, Pat Neal for best actress, Melvyn Douglas for best supporting actor, the Ravetches for best script, and James Wong Howe for best cinematography. It was quite a race for the Oscar that year. Sidney Poitier was a strong contender for best actor with his performance in *Lilies of the Field*. Albert Finney was superb in *Tom Jones*. Richard Harris was flamboyant and dramatic in *This Sporting Life*. And Rex Harrison was up for his role in the celebrated Elizabeth Taylor–Richard Burton opus *Cleopatra*, which had finally hit the theaters. Liz and Richard hadn't copped nominations, but they certainly had replaced the Newmans as the team of the moment.

While in rehearsal for *Baby*, Paul said of the Oscar nominations, "I'd like to see Sidney Poitier get it. . . . I'd be proud to win it for a role I really had to reach for." His implication was that *Hud* had been a breeze; his parts in *The Hustler* and the soon-to-be-released *Outrage* were ones he was prouder of.

Newman later said, "Which do you take more credit for, a movie that has everything, or something like *The Outrage*, which wasn't successful but in which I probably came closest

to crawling out of my skin?" For Newman that was the ultimate accomplishment for an actor—crawling out of his own
skin.

In New York the Newmans were living in their East Side
apartment where a new feature had been added: a sauna, which
Paul called "the rehearsal steam room . . . the living end."
Paul and Joanne said they rehearsed in the steam room,
but Paul wryly noted that, after the steam, he didn't feel like
going to sleep; rather, he felt like going to a party.

The family would be moving to their Connecticut house as
soon as the play opened and the summer began, and would
commute to the theater in Paul's Volkswagen with its Porsche
engine. (He later explained how that souped-up car came
about: "I was complaining to my mechanic about driving the
VW back and forth between the theater in New York and my
house in Connecticut. There was a lot of shifting, downshifting
in traffic. He said, 'Why don't you dump a Porsche engine in it,
and you'll still retain your backseat but have the power you
need?' So we dropped in a stock Porsche engine, installed
Konis, and Dunlop Super Sports tires. The car handled so well
that we put in a Porsche Super 90 to 1800 cc and put a hot cam
in it. It was a neat little bomb. I guess that was my first so-
called hopped-up street machine.")

Newman actually appeared in an ad for Volkswagen in the
nineteen sixties. When an interviewer asked if he really owned
fourteen or fifteen Volkswagens, he answered, "No, I did [the
ad] just for a lark. I don't endorse products very often, but I do
like that little bug."

On Oscar night Sidney Poitier did win for his performance
in *Lilies of the Field*. Ritt and the Ravetches lost also (*Tom Jones*
won in their categories) but Patricia Neal, Melvyn Douglas,
and James Wong Howe won Oscars for *Hud*, and the film was
one of the top money-makers of the year.

*Baby Want a Kiss?* was having problems in rehearsal. Frank
Corsaro, who directed the play and was a friend of the Newmans, subsequently said: "Paul and Joanne wanted to shine in a
little vehicle, and this was the play they really wanted to do.
. . . We had fun with it. I think it had a certain appeal as an

absurdist piece, but it really was not a good choice; it exemplified a fallacious side of the Studio."

David Garfield says Paul and Joanne wanted to do the play "because Costigan was a friend, and because the notion of playing a glamorous Hollywood couple amused them."

According to reliable sources, Corsaro thought the play had merit, but was upset that once they went into rehearsal, the author was "obdurate and unwilling to change things." Corsaro has observed: "The truth was he couldn't change it. The last ten minutes, the play sank like the *Titanic*." (Patrick O'Neal, who'd also worked with Corsaro, makes an interesting observation: "I think Frank kind of soured on the theater because he took the fall on a couple of things.")

*Baby* opened at New York's Little Theater on April 19, 1964. One of the plot points the audiences undoubtedly found a bit shocking was that Newman's character makes homosexual advances to the writer-character portrayed by Costigan—this character was not the macho Paul Newman of *Hud* and *The Prize*. The reviews were not good, but nonetheless thanks (one would assume) to the presence of Newman and Woodward, the play would be performed to sold-out houses for four months and was the only Actors Studio production to show a profit.

Foster Hirsch, in his analysis of the Actors Studio, noted that while the play was a moneymaker, "*Baby* . . . probably did more damage to the Actors Studio Theater than any other production. To have sold a cheap bill of goods on the basis of attractive star names was a betrayal of the kind of theater that Strasberg had always talked about, and when the Ford Foundation saw this production, it began to re-evaluate its commitment to him."

Joanne got better reviews for *Baby* than Paul did. She later said, "The critics were just not bright enough to understand his performance. . . . It was a funny, funny play, but somehow it was as if the audience disliked their lovely blue-eyed Paul in that role." Woodward said that Newman was marvelous onstage, and that she preferred him in theater rather than in film, because as an actor, he was larger than life, and onscreen that quality had to be contained.

Meanwhile *What a Way to Go!* was launched with a glitzy Manhattan premiere. New York was "star city" at this point in time—the New York World's Fair had opened and celebrities were flying in from all over the world. Naturally, one of *the* places to be seen was at the theater, to catch "Paul and Joanne."

That summer, while he was on Broadway, Newman took time to go down to Atlantic City to the Democratic National Convention, to support President Lyndon Johnson. At the time Barry Goldwater, the Republican contender, was openly advocating escalation of the war in Southeast Asia, and the Democrats were promising de-escalation. The president, of course, received his party's nomination, and Newman later campaigned for Johnson.

In August, when the Newmans had fulfilled their commitment in *Baby Want a Kiss?*, they packed up the family and left for Paris, where, amidst a fanfare of publicity, Paul would star opposite Sophia Loren and a host of international stars in Carlo Ponti's production of *Lady L*. Peter Ustinov was set to direct.

"Anything wrong with *Lady L* was the fault of Paul Newman," Newman subsequently said, referring to his performance. "I have a very American skin, and when I try to go out of my skin, like playing a French anarchist in *Lady L*, I go wrong."

Despite the chivalrous assessment, Newman was not the cause of the picture's failure. There was virtually no continuity to the script, and many scenes simply did not play at all. No one could have salvaged this fascinating mess—fascinating because it illustrated how, without a script and well-written characters to play, even the most charismatic actors in the world could flounder.

*Lady L* had been a doomed, and very costly, project long before Paul Newman became involved. MGM had bought the property as a vehicle for Tony Curtis and Gina Lollobrigida a few years earlier. George Cukor had actually begun directing. Then the project was shelved. The studio had wanted to team Loren and Newman, with whom it had commitments, and someone had suggested dusting off this vehicle. Studio thinking was that the investment to date might be salvaged—but the ship was sunk before it left port.

Though the picture was not coming together, and certainly one and all knew it, Paul and Joanne became friends with Peter Ustinov, one of the wittiest and most intellectual of people. Ustinov observed, a few years later: "Paul is overly cerebral about a role. As a result, he's a superb actor who has not yet hit his zenith. I believe Paul's true destiny is *behind* the camera, as a director. There he will have all the room he needs to buttress his intelligence with his instinct. Luckily for all of us, Joanne will remain an actress."

While the Newmans were in Europe, the producer Elliott Kastner sent over a script for Paul to read. Kastner, on the suggestion of the novelist-turned-screenwriter William Goldman, had optioned Ross Macdonald's book *The Moving Target*, the first in a series of Lew Archer detective novels. Goldman had written a tight script, and Frank Sinatra had been close to signing for the part of Archer, but the deal fell through.

Goldman has said that Newman showed quick interest in the script, probably because Paul knew "he was making a dog of a period piece, *Lady L*." The Goldman script, which was "very much in the American tradition," appealed to Newman.

Kastner, with a director Paul had okayed, flew to Paris to discuss the project. But when they had their meeting, the director revealed that he hated the script, that they should do a different script, not this one. The deal almost fell through, but Kastner salvaged it, retaining Newman's interest, getting rid of the original director, and signing Jack Smight, whom Newman also okayed. The project seemed to be a go again.

Newman's two biggest personal hits, what he referred to as his "H" movies, *Hustler* and *Hud*, inspired a title switch for *The Moving Target*. It was Newman's suggestion to change the detective's name to Harper.

Production on *Lady L* ground on, but the Newmans' time in Paris was not unpleasant. Joanne, however, had her hands full, so she sent for her mother—something she rarely did, because her mother was not an organized, "take charge" woman but often needed to be looked after herself. At one point, all five of the children were with Paul and Joanne, and the nanny had suddenly taken ill. To Joanne's relief, her mother flew to Paris to help with the children. There was another reason she wanted her mother there. Joanne was pregnant again. The Newmans were obviously making good on their promise to have eight in the family.

Back in the States the first order of business for Paul was to meet with Kastner and the screenwriter Bill Goldman. A final version of the *Harper* script had yet to be completed, and Goldman later revealed that he knew that if he could not accommodate the script changes Newman wanted, Kastner would have found someone else who would. The producer's main concern was to hold the star's interest. According to Goldman, "If a situation begins to get messy, they can get turned off quickly."

One thing that stands out in Goldman's memory of Newman in those days is that Paul had devised small ways of maintaining his privacy. On their walks along the roads in Westport, Connecticut, Goldman recalled, Newman "carried a handful of pebbles, and . . . whenever a car drove by, he was always in the act of tossing a pebble into the woods."

The men hit it off, and the script changes were agreed upon. On the trip back to New York City Kastner said to Goldman, "You don't know what happened, do you?" Goldman said he didn't. "You just jumped past all the shit," Kastner told him. And Goldman realized later what Kastner meant. In the Hollywood market he was no longer just a novelist from New York —he was now the screenwriter of a Paul Newman picture.

*Harper* would be a Warner Bros. release. At the start of production Newman was photographed on the lot with his former nemesis, Jack Warner. This time Warner was paying Paul $750,000 plus ten percent of the gross. The actor had been rated the number nine box-office attraction in the nation the previous year, and his price reflected his status.

Status, however, did not translate into big box office if the vehicle wasn't right, as indicated by returns on *The Outrage*. "The public certainly didn't like it," noted Newman, "but with the exception of the ending, I thought it was a good script." He was referring to the last version of the four stories, wherein the rape was played for broad comedy. This completely confused and negated the three previous versions, which were heavily dramatic.

Although he personally enjoyed the characterization, because it had been a stretch and an acting challenge, it was obvious the public was unwilling to accept their blue-eyed, all-American hero as a swarthy Mexican rapist. In *Harper* there would be no such physical change in Paul Newman's appearance.

An all-star cast was assembled for *Harper:* Lauren Bacall, Julie Harris, Shelley Winters, Janet Leigh, Robert Wagner, and Pamela Tiffin. Tiffin was then one of the young female stars-on-the-rise, having made a memorable screen debut a few years earlier in Billy Wilder's *One, Two, Three*, in which James Cagney starred. Tiffin had also appeared with Laurence Harvey and Geraldine Page in the film version of Tennessee Williams's *Summer and Smoke*.

Ms. Tiffin, today the mother of two children, vividly recalls the *Harper* experience: "I never understood the script of *Harper* —I did the whole movie without understanding what it was about." But she liked Paul Newman immensely. "Paul is a very 'normal' man who happens to act," Tiffin observes. She describes a reserve that can border on shyness; but she says, "he won't permit himself to be shy." Newman, unlike many other actors, is, according to Tiffin, "not the narcissistic type." She adds, "There's a core of masculinity, a *tough* quality—it's very attractive in a man—when you're around them, you feel protected in some way."

She also recalls: "Paul put up with a lot of nonsense during the filming of *Harper*, but he was very methodical and careful in fashioning his performance. He'd make a great surgeon or business executive," the actress states, remembering that he was a *good* businessman. Another Newman trait she admires: his loyalty (she recalls Newman's brother worked on the film) and conscientiousness.

"He has the best relationship with movie people," she has observed. "He is at ease with everyone. He sees everyone as vital on the movie set—doesn't take it *too* seriously. He knows the electrician's as important as he."

Janet Leigh, who played Harper's former wife in the film, had this to say about Paul Newman: "When Paul looks at you with those eyes of his, he commands you to look at him and listen. He *makes* you respond to him. That's the basis of his sex appeal."

Woodward came to the *Harper* set one day. Tiffin sensed, with what she calls a "woman's perception," that Joanne was a woman of strong character ("Stronger than I," Tiffin notes). Tiffin describes Woodward as "sober": "Joanne doesn't have a great sense of humor." Of the couple's marriage, she says it appeared to be a "working" one, "steady," "not capricious or flighty."

Tiffin speaks admiringly of Newman's "remarkable" concentration: "When he decides to do something, he does it." This ability to concentrate and perform, she believes, helped him to become a successful racing car competitor. Tiffin recalls that even at the time of *Harper* he liked cars. "I think his *true* interest is racing," she says.

Newman has not tried to downplay his love of automobiles. "It's the one thing that I can be genuinely adolescent about; automobiles. I love 'em!" He has recalled: "They had an old beat-up Ford that they were going to use in *Harper*, and I wanted to use the Porsche. I thought that was much more indicative of his character. And I also wanted that one fender which was just primered. So that was my suggestion for a change in the movie, and they made it."

In a car scene one day with Newman, Pamela Tiffin experienced a near accident. Both actors were in a real car on a real street in real traffic when, Tiffin says, "some people discovered that Paul Newman was in the car and an accident almost occurred." Newman remarked to Tiffin at the time, "They don't see you as a person but as an icon or object."

One icon wasn't reluctant to borrow mannerisms from another if it would fill out a characterization. Paul knew Robert F. Kennedy and had observed how the politician had a habit of listening sideways—a person might be seated next to Kennedy and think he wasn't listening, but he was—he was simply listening sideways. Newman incorporated this trait into the character of Lew Harper.

After completing *Harper*, Newman signed with Universal for what everyone assumed would be yet another landmark film. Newman would be directed in *Torn Curtain* by the master, Alfred Hitchcock. His co-star would be a person who was currently even more popular at the box office than he, Julie Andrews, fresh from two huge triumphs—*The Sound of Music* and *Mary Poppins*.

Years later he discussed the experience: "I was asked if I'd like to do a film with Hitchcock, and I said, 'You bet your sweet ass.' So they said, 'Go on over and talk with him.' Usually that doesn't turn out very well, but because it was Hitchcock, I went over. We talked about the story, and he said, 'I can't give you a script, because there won't be one ready for eight or ten days.' "

Hitchcock added: "That's the best I can do. I know you should have script approval and everything else, but I don't want to show you the script we've got now, because it's not very good."

Since the plot sounded okay to Newman, he agreed.

Other sources contend that Hitchcock and Newman did not hit it off. Newman said in retrospect: "Well, I think I could have hit it off with Hitchcock if the script had been better. That was the main problem. It was not a lack of communication or a lack of respect. The only thing that constantly stood in our way was the script."

Many of Hitchcock's biographers contend that the relationship between actor and director went awry not on the set but in the director's home. Hitchcock had invited Newman to a formal dinner party. Paul dressed casually for the occasion, requested beer instead of the vintage wine that was being served, and even said, "I'll go get the beer myself." The implication was clear. If a well-brought-up young man from Shaker Heights, Ohio, who certainly knew how to behave at a formal dinner party, did this, it could only be that he was trying to show Hitchcock how pretentious he thought the director was.

The men had different styles of working. For Hitchcock, once the picture was storyboarded to his satisfaction—that is, once the key scenes were sketched out by an artist so the cameraman knew exactly what the director wanted him to shoot—the picture was finished. Actually making the film, for Hitch, was drudge labor.

Newman, of course, was a method actor and was constantly working on his character. One of Hollywood's legendary and perhaps apocryphal tales is that one day Hitchcock, after a lengthy conversation with Paul regarding character motivation, became exasperated and exclaimed, "Your motivation, Mr. Newman, is your salary."

Woodward has always been candid in her comments on life with Paul when he's involved in filmmaking: If he's pleased with the material and with the way things are going, he's "wonderful and happy and relaxed." If, however, he is making a picture he does not like, "he can be an absolute pain in the neck. He'll work much harder on a script he hates, and, at the same time, he'll drink too much beer." One can imagine what life was like for Joanne while Paul was making *Torn Curtain*.

In the spring of 1965, on April 21, Paul and Joanne's third daughter, Claire (whom they dubbed Clea), was born. For the occasion Paul gave Joanne a gift—a diamond tiger pin from Cartier's. Although years later Joanne stated, "She is the only child I didn't immediately turn over to a nanny while I went off to make a movie," the facts indicate her memory is faulty. While it is true that she breast-fed the baby and committed herself to bringing this one up herself, there were film commitments. And others had to be employed to care for the children. Paul was obviously of little help with the day-to-day care of babies. (Joanne later confessed, "My husband takes pride in being a father of six children and having never changed a diaper.")

Woodward was intent on regaining her figure: she would not get out of shape as she had after the birth of her second daughter, Melissa. So after Clea's birth Joanne took up ballet. When her six-year-old daughter, Nell, had started to take lessons, the teacher had said to Joanne: "Why don't you take some lessons?

We have adult classes." In Woodward's words: "I was thirty-five, really kind of plump around the middle, decidedly middle-aged looking, and I had just had Clea and was nursing her. So I started taking ballet, and it was like a drug. I got hooked." Lessons three times weekly became lessons five times weekly.

Woodward's last film, *Signpost to Murder*, finally went into release and received disastrous reviews. Some critics even implied that Woodward took this terrible part because she was not getting any other offers, a patently ridiculous assertion. Joanne was already set for two important films. One would present her as the wife of Henry Fonda in a western comedy, *A Big Hand for the Little Lady*. The other was an offbeat comedy, *A Fine Madness*, which would co-star Woodward with the hot new sex symbol of the day, Sean Connery, who was enjoying great success with his portrayal of Special Agent 007, James Bond.

In *A Fine Madness* Connery would be stretching, playing a very non-Bond-like character—a poet maintenance man. Like Paul Newman, Connery was an actor yearning for roles that would enable him to crawl out of his own skin. In *Madness* Patrick O'Neal, Jean Seberg, and Diane Cilento (Connery's wife) would co-star. Part of *A Fine Madness* would be shot in New York City, but most of it was to be filmed on the Warner Bros. lot in Burbank.

Patrick O'Neal remembers: "When we did *A Fine Madness*, every Friday night we watched a film. [Joanne had organized the cast and director into a movie fan club.] Paul rented the screening room at the Beverly Hills Hotel. Every Friday there was Sean Connery, Sean's wife, Diane, Paul, Joanne, Jean Seberg, and [her husband] Romain Gary—that was the group. Paul brought the beer and popcorn—made it himself. It was just a social evening after work—we all felt very close. I have a wonderful memory of all of us being warm, close. Each of us got to choose our favorite film. I chose *Singin' in the Rain*. Jean chose a Russian film about a little dog, which I thought was wonderfully appropriate—you know that Jean was a little girl from Iowa. I don't remember what Paul and Joanne chose." (Joanne chose Hitchcock's one and only comedy *Mr. and Mrs. Smith*, starring Carole Lombard and Robert Montgomery.)

O'Neal continues: "Working with Joanne was always a pleasure. She always kind of amazed me the way she dives in and creates a character. She's not laid-back. *Fine Madness* was a very broad kind of comedy. I always got the sense of her being a hard worker—willing to take chances and create."

Early in 1966 *Harper* was released and proved to be a big success. MGM then released *Lady L* to capitalize on *Harper*'s success, but to no avail. *Lady L* was a turkey.

Joanne was still part of the Hollywood crowd and agreed to appear on the Academy Awards telecast in April. After all, she had two major films awaiting release and the exposure wouldn't hurt. Along with George Peppard, she presented the Oscar for best screenplay. Speaking of her gown, a Travilla creation, she quipped, "I hope this makes Joan Crawford happy."

When *A Big Hand for the Little Lady* and *A Fine Madness* were released (almost simultaneously), the public stayed away. Just as fans preferred Paul Newman in a certain type of role, looking a certain way, the same applied to Sean Connery, only much more so. In *A Fine Madness* he was playing a character role, and even the combined star power of Connery and Woodward could not stir up box-office interest. The pairing of Fonda and Woodward in a western didn't ring box-office bells either.

Universal went all out for the world premiere of *Torn Curtain* in Boston that summer. It was Hitchcock's fiftieth film, and the great director was to be on hand (although neither Newman nor Julie Andrews would be there). Through his hugely successful television series, Hitchcock's face and figure had become as well-known as any superstar's. Hitch eagerly publicized the picture, and although it received disastrous reviews, it was a money-maker. In truth, it was a terrible film, and a major disappointment for all concerned.

After his unsatisfactory experience working with Hitchcock, Newman returned to his screen family—Ritt, Ravetch, and Frank—again in an "H" picture. With Ritt and Ravetch, Newman produced and starred in *Hombre,* a film based on an Elmore Leonard novel.

The inside story on how this deal was put together was re-

vealed by John Gregory Dunne. He reported that the agents
Evarts Ziegler and Richard Shepherd presented the package to
the 20th Century-Fox production chief Richard Zanuck. The
specifics: Newman, Ritt, and Ravetch and Frank's services for
$1.3 million. The figure breakdown: Newman's price, $750,000,
"against ten percent of the gross until the picture showed a
profit. After that, a piece of the profits."

Zanuck was agreeable.

The Ravetches were to receive $150,000.

Zanuck was agreeable.

But when the agents proposed that Ravetch should receive
an extra $50,000, since he was going to co-produce, Zanuck
balked.

"It was twenty-five the other day," Zanuck replied. "You
changed the figures."

"Not changed. Corrected," replied Ziegler.

According to John Gregory Dunne: "The longest discussion
was over Ritt. He had once been under contract to Fox, and the
studio was now suing him for failure to live up to that contract's provisions. All film companies file charges almost pro-
miscuously, since a lawsuit is a potent bargaining tool in any
subsequent negotiations. Few of the suits ever come to trial."

The agents stated $350,000 as Ritt's price.

Zanuck pointed out the director was earning $300,000 for his
"current picture."

Ritt's price would be $250,000, *if* "Fox dropped the lawsuit."

"If we drop the suit, he only gets one-fifty," replied Zanuck.

After some "friendly" negotiating, Zanuck was agreeable to
$200,000.

"I'll have to check Marty's financial needs for the rest of the
year," replied Shepherd.

The deal was made.

Ritt says 20th was angry with him, because he had gone over
to Paramount. "They felt I owed them a picture—so we
brought Paul over for this project."

Filmed on location in Arizona, the picture had an outstanding cast: Fredric March, Richard Boone, Barbara Rush, Cameron Mitchell, Martin Balsam, and Diane Cilento.

*Hombre* was the kind of picture Fox's sales department could get exhibitor enthusiasm for: a true western with Paul Newman. In the film Newman plays a man who has been raised by Indians. "I remember for *Hombre* I went down to an Indian reservation for five days and brought back one thing," recalled Newman: "I drove past a general store, and there was this guy standing there in front with one foot up and his arms crossed. He was in exactly the same position when I drove back four hours later. That whole character came out of that."

Meanwhile, through the years Jack Garfein had kept up his efforts to get *The Wall* project off the ground. As Garfein relates: "Hollywood just didn't want to do it. So I sat on it. One day I got a letter from Martin Ritt: 'Dear Jack, I know you are having difficulty putting the project together. I went to Paul, and Paul said he'd like to do it, but his commitment is to you. So if you can't put the project together, will you release Paul from his commitment so I can proceed and try to put it together?' "

Garfein was again impressed by Paul Newman's integrity. He explains: "Marty Ritt was a big, hot director. I had two films which artistically had gotten a lot of notice, but commercially they didn't mean anything. And yet Paul said to Marty Ritt—even though we didn't have a contract—my commitment is to Jack."

Since Garfein's problem in selling the project was the subject matter, not his credentials as a director, he of course released Paul from the commitment and said to Ritt, "Go ahead and try." Garfein recalls: "Well, Marty Ritt couldn't lick the problem either. He came up against the same problems as I did. So the project went by the wayside."

Another project for Paul Newman had materialized, however, and Newman was off to the San Joaquin Delta area in northern California to begin shooting *Cool Hand Luke*. When a film is beginning production, the people involved never know how well things are going to turn out, but from the outset Newman was very happy with the script of this film. He was portraying an outsider, a loner. With this character Newman returned to the rebels he had portrayed earlier in his career.

The director, Stuart Rosenberg, said, "Luke is the perfect existential hero." And Newman himself described Luke as "the guy who beats the system . . . the ultimate non-conformist and rebel." Whether in jail or in the army, "he's still a free agent."

Offscreen, fans were beginning to *boldly* intrude on Newman's privacy. Newman didn't exactly invite polite conversation, but the public was oblivious. Newman has explained: "People come up to me, perfect strangers, and ask me to take off my dark glasses so they can have a look at my eyes. My answer is simple. I just say, 'Is that all you think of me?' Are they going to write on my tombstone, 'Here lies Paul Newman, who died a failure . . . because his eyes turned brown'? If blue eyes are what it's all about, and not the accumulation of my work as a professional actor, I may as well turn in my union card right now and go into gardening."

Paul and Joanne were nonetheless trapped in the web of celebrity: Newman, especially, could not escape it. Joanne might avoid it, and even if she was recognized, she would not engender the kind of response Paul did. It was extremely hard on the children, however. Paul and Joanne could cope, but they were not comfortable about the pressures fame placed on their family. It was said they allowed no photographs of the children for fear of kidnapping, but Joanne countered, "It's not because we fear kidnapping, but rather that we want to rear normal children whose sense of importance is for and within themselves, *not* because they have parents who are movie stars."

"Normal" was impossible. The Newman children, like all children of famous and recognizable people, had to contend with seeing their parents gaped at and fawned over in public.

Scott was now a troubled teenager, and although none of this was revealed at the time, there had been tension whenever the three older children stayed with their stepmother and half-sisters. The discrepancy between the life-style of their very wealthy father and the hardly extravagant life-style of their own mother was creating problems for the three older Newman children.

In addition, Scott had not adjusted to his parents' breakup, and there were frequent clashes with his father. A family friend says that the troubled boy was a disruptive influence. Scott's feeling was that his father had deserted them, and now he was entitled to all Paul could give.

Scott resented Joanne, and there were long periods when he would not speak with her. Naturally, the older girls were caught in the middle, between loyalty to their brother and their desire to build a relationship with their stepmother.

Through it all, Paul and Joanne were determined to keep the family together. They defended their practice of taking their kids wherever they went. "We move around a lot," Newman observed at the time, "but we figure home is where the family is, and having both parents there is more important than always being in the same house. If I go on location for more than two weeks, Joanne and the kids come with me."

"I don't spend as much time with my children as some fathers," he said on another occasion, "but when I am with them, I enjoy it, and so do they. But I don't have a lot of patience. They know that, and they try me. But at a given point, they flee in terror!"

His relationship with Joanne was not harmonious all the time either—there were plenty of arguments. "I'm all in favor of a good screaming free-for-all every two or three months," he said. "It clears the air, gets rid of old grievances and generally makes for a pleasant relationship. Joanne has a habit of rationalizing, and when she starts that, that's when I turn ugly! But when she tells me what she instinctively *feels*, I pay very close attention."

Newman was doing another movie for Universal. The film was standard stuff, the wartime comedy-adventure *The Secret War of Harry Frigg*, but it gave him the opportunity to play a con man, and would be directed by *Harper*'s Jack Smight. European sex symbol Sylva Koscina was co-starring, and it was hoped the pairing might bring some interesting new chemistry to the screen.

The outspoken James Gregory was in the cast, and during production he detected a dissonant quality in Paul's characterization: "I didn't think he was playing it right. He was playing it like *Somebody Up There Likes Me*. How was this Italian count-ess supposed to fall in love with Rocky Graziano?"

But the studio had high hopes for the film. Buzz around the lot was that it was going to be another one of Newman's "H" hits. It would, however, turn out to be an "F."

The task of acting in films had worn thin for Newman. Paul was too intelligent not to see his work in films objectively: "Every time I see myself on the screen lately, I think, 'There's Hud. And, oh, yeah, that was a little 'Harper.' It's all getting pretty familiar. The more I do, the more I duplicate. I'm not inexhaustible, like an Olivier. I don't have that kind of talent."

The Newmans were returning East for a project that defi-nitely would not duplicate anything. They were going to com-bine her need for a good script with his ambition to challenge himself. He would direct a film. Paul noted, "Why merely be a first violinist, if you feel you can conduct?"

# BOOK II

# 8

None of the studios had wanted the project. In Hollywood, even when they do *want* you, it's got to be on *their* terms, and to fit in with *their* idea of what is best for you. This is true even if you're Paul Newman, one of the top box-office attractions in the industry, or Joanne Woodward, an Academy Award–winning actress noted for her talent, not her temperament.

At this time, only Elizabeth Taylor and Richard Burton in tandem and Cary Grant were bigger box-office draws than Paul Newman. Paul's price per film was now over $1 million—when he was acting, that is. The problem was, Newman was not going to appear in *Rachel, Rachel;* he would only direct. So even though the film promised to give Joanne her most vivid role since *Three Faces of Eve,* and the financial risk was minimal (the Newmans were willing to work for no salary; *Rachel, Rachel* was a contemporary story and required no expensive sets or locations), it was tough to find an interested party.

Newman was bitter about the studios who turned down the project. "There's not much loyalty in movie-making," he noted years later, referring specifically to a studio that once had him scheduled to do a film. There was a play-or-pay clause in his contract with the studio. What the clause meant was that if a certain actress was not free to be Newman's leading lady in the project, the film would not be made, but Paul would be paid anyway. As it turned out, the actress was not available, but Newman did not hold the studio to the contract and refused to take their money for not making the picture.

"There was a lot of gushing from them, multiple thank-yous," recalled Newman. "Then I wanted to direct *Rachel, Rachel* with Joanne in it, and I went to those producers and said, 'If you finance this, the total cost to you will be $350,000. That's for the script, me directing, Joanne—below-the-line costs, above-the-line, everything.' They said, '*Sor*-ry.' So much for loyalty."

The response from other studios was uniform: "We love the idea, but it's not for us."

When he was trying to sell the package, Newman was astonished at the unreceptiveness he encountered. He subsequently told Roger Ebert, "I finally had to go off in a corner and say, no, my taste is better; ultimately, I'm more perceptive than they are." One can speculate on what else he said, in private, about the industry biggies who were so eager to be his best friend—as long as friendship did not extend into the realm of taking a chance on Newman the director, as opposed to Newman the actor.

On the face of it, *Rachel, Rachel* was not the kind of film the studios had reason to believe in. It was a simple tale of a New England schoolteacher discovering truths about herself, a serious, slice-of-life story, with no violence, no action-adventure, no glamour.

"People who want to see James Bond or *The Guns of Navarone* aren't going to be interested," admitted Newman at the time. "I don't expect them to be, and I don't really *care*. That's why we're not taking any salary. If you want to make films like this nowadays, you've got to be prepared to make a sacrifice."

There is a kind of *Rashomon* situation surrounding the genesis of the *Rachel, Rachel* project. Was Paul involved from the beginning or not? Whichever version of events holds the greatest truth, it became apparent sometime during the story conferences and preproduction meetings that Paul was going to take over as the director, and he began fashioning the script with Stewart Stern. There were many differences of opinion on the story. At one point Paul, Stern, and Joanne were arguing, and Stern left, saying he could not deal with both of them at once. (This particular argument concerned whether the character Rachel would masturbate lying on her stomach or on her back.)

The following day Paul showed up at Stern's home, dressed head to foot in a Nazi SS uniform. The actor banged on the door, marched in, stared at Stern, and said, "I just wanted you to know who's boss." It was obviously this kind of crazy humor that kept the two men's friendship intact and their collaboration alive. From then on, Newman and Stern worked on the script without Joanne. (In the final film Rachel masturbates both on her back and on her stomach.)

Paul and Joanne finally decided to produce the picture themselves. Their production company was named Kayos (pronounced *chaos*) Productions. Frank Corsaro, who had directed the Newmans in *Baby Want a Kiss?*, was going to be in the picture, and so was Newman's auto mechanic. Paul and Joanne's eldest daughter, Nell, was set to play Rachel as a child. The film would be shot in Connecticut.

Meanwhile Newman's agents were frantically trying to line up financing. Newman has recalled: "Finally Warner Bros. called and said they would finance the picture for $700,000 plus ten percent overcall—if I would sign for two pictures, as an actor, at half my regular salary, and if Joanne would sign another commitment at less than she had been accustomed to making. They really had us over the barrel. We said okay. Then they had this really complicated way of assigning those pictures to myself and Joanne. But I said the deal would be okay only if the guy who was in charge of the studio—whom I trusted—would still be in charge, because I didn't want some idiot to be submitting scripts. Suffice it to say that the guy who was in charge of the studio then was not in charge when the picture was over—so we didn't have to go through with those commitments."

The Newmans were risking a lot by tackling this project— their self-esteem, for one. "It just had to work," Joanne later admitted. "If *Rachel* had been totally unsuccessful, I would have been heartbroken."

"Joanne really gave up her career for me, to stick by me, to make the marriage work. That's one of the reasons I directed this film with her," Paul candidly explained.

Stewart Stern offered insight into Paul and Joanne's relationship and the genesis of *Rachel, Rachel* when he observed, "He's constantly trying to provide a setting where the world can see what he sees in her."

The project also came along at a time when Newman was anxious to explore new territory. The forty-two-year-old actor was experiencing a mid-life crisis. He felt that he was burning out creatively, that he was no longer inventive as an actor. As far as he was concerned, he had been at it for too many years, and a major change in his life was essential.

*Could* Newman make it *behind* the camera? It was a real challenge for both him and Joanne, and—more significantly—it was one they could share. "I'm curious about my taste, my dramatic selection, my technical ability with the camera," Newman explained when he took on the challenge. "There's no way to find out but to get up there, and do it, and then let people hit you with baseball bats. I've always wanted to direct, because I've always enjoyed most the peripheral things about acting, the rehearsals and the field trips, the exploration of character, and the whole intellectual exercise of the thing. I enjoy this more than actually getting up on a stage or in front of a camera. That has always been more painful to me than enjoyable. I guess I've never been that much of an exhibitionist."

According to Stewart Stern: "Directing was a tremendous challenge for him. He was untried. He had made an enormous reputation as a superstar and thought that if he directed, people would be lying in wait hoping he wouldn't come through. But mainly he was willing to face his own fear. He knew he would be challenged every moment. Paul seeks out those situations which frighten him most. Even acting for Paul is not playing. Joanne is much more of a player. Any task for Paul is a gunfight at high noon. Directing was like that. No shadow out there to hide in."

Joanne was at a point in her life where *she* had ambivalent feelings about parenthood and the pursuit of her career. She, like many women of the day, was trying to do it all. At thirty-seven, she realized there were certain things she could no longer accomplish (it was too late to be a great ballerina), but she was discontent merely being a wife and mother.

She said at the time, "Now I'd like to be more active, principally because I feel I've done my bit for the population explosion and raised the children to where I feel I'm not depriving them if I'm working."

A decade later she conceded: "If I had it to do all over again, I would make a decision one way or the other. My career has suffered because of the children, and my children have suffered because of my career." It was an unfair, frustrating predicament which apparently extracted a heavy inner toll in the form of dissatisfaction and unhappiness. Joanne found herself unable to devote herself wholeheartedly either to her work or her children. She wasn't alone in this predicament, for many of her friends who were working mothers had also been unable to resolve the dilemma. Joanne later said she had left her children with well-intentioned women and she was not there: "I was afraid to take the total responsibility."

Newman was keenly aware of his wife's career sacrifices for their marriage. In an interview with feminist Gloria Steinem, he said, "I know she misses out on things, Broadway plays for instance, but if she had to be at the theater every night and I was on the coast, there would be no marriage at all. I think I feel worse about it than she does, but it bugs her, too. Sometimes, I come home and here's this woman wandering around the house muttering, 'What-am-I-doing-cooking-for-seven-people-what-the-hell-am-I-doing?' "

*Rachel, Rachel* was an opportunity for them to work together again, only this time they would have major artistic control over the production, and—more significantly—Joanne would be the one in the spotlight.

And so, with much riding on it, production began on *Rachel, Rachel* in Connecticut in the summer of 1967.

"There we were, off in our own little corner creating," recalled Joanne. "It was not at all like working in Hollywood where the grips play poker and have no idea what the movie is about. Everyone from the little boy who helped the grips was involved."

But no one was more involved than Joanne. "I wanted to do a film, a little film that meant something to me," she later explained. "I feel uneasy in big productions. We kind of talked Paul into it. He put the production together in five weeks."

At the time Newman said that if he went over the $700,000 budget, it would come out of his own "after tax" pocket. He and Joanne took no salaries, but if the movie made money, they would split the profit three ways with Stern.

Certainly foremost in the couple's minds, beyond possible profits *or* losses, was the challenge of working together in this new relationship, not as co-stars, but as director and actor. As for how Joanne felt being directed by her husband: "Who could direct better than the person you live with? He knows all there is to know about you. Paul is an actor's director in that he is very specific, clear, he talks in shorthand. . . . I just wish Paul could direct every movie I'll ever do again." (She prefaced that final comment with a polite acknowledgment of the great directors she had worked with.)

Newman said that his ego did not intrude into the process of directing. In his opinion, it was simple for a director "to inflict his own personality on an actor," but if one was confident about the material and the actors, it wasn't necessary. He acknowledged, however, that he would have been in trouble "if Joanne had been an untalented lady." Likewise, the couple's daughter Nell proved to be a natural actress in the part of the young Rachel.

Newman knew what Joanne was capable of as an actress, and she almost always deferred to his perception. In the rare instances when they violently disagreed, he would say to her,

"Fine, show me what you want to do." And then, as Joanne has said, he would let her do the scene her way.

Another actor in the *Rachel, Rachel* cast was equally enthusiastic about Newman's directorial ability. "I don't, as a rule, communicate too well with directors, but he's wonderful," said Estelle Parsons. "It's all been so relaxed and easy."

The production progressed smoothly, with Newman learning the art of directing in the process, as well as learning just how applicable his talents as an actor were to the requirements of directing. In fact, he found the art of directing less emotionally and physically draining than acting. "I didn't get anywhere near as tired directing as when I act. As an actor you stop and start the motor all day. It's like running a hundred yards two feet at a time. When you're involved with every facet of the production—script, attitudes, lighting, makeup, wardrobe—you're constantly pumped up, and you don't have an opportunity to slow down."

Filming was completed in six weeks; then Newman and the film editor DeDe Allen spent eight months putting it all together.

In the case of *Rachel, Rachel* the editing was an especially crucial phase in the film's development. *Rachel* was neither a suspense story nor an action adventure; this film was a *character* picture, a *mood* piece. In many respects the editing was as important as the performances.

Fortunately, it was in perfect hands. DeDe Allen (*Bonnie and Clyde, The Hustler*) is one of the most creative and talented editors in the business. Her sensitivity in putting a picture together is legendary. Newman gave Allen all the footage on *Rachel* and left her alone, consulting with her only occasionally as the film took shape.

As Stewart Stern has recalled: "We kept looking at cut after cut. . . . It seemed it could never get right. Then one day it was there! We were in the projection room, and I looked over at Paul, and he was crying. So was I, because he and DeDe had somehow brought Joanne's performance into proper focus. . . . And we saw what magic it was. Joanne has the capacity to be invisible to everything but the camera and Paul's eye on the set."

There was further postproduction work to be done, and all concerned remained highly protective of the picture and cautious about showing it to anybody.

*Cool Hand Luke* was released late in the fall of 1967, just in time to be in the running for that year's Academy Awards. The film received sensational reviews and reclaimed for Newman his position as a rebel hero. Judith Crist wrote that *Luke* was "the natural-born martyr, the man in revolt for whom the revolution is all."

When the film was released the country was in the midst of a social revolution. The flower children, the hippies, the discontented young of the day, were all looking for a hero like Luke, who would flout convention and take beatings, if necessary, to retain his integrity as a rebel.

Newman was widely praised by critics for his performance. Outstanding in supporting roles were George Kennedy as the leader of the chain gang; Jo Van Fleet as Luke's dying mother; and Strother Martin as the sadistic warden. It is Martin who delivers the much-quoted line: "What we've got here is a failure to communicate."

The film was a huge box-office success, and Newman was again nominated for best actor by the Academy. The competition for the award was particularly keen that year: Warren Beatty was nominated for *Bonnie and Clyde;* Dustin Hoffman, for *The Graduate;* Spencer Tracy, for *Guess Who's Coming to Dinner;* and Rod Steiger, for *In the Heat of the Night.* George Kennedy was nominated for best supporting actor. But Van Fleet was not recognized for her role. The screenwriters, Don Pierce and Frank R. Pierson, were nominated for their screenplay (which was based on Pierce's novel).

Universal released Newman's next feature, *Harry Frigg,* in the midst of all the *Luke* excitement, but it bombed both critically and commercially, proving once again that a star could only draw if he or she was in a *good* movie.

Once again, Newman lost the Oscar. But not to Tracy or Beatty—to Rod Steiger. Joanne later stated, "Paul didn't mind losing to Rod Steiger for his role in *In the Heat of the Night*. Rod has given a number of brilliant performances, and it was like losing to a real pro."

Paul attended the Oscar ceremonies that year with his daughter Susan, who had grown into a strikingly attractive young woman. Now in her mid-teens, Susan was something of a problem child (as was her brother, Scott). Susan later conceded that between the ages of fourteen and seventeen, she was "intolerable."

Paul was deeply concerned about his children, and committed to helping them adjust as best they could. Susan once noted: "Scott and Stephanie and I had a very normal, middle-class upbringing. I guess you could say we saw as much of our father as any children in a divorced family." However, she often referred to her father, her half sisters, and Joanne as "their" family, and like most children of divorce, she, Scott, and Stephanie would always have to contend with two families.

It was certainly a busy period in Paul Newman's life. In addition to his family responsibilities and his professional responsibilities (he was editing *Rachel, Rachel* and preparing it for an autumn release), this year he had taken on political commitments.

Newman spent a great deal of time in 1968 working in support of several candidates for public office, with his primary effort directed toward backing Senator Eugene McCarthy, who sought nomination as the Democratic candidate in the upcoming presidential election. Newman was even elected a delegate to the Democratic convention, which was to be held in Chicago that summer.

Joanne observed: "We've always been politically active—Paul more so than I, although I did work on the first Stevenson campaign. But in this instance, he just felt so strongly about Senator McCarthy that he wanted to take an active part. He's very good at it. I'm no speaker, so I just open discotheques and host dinners."

"In supporting Senator McCarthy I was just a citizen doing what I felt was right, just as thousands of other volunteers all over the country did," said Newman. "I chose Senator McCarthy as my man, because I admired his courage and his convictions. He stood firmly for what I believe in." Newman also revealed, "There were moments during that McCarthy campaign when I would be thinking, 'What in the name of God am I doing here?'"

Newman had to confront his innermost feelings about taking a stand on candidates and issues after a dramatic incident that occurred during the New Hampshire primary in March 1968.

"The thing I'll always remember about that whole McCarthy campaign," Newman told Roger Ebert, "was this cop in New Hampshire. We were going somewhere with a police escort, and one of the cops pointed to his partner and said he'd received word the night before that his son had been killed in Vietnam. And you have to remember that this was before Lyndon Johnson pulled out of the race.

"At a moment like that, it took every ounce of conviction to know the war was wrong. The man's son was dead, and that was a hell of a thing to put against a political theory.

"I offered the cop my sympathy, and he thanked me. Then we stood there. Finally, I blurted out something: What did he think about some creep, some Hollywood peacenik, a functioning illiterate, coming in there and telling him about the war? And the cop said, no, he didn't resent what I was doing. Even if a war takes your boy, he said, that doesn't make it right."

McCarthy won the New Hampshire primary, and Newman began to look forward to the Democratic convention in July. That was several months away, however, and in the meantime Paul was about to take a major step in the direction of turning an old interest into a full-time obsession.

# 9

Paul Newman's interest in cars, and in racing, was well known to film executives; other stars, like Steve McQueen and James Garner, were already into the sport. For the last few years Newman had attempted to arrange his schedule so that he could attend the Indianapolis 500 car race on Memorial Day. So far, however, he had remained primarily a spectator.

MCA-Universal was at the time presenting the Indianapolis 500 as an annual closed-circuit TV attraction in theaters, and intended to incorporate footage from actual races into a made-for-television movie to be called *Winning*. The picture turned into a big-screen venture when Paul Newman took an interest in it, seemingly overlooking the fact that the script was far below his usual standards. What would have been a movie of the week escalated into a major production, with Joanne as co-star, and with Robert Wagner signed for a key role (Newman and Wagner would be playing rival race car drivers). Teenage newcomer Richard Thomas also joined the cast.

Newman and Wagner went to the famous Robert Bondurant Racing School to prepare for the racing sequences. "Two of my first pupils were actors James Garner and Yves Montand for the picture *Grand Prix*," recalled Bondurant, "but that training job was a lot easier because I had more time available. I only had a few weeks to teach Newman."

At the school Newman and Wagner first attended classroom sessions, studying fundamentals, learning how to handle racing cars before they were allowed to drive them. Then they went onto the track and walked around it many times. Finally the two famous "student drivers" rode with an experienced racer in a training car.

Within a week Paul had advanced to driving his own car. Newman went to Phoenix with Bondurant, and, according to the famed teacher, Newman made incredible progress and actually began filming *Winning* with less than two weeks of high-performance driving experience.

"I guess I've been interested in sports cars and bikes for about ten or twelve years," Newman explained at the time, "but it's always been kind of Mickey Mouse with me. I've never really had a chance to do anything seriously. So when the movie *Winning* came up, even though I had some quarrels about their script, it was just sensational for me to be able to drive the big stuff and to have the luxury of going to Bob Bondurant's driving school. I get 'stoned' on automobiles . . . for me it's a natural high, which is marvelous."

Universal was filming location scenes at the track in Elkhart Lake, Wisconsin, and they set up a studio in a garage where they could also film many of the indoor sequences. The cast and crew ate at the local restaurants with all the other race car drivers and crews (typical non-"star" behavior for Newman who, to this day, enjoys being "one of the guys").

James Arnett, stunt coordinator for *Winning,* observed: "Paul took to racing as though it were second nature to him. We had a lot of experienced drivers on hand, but Paul turned out to be better than any of them."

Paul loved racing cars because it fit his personality perfectly. "Like a terrier, I keep gnawing at it, just trying to go faster and faster," he has said.

Although he, in his words, "had never done anything more dangerous than drive into New York," during *Winning* his inclination to race intensified. He noted at the time: "The sensation of fast driving on a track is in doing it right, if you can do it right. Or at least driving within your own limits with skill. I obviously started much too late . . . I could never be a competitive driver. But look at my type. I'm reminded of Joanne, who took up ballet and went on points when she was thirty-five. So there must be something kinky that she gets out of it. She's not going to be another Margot Fonteyn, but she still gets her kicks from it."

He wanted to share his new passion with Joanne. She agreed to take a run around the track, with Paul at the wheel. "We didn't get out of second gear," she laughingly related afterward. "I was holding on so hard Paul said, 'You're leaving fingerprints.' "

During production Joanne drove one lap around the Indianapolis track. "Sure, she may be the only person who ever drove it at forty miles an hour," her husband remarked, "but she tried. She wanted to find out what *I* love about it. I don't suppose she understands any better, but at least she did it."

Newman told a friend: "She thinks competitive driving is the silliest thing in the world. It is also very scary to her, and she doesn't much care for it."

What little plot the film *Winning* had concerned the driver's neglect of his wife, and her relationship with his pal and rival (Robert Wagner). John Foreman, the producer, has recalled the time Robert Wagner and Joanne played a love scene. The couple were in bed, and the action called for Paul to discover them making love. The scene was filmed many times as Newman observed his wife and Robert Wagner endlessly enacting the intimate tableau. During a pause in filming, Wagner eagerly sought Newman's advice on how he thought the scene was going—Wagner wanted to know if Paul thought he was doing a good job. Foreman saw that Newman was on the verge of breaking into laughter, but Paul managed to remain serious and soberly talked the matter over with his fellow actor. Foreman relished the irony of the situation— "I mean, here's Paul giving Wagner several good points about how to behave in bed with his wife."

While on location, the Newmans were sent a print of *Rachel*,

*Rachel* to review. Stewart Stern recalls that Paul arranged a screening for the racetrack driver: "He called me up, very bewildered, to say they had all cried. They had come up and shaken his hand and told him what a beautiful, moving film it was. He said he tended to believe they only did it because he and Joanne were there. He asked me to have a screening in Hollywood. He wanted to know if people would cry if he wasn't in the audience. They did. Then he was worried because the Hollywood audience were friends of mine and perhaps they cried because *I* was there!"

The *Winning* company returned to Hollywood to film final scenes. Meanwhile, Paul and Joanne were starting to publicize *Rachel, Rachel*, which was set for a summer launching.

A volatile climate was engulfing the country, and 1968 was to be one of the most violent years in American history. In April Martin Luther King, Jr., was assassinated. There were well-founded fears of race riots, since it was only the previous year that paratroopers and national guardsmen had had to quell riots in Detroit, and there had been riots in the black neighborhoods of Newark, New Jersey, as well. Fortunately, however, the country dealt with King's death soberly.

Paul and Joanne were now more committed than ever to civil rights causes, to an end to the war in Vietnam, and to the nomination of Senator Eugene McCarthy as the Democratic candidate for president. Senator Robert Kennedy, however, was the front runner in the Democratic race. His murder in June of that year was another stunning blow to the American public. In the midst of all the protest and unrest, President Johnson decided to withdraw himself from the presidential race, leaving as the new front runner Vice President Hubert Humphrey.

That summer, in Chicago, there was another ugly explosion of violence. All the pent-up frustration about the King and Kennedy assassinations, along with the growing distrust of government and anger over the escalation of the war, had produced an atmosphere of revolt. Paul Newman was in Chicago at the Democratic convention when rioting broke out in the streets, and the city's mayor Richard Daley squelched the dissidents harshly.

Newman had given about twenty-five days that year to the McCarthy campaign—full campaign days with four or five or six speeches a day, at airports, at college rallies. His efforts were to no avail; McCarthy did not stand a chance. Hubert Humphrey was nominated as Democratic candidate for president.

A shoo-in for the Republican nomination was the former vice-president, Richard Nixon, who had made a spectacular political comeback. He won his party's nomination and was pitted against Humphrey.

The mood of the country was serious and introspective, and a motion picture exploring a serious and highly personal theme could have a wide appeal. *Rachel, Rachel* did open to glowing reviews.

"We hated to release it," said Joanne. "It's like breaking the umbilical cord. We actually toyed with the idea of making a sixteen-millimeter print to show only at home."

Stewart Stern echoes this sentiment in his recollection of the gala New York premiere: "As we got into the limousine to go to the Plaza Theater, Joanne all gowned and beautiful, we three all looked at each other and said, 'Well, now we have to show it to strangers!' It was something we didn't want to let go of, because it was so personal. The fact that strangers identified with it and liked it was a great surprise to us and a tremendous affirmation of the private faith we had."

There had been a major behind-the-scenes controversy concerning the director's credit. In every movie the director's name appears in the opening credits. For *Rachel* Newman had a fresh and very sensible idea: He wanted his name to appear at the end of the picture. That way audiences would not be distracted by the fact that what they were about to experience was "directed by *Paul Newman*."

A battle royal, involving Newman and the all-powerful Directors Guild, ensued. Joanne has recalled: "He wanted his credit at the end of the picture. It opens with 'Joanne Woodward in *Rachel, Rachel*,' then all the other credits are at the end, with Paul's name last. But the Directors Guild said no. All the credits must come before the film. He was like a scolded school-boy. They made him wait outside the door, then called him and said, 'The director's credit must come before the film,' so Paul said he wouldn't show the film. He called up friends like Wyler and Kazan to support him, and he did finally win the case."

Meanwhile publicity on the film was tremendous, with *Rachel, Rachel* garnering perhaps even more media coverage than the big-budgeted blockbusters of that year, such as *Funny Girl*, *Camelot*, and *2001: A Space Odyssey*.

Warren Cowan, the Newmans' public relations agent, explains how *Rachel, Rachel* was marketed: "First we set up a great many trade screenings for eight people at a time, usually in the Cinema Room of the Beverly Hills Hotel. Often Paul would join us afterwards for coffee. We had a big premiere in New York, and we put Newman and Woodward on all of the TV talk shows. Then the Newmans spent all of Labor Day weekend posing for the cover of *Life*."

The *Life* cover was striking: a closeup photograph of a bronzed, blue-eyed Newman and magnolia-skinned, light-eyed Joanne, lying on the carpet of their rented Malibu beach house. The cover line said it all: "Director and Star: The Newmans Triumph with *Rachel, Rachel*."

The *Life* cover attracted the attention of Richard Nixon. John Foreman has recalled that he was looking at the magazine in his New York hotel room when he received a message to phone Barry Goldwater in Richard Nixon's apartment. Foreman suspected a mistake, but he made the call and was amazed when Nixon answered the phone. It turned out the call actually had been a mistake, that Goldwater had been trying to reach someone else. Nixon, however, on learning that Foreman was partners with Paul Newman, took the opportunity to try to find out how Newman had made the cover of *Life*, a distinction Nixon apparently was seeking. Then, according to Foreman, Nixon added, "By the way, tell Paul I think he's a first-rate actor even if he thinks I'm a lousy politician."

The reviews were overwhelmingly favorable, with the critics citing Newman as a first-rate director. Hoping to capitalize on the media attention, Paul and Joanne concentrated on promoting *Rachel, Rachel.* Since the Newmans prided themselves on keeping their private lives private, and as a result rarely did talk shows or gave interviews, when they did make themselves available for publicity, they were, of course, snapped up.

Joanne was clear about why the picture had turned out so well: "With all due respect to the other wonderful directors I've ever worked with, it was just heaven to work with Paul. . . . He's the best director I've ever had. . . . I kept thinking it must be like the rapport Bergman has with his actors. . . . About halfway through the film, we began to feel like the Moscow Art Theater."

Joanne expounded on Paul's patience: "I know he has a temper but he never lost it once. It must have been difficult for him working with me and Nell."

Although reviews for the picture were spectacular, and initial business in New York and Los Angeles was strong, the distributor knew it would be difficult to sustain these grosses in the hinterlands.

"Who cares about a thirty-five-year-old virgin?" exclaimed a headline in *Women's Wear Daily,* handily summing up the problem. (Actually, this had been Paul's line to Stern and Joanne when they were working on the script.) But what thrilled the Newmans was that *young* people were responding enthusiastically to the picture. "Young people seem to like *Rachel, Rachel* enormously, which is very strange," Woodward observed. "I wouldn't have thought they understood Rachel's problem—yet. Of course, in the larger sense, the problem is always there —people should not stagnate, they should move in some direction. That problem can exist at any age."

Newman discussed the picture with a group of students. "I think that this film went over because it dealt with the values we all deal with: loneliness, birth, death, change, despair," he told them.

When Joanne was asked if *she* now wanted to direct, she answered that she did not have the attributes of a director and usually actors *did not* make good directors. She explained: "An actor has such a strong sense of personal identity and ego. It must be difficult to have the patience and kindness to allow someone else to do a thing his way." She was impressed that her husband was able to "take everything from his acting experience and to use it as a director. I love to act. Paul loves to rehearse."

Newman, meanwhile, was back working as Paul the actor. Unlike some of his peers, who spent years working on one project, Paul often was preparing one movie while filming another and promoting a third. For example, negotiations for the film he was about to begin had gone on for a very long time.

William Goldman had researched the lives of the Sundance Kid and Butch Cassidy for eight years before writing the story of these two legendary characters. Richard D. Zanuck, then head of production at 20th Century-Fox, and his vice president in charge of story operations, David Brown, bought the screenplay, originally titled "The Sundance Kid and Butch Cassidy," for $400,000—at the time a new high for a screenplay. From the start Goldman had wanted Newman for the role of Sundance. As the writer noted, "I had seen Jack Lemmon in the film *Cowboy*, and Newman in *Billy the Kid*, and I thought they'd be great together."

Zanuck wanted Newman, too, but with Steve McQueen as Butch. The deal seemed to be falling into place. However, George Roy Hill, fresh from the success of *Thoroughly Modern Millie*, was picked to direct, and he wanted Newman for the role of Butch, not Sundance.

Hill talked to Newman about the part, but the actor was not interested. Paul was convinced, after the failure of *The Secret War of Harry Frigg*, that he was not good at comedy. Hill had to convince him that the *part* was not comedic, the *situations* were.

McQueen was upset when he learned that, whichever part Newman played, Paul would receive top billing. McQueen's dissatisfaction did not concern George Roy Hill, because Hill already knew who he wanted for Sundance—Robert Redford. He had known the young actor since 1962 and knew what Redford could do with the role.

At first Newman had doubts. He saw Redford as "a Wall Street lawyer type." But, according to Hill, Newman "hates to get involved in casting decisions," so he left it to Hill, Foreman, Zanuck, and Brown to select his co-star. Newman later contended that Redford was Joanne's idea!

Zanuck and Brown had their own ideas. The duo were holding out for Marlon Brando. When Brando could not be found, Zanuck was reportedly ready to "cancel the production rather than use Redford" and apparently phoned Warren Beatty and "offered him the part."

Redford had been assured by Hill that he would get the part. He had cleared his schedule and was waiting. According to Hill, "that takes guts." If Hill didn't win out, all of Hollywood would know that Redford had been rejected by Fox. (Redford's screen credits up to that point were not particularly impressive —*The Chase*, *Inside Daisy Clover*, *This Property Is Condemned*, *Situation Hopeless but Not Serious*, and *War Hunt*, all of them losers at the box office. Only *Barefoot in the Park* had been a hit, and that, everyone reasoned, was largely because of the Neil Simon property, and not the presence of its stars, Redford and Jane Fonda.)

Newman and Goldman intervened in Redford's behalf, since Hill had asked both of them for support. The writer sent Zanuck a telegram. Newman did something a bit more direct: "He called Zanuck and stated very forcefully that Redford was the man he wanted," Hill has said.

Katharine Ross, fresh from *The Graduate*, was signed to play "the girl," a role that Newman would later describe as "incidental." "You know," he explained, "I don't think people realize what that picture was all about. It's a love affair between two men."

Hill remembers that Paul and Redford became pals almost instantly: "It was a rare kind of relationship between those guys on and off the set." They bantered a great deal; indeed they were, in Hill's words, "very fond of each other."

They rehearsed scenes before shooting them, something Redford was not in favor of. Redford later said, "Paul really is a good guy. I really like him. Otherwise, I would have balked at the whole rehearsal thing. I believe rehearsal cuts into the spontaneity of what you're doing. . . . But I rehearsed. Newman was calling the shots, so I rehearsed."

It seems logical that Redford would go along with whatever Paul suggested, though Redford did have his own way of doing things. Newman often kidded his new pal about his habitual lateness, and has commented: "You know Redford's left-handed. I wanted to change the name of the picture to 'Waiting for Lefty.'"

Even though it has been reported that all went well on the set—since Newman respected Redford as an actor, and both actors respected Hill—and even though Newman later referred to this picture as "a perfect example of filmmaking as a community experience," one in which "nobody had to defend his position, and everybody was geared to invent and create," it was not all smooth sailing.

Newman and Hill disagreed on one scene, dubbed "the Bledsoe scene." Each day their arguments became more heated. The screenwriter, Bill Goldman, got into the fray, but Redford stood apart, though at one point, Goldman has recalled, Redford suggested they retitle the movie "The Bledsoe Scene."

News of the arguments filtered back to Los Angeles. Because of the dispute, it was rumored, the film was going to be postponed. It wasn't, of course, although Newman never gave up the fight and Hill stood his ground. Both men were tough, but neither of them would permit professional skirmishes to degenerate into highly negative and personal confrontations.

There were many light moments during the making of the film. Newman, ever the practical joker, found a perfect target in George Roy Hill: "I sawed his desk in half in his office because he wouldn't pay his bill for liquor which he had borrowed from my office. That was kind of the beginning of everything."

Hill and Redford apparently shared Newman's liking for practical jokes. One story involves the trio contemplating a cross-country race. Newman was going to drive his Volkswagen with a Porsche engine, Redford his Porsche, and Hill was going to fly his biplane (which required refueling mid-race, so the vehicles were regarded as "equal").

Pier Angeli starred with Paul Newman in his first film, *The Silver Chalice*, which he regards as one of the worst movies ever made.
*(Phototeque)*

Joanne Woodward in her first film, *Count Three and Pray*. It remains one of her favorite films.
*(Phototeque)*

Joanne Woodward posing pin-up-girl style to publicize a movie? Yes, for *A Kiss Before Dying*. *(Wide World)*

Newman as Rocky Graziano in *Somebody Up There Likes Me*. The film made him a star. *(Phototeque)*

Joanne Woodward portrayed a girl with multiple personalities in *The Three Faces of Eve*. *(Phototeque)*

Woodward in *The Three Faces of Eve*. The film made her a star. *(Phototeque)*

A rare "cheesecake" photo of Joanne Woodward taken the year she married Paul. *(Wide World)*

Paul and Joanne right after their marriage in Las Vegas. She was twenty-seven; he was thirty-three. *(Phototeque)*

On their honeymoon, in their suite at the Connaught Hotel in London. *(Phototeque)*

Backstage, Oscar night, 1958. Joanne won the best actress award for *The Three Faces of Eve*. Miyoshi Umeki and Red Buttons won in the best supporting category for *Sayonara*. Jean Simmons accepted Alec Guinness's Oscar for *The Bridge on the River Kwai*.
*(Phototeque)*

Newman and Elizabeth Taylor in *Cat on a Hot Tin Roof*, a box-office blockbuster. *(Phototeque)*

Newman with Lita Milan in *The Left-Handed Gun.* Arthur Penn directed. *(Phototeque)*

Newman on location for *Exodus* in Israel. His biggest box-office hit until *Butch Cassidy and the Sundance Kid.* *(Phototeque)*

Newman with Jackie Gleason in the now classic film *The Hustler*. Newman was nominated for an Oscar. *(Phototeque)*

The image that seduced audiences around the world: Paul Newman as Hud. Newman received another Oscar nomination for best actor. *(Phototeque)*

*Left:* Joanne in *The Stripper*—neither a critical nor a box-office success. *(Phototeque)*

*Below:* Paul and Joanne in a unique publicity shot for *A New Kind of Love*. *(Phototeque)*

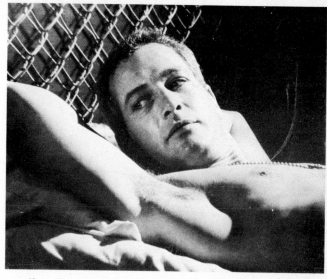

*Above:* Newman as the ultimate loner in *Cool Hand Luke*. The picture was a smash. *(Phototeque)*

*Below:* Paul and Joanne on the set of *Rachel, Rachel. (Phototeque)*

The most popular screen team of them all: Newman and Redford in
*Butch Cassidy and the Sundance Kid*. *(Phototeque)*

Paul and Joanne in
*Winning*, released the
same year (1969).
*(Phototeque)*

Joanne, daughter Nell (left), and Roberta Wallach in *The Effect of Gamma Rays on Man-in-the-Moon Marigolds*, which Newman directed. *(Phototeque)*

A beaming Paul with his radiant wife at the New York Film Critics Circle awards ceremony in 1973. She was named best actress for her performance in *Summer Wishes, Winter Dreams*. *(Phototeque)*

Newman in his biggest box-office film to date, *The Sting*. *(Phototeque)*

With Steve McQueen in *The Towering Inferno*. Getting billing over Newman was *the* high point in McQueen's career, according to McQueen. *(Phototeque)*

With daughters Melissa and Nell in "The Wild Places," a TV special about nature (1974). *(Phototeque)*

Susan Newman at the time of her appearance in *I Wanna Hold Your Hand*, a movie produced by Steven Spielberg. *(Phototeque)*

Scott Newman in a scene from *Fraternity Row*, released a year before his death. *(Phototeque)*

Newman, totally exhausted, had just won the Sports Car Club of America GT-1 national race (1982). *(Wide World)*

Newman's damaged auto after a collision at the Road Atlanta race in Flowery Branch, Georgia, in 1983. *(Wide World)*

Joanne and Paul leave the pits after the collision ended Newman's bid for a third national SCCA driving championship. *(Wide World)*

*Left:* In *The Verdict* Newman triumphed in his first all-out character role. There was another Oscar nomination—but no Oscar. *(Phototeque)*

*Below:* Tom Cruise and Newman in the highly praised *The Color of Money*. The performance won Newman an Oscar for best actor. *(Phototeque)*

Joanne and Richard Kiley starred in the memorable *Do You Remember Love?* in which she portrayed, with devastating impact, a victim of Alzheimer's disease. *(Phototeque)*

Joanne and Karen Allen in *The Glass Menagerie*, directed by Newman. *(Phototeque)*

However, Newman was going to secretly charter a transport plane to beat out the others, and, according to Hill, Redford was taking the whole thing too seriously, so the stunt was called off.

Newman later observed that planning and executing various jokes was a clever tactic on Hill's part; it enabled the actors to really get into, and go with, the picaresque characters they were playing.

"I knew that was going to be the biggest film I'd ever been in," stated Newman in retrospect. "There was no way of missing with it. When we began discussions, I said to Robert Redford, 'You're in your first twenty million dollar picture.' He told me afterwards that he thought at the time, 'God, this is an arrogant snob.' But I was sure about it. Because it had that kind of male *camaraderie* which you don't see very often now—that kind of stuff that Gable and Tracy had. And a lovely kind of hit-and-run sense of humor, a contradictory sort of sense of humor. Then George Roy Hill is a sensational man, and a great director. And, also, it was placed inside the envelope of the western, which is the most successful kind of American film."

On the set of *Butch Cassidy and the Sundance Kid*, at dinner, Paul would fill a coffeepot with Scotch and ice. The future king of salad dressing made a big salad at his table every night, sending portions to other tables. After dinner the group watched the rushes of the day's filming. Newman's hands sweated: "It always happens when I watch rushes."

Hill was making the most of Newman's on-screen charisma by using many close-ups. A number of scenes had no dialogue at all; they were simply reaction shots—of Newman alone or of Newman studying someone or something. Hill used Newman in much the same way that an earlier generation of directors had used Greta Garbo; he constantly filled the screen with the actor's unique and expressive face.

When Rona Jaffe interviewed Newman on location, the actor discussed his daily routine before the start of filming. According to the actor, he got up at five-thirty every day, spent an hour in the sauna and pool, and was on the set by seven.

Jaffe observed: "The thing about the famous Paul Newman

eyes—after the first few minutes, you don't notice them because his personality takes over. You notice his whole face and
what he's saying. He never pushes, never plays the star. Just a
supernice, intelligent guy with charisma. Always refers to
women as ladies, never women, girls, broads, or chicks. A gentleman, but humorous with it."

Newman told Jaffe that he phoned Joanne about three times
a day. At the time Woodward was in London to receive an
award from the Royal Academy of Dramatic Arts for *Rachel,
Rachel*.

*Rachel* was continuing to garner impressive recognition, and
the National Board of Review named it one of the best English-
language films of the year. Both Paul and Joanne received
Golden Globes from the Foreign Press Association. (It should
be noted that the Golden Globes honored two categories of
actresses: best actress in a drama and best actress in a musical.
Barbra Streisand, making her film debut in *Funny Girl*, won in
the latter category.)

The New York Film Critics Circle gave Newman its award
for best director. "Four critics walked out when the vote was
counted," Newman noted. "Being perverse, I take a good deal
of the credit for that." He later said that he was so pleased
about winning the award that the high lasted two days! But
then a terrible depression set in. He hated himself when he
realized how much the award meant to him. He wanted to
believe that how a picture was received was not important; the
important thing was *making* the picture.

The New York Film Critics Circle had voted Joanne best
actress. Woodward herself was vocal about the upcoming Oscar
nominations: "You know what I'm hoping? That Paul gets an
Academy Award as best director. . . . He's been nominated so
often as an actor that it would be a crack-up for him to win as a
director."

When the Academy Award nominations were announced,
*Rachel, Rachel* was not overlooked: Joanne was up for best actress; Estelle Parsons, for best supporting actress; Stewart
Stern, for best screenplay adaptation; and the film, for best
picture. But glaringly absent from the list of nominees was the

name of Paul Newman, who had not been nominated for best director. The directors, who named the candidates in their own category, had had the last word.

Woodward was furious, and stated flatly, "I'm not going to go."

"You're being emotional," Newman told her. And he reminded her that *Rachel, Rachel* had been nominated for best picture. Joanne relented: "My husband decided that I should go, and I do what he says."

Joanne's competition in the best actress category was, to put it mildly, formidable: Katharine Hepburn was nominated for *The Lion in Winter*; Streisand, for *Funny Girl;* Vanessa Redgrave, for *Isadora;* and the Newmans' old friend Patricia Neal, for *The Subject Was Roses.* Neal had made a remarkable recovery from a series of strokes and was easily the sentimental favorite, but it was a hard year to pick an obvious likely winner.

Stern's screenplay lost to James Goldman's script for *Lion in Winter.* Parsons lost to Ruth Gordon for *Rosemary's Baby.* When Ingrid Bergman opened the envelope announcing the winner of the best actress award, she was shocked. It was a tie—Hepburn and Streisand. The final disappointment came when *Oliver* won the best picture award.

Paul and Joanne skipped the post-awards ball, and attended a private party given by friends. They were not snubbing the Academy—the Newmans have never been avid partygoers under any circumstances. Newman is bored by small talk. Joanne can deal with it, but, surprisingly, she dislikes parties more than he does.

At a party, though, when Paul is discussing something that interests him, he can be fascinating. Their pal Barbara Rush (who, incidentally, was married to the Newmans' public relations agent, Warren Cowan) has noted how, at a party, Paul stays very close to Joanne, seeming to rely on her. She noted how people often said he was lucky to be married to her. Rush also noticed how, at a social gathering, Paul would stroke Joanne's arm, or her hair, or sometimes whisper in her ear. He would also look to her for approbation after telling a story. His favorite topics were film directors or automobiles; hers usually

involved the children or something pertaining to them. Regardless, it was obvious to everyone that Paul and Joanne were,
to quote Rush, "in tandem."

*Rachel, Rachel* had served its important purpose. The film had
reestablished Woodward's reputation as a major movie star.
Even she admitted, "I guess *Rachel* has revived my career. I feel
rather like Richard Nixon. Some people thought I'd gone un-
derground."

For *Rachel, Rachel*, the Newmans had used their daughter's
nickname as her professional name, and she had been billed as
Nell Potts. "Now that Nell is a movie star," mused Joanne,
"Stephanie wants to be one too. The kids are all marvelous and
beautiful and slightly insane—five beautiful blond ladies and
Scott, who is eighteen and looks like a French film star."

Scott was indeed a handsome young teenager, but he was
deeply troubled. Paul had sent the boy to private schools,
where he got into many scrapes, and was disciplined for drinking. He had been expelled from some schools because of his low
grades. In general, he seemed unable to cope. His mother had
remarried and was expecting another child. Although they
tried virtually everything, apparently neither of his parents
could help him. They wanted him to continue his education.
He wanted to be free of their parental directives but had grown
used to a comfortable, materialistic life-style. There were no
easy answers.

Joanne and Paul were working together in a new project. To
fulfill an old commitment he had to Paramount, Newman, via
his Newman-Foreman production company, was making
*WUSA*. Stuart Rosenberg (of *Cool Hand Luke*) was directing and
co-producing with Newman-Foreman.

Without the clout of the Newmans, this script would never
have been produced—nor would it have made it to the screen
before the "new" Hollywood was firmly in place. John Gregory Dunne understands this: " 'The deal, that's all this business
is about,' a studio producer told me. . . . 'Who's available,
when can you get him, start date, stop date, percentages—the
deal, it's the only thing that matters. Listen, if Paul Newman

comes in and says he wants to play Gertrude Lawrence in *Star!*, you do it, that's the nature of the business.'"

Newman—and Joanne, a hot property again—wanted to do *WUSA*, and by the spring of 1969 the film was in production. Newman was going for something meaningful with this venture: "I think films can change the way people think in a very, very small way. They are more a reflection of our times. Some people are going to watch *WUSA* saying, 'Treasonous, self-defeating. You indicate that our society is brutalized, that there's no room for a vulnerable human being.'"

The script concerns political corruption and a fascist conspiracy in a southern city. It offered a gritty role for Joanne— that of an ex-prostitute who is framed by the police and sent to prison, where she commits suicide. Newman plays a hard-drinking disc jockey at a right-wing radio station with the call letters WUSA; he is caught up in the political corruption. The rest of the cast was strong: Anthony Perkins (as a welfare worker), Bruce Cabot and Pat Hingle (as politicians), and Cloris Leachman, Lou Gossett, and Don Gordon.

Stuart Rosenberg has compared Newman's and Woodward's differing approaches to acting. He found Joanne so controlled that he virtually never needed to repeat a direction, although sometimes it was necessary to prod her to try a different approach. Paul, on the other hand, was the exact opposite, always analyzing his character and searching for motivation for virtually every gesture. "You must do everything you can to try to relax him," explained Rosenberg, adding that Newman and Woodward were, in his opinion, both virtuosos. However, still it amazed the director to observe the varying paths Paul and Joanne took "to reach the same brilliant performance level."

While Newman, Woodward, and company were enthusiastic about *WUSA* and its political statement, the powers-that-be at Paramount had their doubts about the marketability of this film, even with the two stars.

With two Newman-Woodward pictures in the can, and *Rachel* in release, the talk, of course, was that Newman and Woodward were *the* current screen duo. Joanne discounted this again and again, flatly stating that the only reason they continued to work together was that it was convenient. There was no doubt that family life was difficult enough without each parent having a different schedule.

In reality, Paul and Joanne were living a pressure-cooker existence. They were reading scripts for future movies, they were committed to publicity and promotion on current movies, and they were in demand for various causes. Through it all, they faced many personal challenges, including the struggle to keep their family close and together.

Their life-style had inevitable drawbacks for the children, and in later years Newman commented on their problems. He acknowledged how hard it must have been for the kids to have gone to so many different schools and to have had to constantly leave behind their friends; inevitably the children reached a point where they were extremely cautious about committing themselves to new friends. A concerned Paul and Joanne also faced the universal dilemma confronting most fathers and mothers: Whatever they did with their children, it seemed to be wrong. "You simply don't know what the right choice is," Newman later lamented. He added that while he was glad their upbringing had made them self-sufficient, it had also made them extremely shy.

Paul Newman was anything but shy about protecting his own interests vis-à-vis his completed, but not-yet-released, films. He had to keep his finger on the pulse of what was happening to a film in postproduction. *Butch Cassidy* was set to open in the fall, but a "distribution hotshot" (the phrase is Newman's) was suggesting that it open in Texas on Memorial Day. "Zanuck says, *Good thinking! We can hurry it a little in the lab.*" Newman's response: "The hell we can." He knew the complicated montage sequences would take months to complete *properly*. Also, the musical score must never be rushed: "I'm expected to stand by and discover that my picture is only going to be sixty or seventy percent realized because some jerk has the bright idea we can take a million dollars out of Texas if we open on Memorial Day. As it so happens, I've already *got* a picture opening in Texas on Memorial Day. *Winning* is opening in Texas on Memorial Day."

In June 1969 *Winning* was released nationally. Hardly a classic movie and not one to further the careers of anyone connected with it, *Winning* was not a critical success. After *Rachel* something important was expected of the Newmans. *Winning* was strictly middle-grade, commercial stuff that betrayed its television roots. Nevertheless, the film was successful at the box office, because the Newmans were in it, and because production costs had been exceptionally low. The big racing movie of the day, *Grand Prix*, had cost a then astronomical $12 million (and the movie flopped). *Winning*, Newman has said, "came in at $5.2 million with overhead"; the film was shot for about $4 million.

That month, Newman, Sidney Poitier, and Barbra Streisand formalized a plan that their agents, managers, and financial advisers had been working on for months. At a ceremony at the Plaza Hotel in New York, the three stars signed incorporation papers for First Artists, a new production company, which would release its product through Warner Bros.

First Artists was hailed as the most important partnership of major stars since the formation of United Artists back in 1919 by Douglas Fairbanks, Mary Pickford, Charlie Chaplin, and D. W. Griffith. The First Artists stars would ostensibly have total control over virtually every aspect of their pictures, with little or no outside interference. It sounded wonderful in theory, and looked good on paper, but anyone familiar with the problems faced by the initial United Artists group knew that things had not really changed that much. Indeed, it was not going to be easy to fulfill the company's lofty goals, assuming, of course, that it would even be possible to do so.

Paul and Joanne, who had managed to elude public scrutiny of their private lives for so many years, were suddenly the subject of talk. Reports were that Paul was drinking heavily during this period, and that there was discord in the marriage.

Those on intimate terms with the couple were stoic. The Newmans had never been a fantasy couple. They had weathered many problems in the course of their relationship, including the inevitable strain that comes from personalities so vastly different. As with most couples, one was grumpy in the morning (Joanne), the other cheerful. She lost her temper easily, he didn't (Paul was more of the "slow burn" type); but when he did lose his temper, he did not forgive or forget easily, whereas she did. Seemingly, at least at this time in their lives, the greatest difference between them was that Joanne, because of her low blood pressure, did not drink anything except an occasional sherry. And Paul drank, in her words, "nearly everything."

She was aware that her dissatisfaction with his drinking, and her inability to accept it unconditionally, sometimes made her into someone neither of them liked: "Often I hear myself saying to him, in a voice which is a cross between a howl of fury and the whisper of a saint, 'You're stoned, you're getting stoned —I can see it in your eyes.' And, you know, nothing is worse than somebody doing that. He's much nicer about the disparity in our natures than I am."

Scott Newman's drinking was also cause for concern. Scott, according to the knowledgeable reporter Bob Thomas, was already "on the edge of danger." At nineteen, Scott was drinking heavily and using drugs; and when drunk, Scott became violent. He had taken up skydiving and was also interested in fast cars and motorcycles.

There was ample evidence, from friends and relatives, that the boy harbored tremendous resentment against his father. The best available professional help was offered, but Scott was uncooperative. Though the family might not have been able to see it at the time, it is clear in retrospect that young Newman was on a path of self-destruction.

Paul was later to say that, from this point on, he lived in fearful expectation of the inevitable telephone call.

Life in a goldfish bowl has claimed many a victim. The Newmans were determined not to let it happen to them, but by July 1969 rumors of an impending split were so widespread that the couple took out a $2,000 ad in *The Los Angeles Times*, which proclaimed, "We Are Not Breaking Up."

Peter Ustinov later commented on why the Newmans had caused speculation in the first place: "They are one of the very few couples who are privileged to be in love, and because they love and quarrel occasionally, they can afford to be quite brash about each other." And he noted, "They have shut the window against the drafts of difference."

The couple left for a much-needed holiday in England, the country where they had spent their honeymoon. On their return, it was back to business.

Professionally, Joanne was again box-office. The National Association of Theatre Owners had named her and Steve Mc-Queen the "Box Office Stars of the Year." She was set for a new film, *They Might Be Giants*, to be produced by Newman-Foreman.

In addition, Newman-Foreman had bought the rights to Arthur Kopit's acclaimed and controversial play *Indians* for $500,000, a walloping price for a far from commercial piece. But *Indians* was legend-shattering stuff and offered the kind of message Paul Newman responded to. "Buffalo Bill—there's a guy who went out and killed all the buffalo that the Indians used for meat. He was really a butcher, and we made him a hero," declared Newman. "But we create legends because that's the nature of our need."

Newman was keenly aware that films created legends that were far removed from historical fact: "I think movies have been important in sustaining heroic images. The legends of the West have left us with great hangovers, like the inaccurate representation of the American Indian. The cowboys were always good guys for killing Indians, and the Indians were always bad guys for killing white folks, even though you know the white folks were encroaching on their land. There have been a series of legends that have been fostered by motion pictures, like the idea that Custer's last stand was glorious. If my memory serves me right, I think he graduated last or second last in his class. Custer was an arrogant ass who made a terrible mistake."

There had been a great deal of speculation about if, and when, Paul himself would enter the political arena. After all, Newman epitomized for many Americans the *involved* star, the star with a *conscience*.

Gore Vidal noted, "He had a chance to run for senator from Connecticut, and I urged him to do so. He declined, probably for financial reasons—he was supporting forty people at the time. I'm sorry he didn't run. He is one of the few people I know who has a good character."

Newman himself tried to squelch the persistent rumors of his political ambitions with a succinct statement: "I don't have the arrogance," he said, "and I don't have the credentials." What he failed to add was that he did not have the personality to deal with all the glad-handing that would be necessary.

One of his pet causes in the late sixties was the Center for the Study of Democratic Institutions, in Santa Barbara, California. Robert Hutchins, a former president of the University of Chicago, was the director. Newman spoke admiringly of the group of intellectuals associated with the center: "When you go there and listen carefully, sometimes you are mesmerized by the magnitude of your own ignorance. There, instead of the separate cloisters of the economist, the theologian, the philosopher, the physicist and the sociologist, groups of thinkers from these fields are all together. They study what they call incidental papers. You see, one of the problems of the world today is diplomacy by crisis. These people study various problems before they become crises. One week they'll murder management, and the next week they'll murder labor. It's marvelous just to be able to sit down with these men and listen."

Back at work, Newman agreed to narrate a TV documentary, *From Here to the Seventies*, scheduled to broadcast in October on the NBC network. Both Paul and Joanne were recognized in 1969 for their contributions to social causes. Jointly they received the William J. German Humanitarian Relations Award of the American Jewish Committee. And that fall Paul was appointed co-chairman of the Citizens for Duffy campaign —the Reverend Joseph Duffy was running for Congress in the Newmans' home state, Connecticut.

On-screen the macho sex symbol now added a new characterization to his belt, the comedic cowboy, as *Butch Cassidy* swept the country. Paul Newman's cinema persona had never shimmered so intensely. His performance was acknowledged to be the anchor of the film—the catalyst that made it all work.

Surprisingly, initial openings had broken no records, but the picture built steadily into a "monster hit," owing to excellent word of mouth. And the surefire, audience-grabbing angle of discovering a new star, Redford, added luster and appeal to the film. Also helpful was that the song from the film, "Raindrops Keep Falling on My Head," became a huge hit. *Butch Cassidy* was offbeat as well as entertaining, the kind of picture that other producers would frantically attempt to duplicate over the next few years.

Newman was named the number-two box-office attraction in films as 1969 drew to a close, with the number-one slot soon to be his. He was at the pinnacle, not only acclaimed as a star, an actor, and a director, but also admired as a man of integrity.

But Newman had reached a crossroads. There were numerous professional obligations and commitments to fulfill, but one fact was undeniable: Newman's enthusiasm for acting was by now, if not dead, definitely dormant.

# ☆ 10 ☆

☆

In the late nineteen sixties Jack Garfein had decided that since he and so many others from the Actors Studio were now based in Hollywood, there should be an Actors Studio West. Paul Newman liked his idea, Garfein said. "Paul had no doubt that something should be done. And he was just as concerned with Actors Studio organizational abilities as I was. He literally gave us the first $20,000 to get the place. He was wonderful."

Paul even helped Garfein in the search for a building to house the Studio, and in the process the two men renewed their friendship.

Garfein recalls: "Paul said to me, 'You know, Jack, I never thought I would arrive at this point in my career as an actor and never have done Hamlet or a major part in a really classic or great play, particularly Shakespeare. I don't know—when I was a young actor [if I had] thought that I'd get to the age of fifty and never play those parts, I don't know whether I'd still be an actor or not—and here I am now, and there's no chance of my doing them.' "

Garfein was emotional: "Well, why not, Paul? Why not do it at the Actors Studio? That's what it's here for."

"No, you don't understand," replied Newman. "Even if I do

it at the Actors Studio, now they come in to see 'Paul Newman' do Hamlet. I don't have the freedom anymore of an actor—just doing it, trying it."

"Paul, I think that's tragic and ridiculous," answered Garfein heatedly. "You certainly have the ability." Garfein pointed out that Paul could take three or four months to work on a part; as an actor he *could* experiment, *explore* his capabilities in any fashion he chose. In Garfein's view, an actor did not need to perform before a paying audience. He could invite an audience or have no audience at all.

The two men were obviously talking about different things —Garfein about stretching oneself as an actor and taking risks; Newman about losing the freedom to take such risks, which is the price the actor pays for stardom.

After several days of checking out sites for the Actors Studio West, Garfein took Newman to a place he thought appropriate. Paul liked the building, and said, "Okay, I think this is the right atmosphere. Let's take it."

"And so Paul took out a checkbook, wrote out a check, and gave it to the landlady," Garfein relates. "But the landlady said, 'I know Mr. Garfein but I don't know you.' I thought it was a joke. She was dead serious. I had to sign next to Paul with my name, address, and phone number! Paul got a great kick out of all this."

Garfein approached Steve McQueen about the proposed Actors Studio West: "I wrote Steve. He called me and said, 'Jack, I'm not really interested in actors. My interest is in delinquents.'

"I said, 'All right, let me ask you something. When you got into the Actors Studio, what did that mean to you? When I did what I did for you, it helped your strength, confidence—you said, "God, this guy really believes in me." '

"There was a pause. Then Steve said, 'Okay, you made your point, you're right. There are others who need help right now. It's very important. If actors don't help actors, who the hell else is gonna do it? Okay, I'll send a check.'

"How much do you think he sent me?" Garfein reflects a moment, then answers his question: "Twenty-five dollars."

Paul Newman, on the other hand, was generous not only with his money but with his time and his commitment to the project (he later became president of the Actors Studio). But though his involvement with acting and the Actors Studio continued, it was racing that really fired Paul's enthusiasm. His interest in the sport had accelerated dramatically after *Winning*, and now Paul wanted to enter amateur meets. Newman moved ahead with characteristic caution. He would incorporate racing into his schedule slowly.

After all, he had many other commitments—financial and personal. He was more than a star now, he was a producer too. Newman-Foreman was in full swing, with Joanne filming the company's *They Might Be Giants* in New York City.

The publicist assigned to the picture was astonished at Woodward's attitude. The actress did not care at all which still pictures of her the studio released; whatever the publicist chose from the contact sheets was fine with Joanne, even though she had approval of any shots taken of her, a contractual privilege actresses generally fought for. In truth, Joanne Woodward cared only about looking *in character*. If the pictures showed the crow's-feet around her eyes, or other imperfections, she couldn't have cared less.

In *Giants* she was playing Watson, a fortyish psychiatrist assigned to the case of a mental patient (played by George C. Scott) who believes he is Sherlock Holmes. Woodward and Scott were certainly a combination of talents that, Universal reasoned, would have strong appeal for the upscale market. Jennings Lang was producing, and Anthony Harvey (*A Lion in Winter*) was directing. For Woodward, the project had great merit.

"I only do films I believe in, and there aren't many of those," she noted with accuracy and candor, adding, "Unless you need the money desperately, it's ridiculous to spend such a large amount of your time with things that don't seem meaningful. I'm involved all the time with Planned Parenthood, peace groups, ecology groups; why, even when my kids and I go to New York, we spend a great deal of time picking up trash in Central Park, hoping that somebody else will too. Nobody else ever does. I am in despair about this country and working very hard to do something about it in as many ways as I can."

One of the ways she could do something was to agree to be interviewed, but both Joanne and Paul often became testy with the press over things they thought had been misquoted, or over questions they thought inappropriate. There was subtle criticism of the Newmans because of their ambivalence concerning publicity. After all, no one forced them to give interviews; they did so to promote their own interests. The couple would discuss their private lives with the press when they felt like it, but not when they didn't feel like it.

Around this time Newman uttered the classic lines that have haunted him for almost two decades. When questioned about fidelity, he said: "I don't like to discuss my marriage, but I will tell you something which may sound corny but which happens to be true. I have steak at home. Why should I go out for hamburger?" He also described Joanne as "the best of the big-time broads." Feminists did not appreciate such comments.

There was no doubt that in some instances the Newmans had cause to be put off by the press. An interviewer once remarked to Paul, "You set a precedent by winning the final TV cut on *Rachel, Rachel*."

"Yeah," Newman acknowledged. "Maybe so."

Then, according to Paul, the interviewer wrote, "Newman says he set a precedent." Newman was furious. "I didn't say it, and it's not the sort of thing I would say; it smacks of arrogance." He said he was going to phone the "bastard" and complain.

Although the Newmans had the Rogers and Cowan public relations organization to field questions from the press for them, in most, if not all, circumstances these two intelligent actors were more than capable of handling themselves. If Joanne was now openly discussing certain aspects of their personal lives, it was because she was dealing with problems of parenthood that she had never envisioned. Sharing her problems was Woodward's way of helping others to cope with similar situations.

On the professional front, Woodward had found another

novel, *Mrs. Beneker*, which had the earmarks of a possible vehicle for her. One of the agent Gil Parker's clients was the playwright Paul Zindel, who had a current Off-Broadway hit, *The Effect of Gamma Rays on Man-in-the-Moon Marigolds*. Parker brought Zindel and the Newmans together, suggesting Zindel as screenwriter for *Mrs. Beneker*.

The Newmans were among the first stars Zindel worked with. The writer recalls: "I was nervous as anything about the meeting. I must admit there were a couple of strange things: Number one, I was not aware of the fact that Paul Newman was handsome. Number two, I also didn't know he had blue eyes, because I'm color-blind. And so I really didn't know why people were fascinated, or why he was such a big star. . . . Joanne Woodward I didn't know very much about. I knew she was a star. That was about it. But I was thrilled to be working for these two big stars, and the more that I saw the impact that these two stars had, and the power that they had, the more impressed I was about working for them."

The writer and the two stars apparently hit it off and began to see each other socially. Zindel recalls an early excursion to the ballet in the company of the Newmans: "She [Joanne] used to handle the ballet tickets, and all the theater tickets, and she has her little calendar, and it's packed full of tickets for every day and everything she wants to see. And so she picked a night we would be going to the ballet."

On the scheduled night, Zindel continues, "I was invited to . . . what they call their 'fuck flat' in New York. A very distasteful term. It was Paul Newman who said that, not Joanne. He said that, and I thought it was out of character. It was on the East Side. But Joanne made me a wonderful caviar omelette. She was into omelettes at that time, learning how to make omelettes from some master omelette mistress in New York. And then we went to the ballet, and the limo pulled up for us, and I really loved getting into the limo, and I was very excited about going to the ballet. . . .

"So we go driving along, and as we are one block from Lincoln Center . . . I noticed Paul taking out a vial, and he's putting his head back, and I said, 'What are you doing?' And he said, 'Oh, it's just a little Murine.' Now, I didn't realize that he's clearing up his terrific blue eyes that the public knows him for."

At the theater, Zindel goes on, "we start walking down the aisle, and the whole place turns around!" A woman asked for Paul's autograph and was stopped "cold." Another woman drew Zindel himself aside and asked if *he* could get the star's autograph. Newman's policy on autographs, Zindel learned then, was an absolute no; he just did not give autographs.

Zindel remembers that no one asked for Joanne's autograph. As he explains it, in public "she supports him, and he's the star. Not in any weak way. . . . I guess it's just choreography."

The Newmans were eager to see the playwright's work. Zindel made arrangements to get them tickets to see *Gamma Rays,* but then forgot to go to the theater the night they were attending, and just stayed at home. "The phone rang. I was avoiding calls at that time, and I picked up the phone to see if it was a call I wanted to take. I hear sounds of a theater mob in the background, but nobody spoke, so I hung up. Then it rang again, and I picked it up, and nobody speaks again, right? And I hear some man's voice say, 'Somebody answers, but nobody talks,' right? Hangs up again. It turns out it was Paul Newman trying to call to say they had seen the play, and they wanna buy the film rights!"

Negotiations began. Meanwhile the Newmans and Zindel continued to mix socially, and Zindel continued to work on the *Mrs. Beneker* project. Zindel was invited to the Newmans' house in Connecticut. "It was poolside, with Ray Stark and Norman Twain, me, and them."

Zindel went to Connecticut again to visit the Newmans. "They were wearing caftans," he recalls, "which shocked me. I didn't know men wore caftans. Edward Villella, the ballet dancer, was there. Joanne was *really* into ballet and taking ballet lessons, and so forth." During the time he spent with the Newmans, Zindel observed Joanne closely. "She was a rather secure woman, and you got a sense of their family life, and you got a sense of their community up there in Connecticut, and what they were protecting."

When Joanne completed *They Might Be Giants*, she attended the traditional wrap party that follows all productions. A publicist who attended the event at Mamma Leone's restaurant in midtown Manhattan recalls that Joanne did not come on as "the star," but instead seemed like just another member of the group. She was mainly interested in talking with the other crew members' about their families and their plans for the future.

"It wasn't an act," the publicist says. "She's a thoughtful and generous person."

Woodward once explained: "I'm probably just as self-centered as most actors, but I'm also southern and your upbringing stays with you. Southern ladies are not rude, and they are not thoughtless. Life is role-playing to a great extent, and that happens to be a very comfortable role to play."

Another role Woodward played was being nice on the set, which she always was. Making this last film, however, almost drove her out of the business. "It was the most miserable experience I ever had," she said. "I hated it." But she quickly pointed out that her dissatisfaction had nothing to do with George C. Scott or anyone else. She was just annoyed that moviemaking wasn't fun anymore: "You get no sense of joy. Too many practical considerations." Production concerns were literally overwhelming, and she was troubled by the fact that good "little" pictures could not be made anymore. Either a picture was a huge hit or a disaster. There was too much riding on every picture, and the pressures overshadowed the creative input.

Still, Paul and Joanne sought "little" properties for Woodward. One source of good material was theater, and of course both the Newmans loved going to the theater. There were too many problems, however: Paul was *always* recognized and pestered for autographs (which he wouldn't give), and the evening would be ruined. Joanne noted that many people had the audacity to *touch* him. Older women tried to pinch his cheek and tell him how cute he was. The Newmans would often have to leave at intermission.

When one of their friends was in a play, Paul and Joanne

would make a special effort to get to the theater. Once, on the West Coast, Barbara Rush was starring in a production of the romantic comedy *Forty Carats*. Rush has recalled how Paul and Joanne, acutely aware of actors' nerves before a performance, hadn't told her they would be in the audience and even took balcony seats so she wouldn't spot them. They came backstage afterwards and it was immediately obvious to Rush that Joanne had adored the play and Paul definitely hadn't. The actress wasn't surprised—the play was pure entertainment, with no underlying message, and she felt that Paul always felt guilty if he either appeared in, or went to see, something without social significance. Joanne, on the other hand, loved light and airy material. She and Barbara had a lot in common—both loved "movie movies," soap operas and comedies that had nothing important to say.

Rush's role in *Forty Carats*, that of a glamorous forty-year-old woman (and mother) who has an affair with a twenty-five-year-old man, was one that Joanne wanted to play on-screen. After all, she reasoned, Ingrid Bergman had just done *Cactus Flower*. But Joanne knew that she had no chance of being cast. "Let's face it," she said, "nobody is going to hire me for a comedy . . . nobody is going to cast me as a forty-year-old sex symbol." This is the only part she has ever really *fought* for.

So, for the moment Joanne returned to the role of housewife and mother while Paul prepared to film *Sometimes a Great Notion*. He loved the Ken Kesey novel on which it was based—"a book about people." But he was torn: "I'd love to direct the film; yet it's also got a great part in it. You reach the obvious question: can I do both? If I could get three weeks of rehearsal instead of two, and if we had enough pre-production work, which we never had with *Rachel*, I might."

Henry Fonda, Lee Remick, and Michael Sarrazin were to play the other leads. It was a dramatic departure for Fonda; he would be playing his first elderly man, a character with grown children. Universal's Jennings Lang was producing, and eventually Richard Colla was signed to direct.

The young character actor Richard Jaeckel's career was revitalized by this film. Today he enthusiastically discusses Paul

Newman and how Newman decided on him for the part—a
couple of years before the film even went into production.

Jaeckel had first met Newman in the fifties. At the time
Jaeckel was appearing in the West Coast stage production of
*The Desperate Hours*, in the role that Newman himself had origi-
nated on Broadway. Newman came backstage one night after
seeing his performance at the Carthay Circle Theater; as
Jaeckel recalls, "He was kind and charming."

In the late sixties, while Jaeckel was visiting friends in the
Malibu Colony, he again encountered Paul. The Malibu Colony is a private enclave where many show business families
own houses. "Someone like Paul could go there, sit down and
actually relax and not have people climbing all over him,"
Jaeckel says.

Jaeckel was on the beach playing with the children of the
people he was visiting. "We were out there throwing a football
around and swimming and surfing and all that." During the
course of the day Newman came over to Jaeckel, discussed the
upcoming film, and offered him a part. Jaeckel conjectures that
the reason Paul picked him was that at that particular time he
had the right build for the part of a logger in the north woods.

He found out indirectly, years later, that when the property
finally got a go, agents began submitting clients for casting.
Fonda was set; Remick and Sarrazin had commitments to Universal. "Now it comes to the character of Joe," relates Jaeckel,
"and they start around the table. Casting agents, vice presidents. 'We think we like this guy—this guy—this guy—' Every
man had three or four different actors to submit. All good
men."

Many of the men submitted, like George Kennedy, were currently hotter, as character stars, than Jaeckel was.

Jaeckel was later told what happened next: "They got around
to Paul, who said nothing. And everybody looked—you could
have heard a pin drop. He got up, and he said, 'You know, those
guys are all good guys, nice guys—they'd all be good. I was
thinking about Richard Jaeckel for this part.' There was not a
sound. Paul looked around—and by the time he looked around

a little bit more, a guy over there says, 'Yeah.' Another guy says, 'Sure.' And another and another."

Jaeckel continues: "The whole point is that Paul Newman could have had Madame Schumann-Heink play the part if he says, 'Fellas, I want this guy.' But he has a directorate sitting there, and he has too much class to force it. So he lays it there in a subtle fashion."

Jaeckel talks about his reaction when Annabel King (a friend who also knew Paul) told him how it had all evolved: "I had chills running up and down, and I just broke into tears. It's not because I was going to get the job or not, but here was a guy who finally followed through and did what he said he was going to do. I told Annabel, 'I don't give a fuck if the picture is ever made or not. That guy couldn't be any higher on my list.' "

That spring, while Paul was in Oregon, on location for *Sometimes a Great Notion*, Joanne and the children were in Los Angeles, a city she didn't care for. Her then-current phrase was, "Eleven years to emphysema in Los Angeles."

Paul Zindel was also in Los Angeles. The Newmans had bought his play for $65,000, and although he did not want to write the screenplay for *Marigolds*, he was still working on *Mrs. Beneker*, so he and Joanne decided to discuss the script over a Chinese dinner.

Zindel recalls: "I hired my first limo. I was staying at the Beverly Hills Hotel. I was a complete nervous wreck as we went to pick her up, and she got in, and she was very nice and, in a sense, a little nervous too. What she did was very unusual. As we were driving to a restaurant on Sunset, we stopped at a light, and some car pulls up next to us. And maybe some people are just simply looking over, right? Which everyone does, right? And Joanne yells out from within the car, 'Yes, there's a star in here! Yes, there's a star in here!' But it was a nervous reaction more than anything else."

Today Paul Zindel is a noted and successful screenwriter, as well as playwright, but he admits that back then he really did not know what actors were talking about when they discussed film scripts. He explains: "In retrospect, I must also say that all the stars I've ever worked with, including the Newmans, were specialists in their acting talents—i.e., they *were* the talent—they could tell when something was missing in a script, but they couldn't tell you how to solve it. They didn't pretend to do that—they knew it just needed more energy.

"They discussed the process and the things that they wanted 'punched up.' I didn't know what on earth they were talking about, because I hadn't been exposed to Lee Strasberg and all that—and I knew nothing about the process."

At dinner, when Joanne began discussing the *Mrs. Beneker* script, Zindel was completely stunned. "She mentioned something that threw me entirely from the point of view of the story. She didn't know *who* Mrs. Beneker was yet. She didn't know *who* the character was. So she said, 'What makes this character laugh? What makes this character cry? What's this character like?' She went down a list of about five things that Stella Adler would ask. And I, of course, couldn't answer. It was too sweeping a question. And also, I didn't have the tools then. I didn't have the training yet in order to answer something like that.

"And so, while the food was delicious, the meeting was clearly unsatisfactory to her, but she was very nice about it when I drove her home. She invited me in for a moment to give me a glass of wine and show me some Utrillos that were on the wall. She had bought nine small Utrillos that she found in a junk heap; the people hadn't known they were Utrillos."

When Zindel left, the limo would not start and he had to go back into the house to phone for a replacement. He remembers that Joanne was "already on the phone with Paul Newman in Oregon." The couple might not spend all their time together, but they were constantly in touch, keeping each other posted and exchanging ideas on the latest developments.

As it turned out, although Joanne had reservations about the script, the Newmans were still interested in having Zindel continue with the *Mrs. Beneker* project. His status had been enhanced when *Marigolds* won a Pulitzer Prize.

Zindel recalls: "I met an actor who had been up in Oregon when Paul Newman came running in with the news: 'Hey, you know that little play I bought Off-Broadway? It just won the Pulitzer Prize, and I only paid $65,000 for it.' "

Zindel did not regret that the Newmans had gotten the play so inexpensively. He knew it would be a difficult film to make. He also felt that *Rachel, Rachel* was a terrific film. "I really loved it," he says. "Artistically, I thought it was sensational. I thought the Newmans were the perfect ones for *Marigolds*."

Joanne and the girls joined Paul on location in Oregon that summer. Scott was there, too, working on the second unit. For two weeks the company prepared; in the mornings they rehearsed scenes in a local high school auditorium, and in the afternoons they would go on location to learn how to run the various saws, cranes, and other logging equipment necessary for the scenes in the film.

Early in the production it was obvious there were "artistic differences" between the young director, Richard Colla, and the veteran star, Henry Fonda. Despite what people thought— that Fonda was such a pro that he did not need direction—in his own mind, Fonda *wanted* a director "who directed."

"Don't tell me just to walk around, move here and there and do what I feel!" Fonda yelled one day. "I have to be directed. It says on the call sheet that you're the director. Now direct me."

Another report, quoting Fonda himself, claims the problem with Colla had resulted from his preoccupation with camera angles and setups. The actors felt that they were unimportant.

Newman would often take Colla aside, and talk with him, presumably about the cast's unhappiness. But the writing was on the wall. Colla was soon replaced.

Henry Fonda later confided, "I think Paul resisted the idea of firing the director, because he felt in his bones he would then have to do it himself." According to Fonda's recollections, Newman did not want to act *and* direct in the same film. Paul then tried and failed to convince his pals George Roy Hill and Paul Bogart to take over.

It would not be easy to get another director who would be acceptable to everyone, not on such short notice. There was a danger that the whole project would have to be scrapped; that is when Newman made the decision to take over the direction himself.

He called a meeting of the cast and crew. He told them that rather than shut down production and stop the momentum they had going, he would take over direction. "I'm gonna need all the help you can give me," he said. "We've got no egos here. Let's just work as hard as we can, and make the best picture that we can."

Richard Jaeckel recalls: "There wasn't a dry eye in the house. It wasn't because he required it or demanded it, but he deserved that kind of reaction."

Professionals like Fonda, Jaeckel, and others in the cast and crew knew that this was really an unselfish act. They knew that an actor would suffer if he starred in a movie that he himself was directing. Jaeckel says, "I think his choice was to put himself second and the picture first."

The task facing Newman was difficult, but he received some help from his friend George Roy Hill. Newman has recalled: "When I took over the direction of *Sometimes a Great Notion*, and was in bad shape . . . he was the first guy to call up and say, 'How are you?' I said, 'I'm terrible.' He said, 'I'll be up.' He got in his airplane and flew up to Portland and said, 'What do you want me to do?' I said, 'I've got fifteen thousand feet of silent footage, and I don't even have time to look at it.' So he sat in the cutting room up there for three days, put the sequence together, and I said, 'What do I need?' He said, 'You need twenty setups, you need a point of view of the kid, you need his walking away shot, and so forth.' And then he got in his airplane and left."

There is a story that exemplifies the problem of being both a film's director and one of its leading players. In one scene the family in *Notion* is at a big dinner table. It was a difficult scene because there was a great deal of dialogue, but they had rehearsed it thoroughly. They began a take, and at first the whole scene went smoothly. Then there was silence; Paul had messed up his cue. After a beat or two he realized what had happened. "Oh shit!" he exclaimed. He'd been directing in his mind, listening to the other actors, and had forgotten he was also an actor, an integral part of the scene itself.

During production Newman broke his ankle in a motorcycle accident. That meant there would be further delays in shooting, and the film was suddenly over budget. However, the team decided to remain and finish the film. "When you're working that close with people who are that good," declares Richard Jaeckel, "and I don't just mean that professionally, but 'that good' personally, you develop a love for them. You develop a loyalty for the project."

Toward the end of production Newman took time out for his new avocation. He was now on the board of directors of the Ontario Motor Speedway in California, and the OMS was launching its first event that September—the California 500. Prior to the professional race the OMS held a celebrity race that August, and Newman was driving a Porsche 914. Among other celebrities in the race were James Garner, Dick Smothers, Roman Polanski, and Robert Redford, and the professional racers Jackie Stewart, Graham Hill, and Mario Andretti.

"I don't plan to do that much driving, and I haven't done that much in the past," Newman said at the time, "because one of the problems has been, until recently, what you would call studio disapproval." That problem had been solved, but there were other considerations: "I would hesitate to drive in competition now. Not because I would be afraid to, but because I'm forty-five years old, I started late, and my reflexes aren't really as hot as they should be. I'd hate to run seventeenth in a field of fourteen. I might run some club races."

At this point Newman owned a Stingray 'Vette and two Volkswagens that were Porsche-equipped.

Production finally ended on *Notion* in mid-fall, but there was considerable postproduction work to be done, at a time when Newman was campaigning for the congressional candidates he supported—the Reverend Joe Duffy in Connecticut and Pete McCloskey in California.

According to Woodward, Newman made "sixty-three appearances in three days" for Joe Duffy. "I don't have Paul's political acumen," she said, "so I stay at home and use the telephone or write letters and try to get out the votes. But Paul is truly a direct-action man."

The Newmans were also on the publicity trail to launch *WUSA* but were frustrated by the fact that Paramount had no confidence in the picture. The critics almost unanimously lambasted the movie, labeling it a pretentious, political diatribe. Joanne argued: "*WUSA* is a fair statement about the country right now. It's difficult to explain what it's about. It is not a film you like or dislike. The young people who have seen it seem to understand the message."

Newman was saddened and angered by the lukewarm reception to *WUSA*: "The thing that the critics don't understand, and sometimes the public does not understand, is, you may start off with a script which you have great hopes for. It may or may not come off. Do you give yourself more points for making something almost good out of something that's mediocre? Or do you give yourself more points for doing a picture like *The Hustler*, where the character was always there, in which it was just a matter of digging? I give myself more points for a picture like *WUSA* than I do for *The Hustler*, because that part demanded a lot more."

Newman was incensed by the *New York Times* critic's reception of *WUSA*: "Vincent Canby had the gall to list that picture as one of the ten worst of the year. If he's right, I don't know my ass from a hole in the ground." The Newmans were hoping that the European critics would recognize the film's import. Despite the Newmans' belief in and enthusiasm for the picture, it did not succeed with any segment of the audience, young or old. It was the Newmans' lowest-grossing film to date.

In person, however, Paul Newman was still a powerful draw for the youngsters in this congressional election year, although his work for the Reverend Joe Duffy in Connecticut was for naught.

Joanne explained why she thought Paul communicated so well with young people: "Most kids are entranced by Paul, not because he's sexy and handsome—he's getting gray around the temples now—but because he represents what they think adults should be engaged in. He doesn't go around to parties carrying on and drinking, he's there with the politics, with whatever causes he feels are valid."

Newman, perhaps because of his own children, was now concerned about the growing problem of drug abuse among teenagers. He narrated a film on drugs, and when it was shown at a local high school in Connecticut, he attended the screening. Woodward later said, "Parents called to tell me it was the first time they ever heard their kids say, 'That really got through to me, because Paul Newman came over to talk to us.' What he said was very pertinent, there was no bull."

Although *WUSA* had disappeared quickly from the nation's theaters, *Butch Cassidy* was continuing to rack up the largest gross of any 20th Century-Fox non-road-show picture to date. And Paul Newman now became the nation's number-one box-office attraction.

On the home front, Scott was to go back to college after working that summer on *Notion*, but such was not the case. He was living on his own.

"Susan, the seventeen-year-old, is in high school," noted Joanne. "Stephanie, the sixteen-year-old, is still a bit of a little girl."

"None of our kids are really involved with movies, not yet, anyway," Paul said. "My oldest daughter might get into it. Lissy might too. She's eight." Clea was five. Nell was eleven now, and supposedly had no interest in acting at all.

The three youngest children were still leading a nomadic life, home being where their parents' work schedules sent them. When in Connecticut, they attended school there. When in California, they attended the Buckley School.

"We thought living in Connecticut was a lot healthier until a proposal came up to bus in disadvantaged kindergarten students from Bridgeport," Joanne said. "The attitude of many was so extraordinary, so biased, that I just wondered whether this was the town we all thought so lovely and marvelous and such a great place to bring our kids up in. We have very high taxes and a lily-white school system because of the very nature of the town. Bringing outside children in would also have helped our children, who are growing up in a very one-sided atmosphere." It is difficult to believe Joanne was so naive about certain attitudes held by the citizens of posh communities like Westport.

She didn't like New York any better than she liked Westport. She was concerned about the air pollution, and that people did not seem to care about it. In this period she, like millions of other Americans, had suddenly became conscious of the environment. She tried to get her grocer to stock certain products, such as biodegradable soaps and pure white paper products, rather than "color-treated" items.

It was at this time, too, that she became particularly outspoken about her private life and made a statement that attracted no particular notice, though in retrospect it is significant. Discussing the future of the world, she said, "Conservatively, I think people have at most two or three generations left. And I'm certainly raising my children not to have any children."

Joanne shocked many wives and mothers in the mid-1970s when she said, "If I had to do it all over again, I would make the decision one way or another. My career has suffered because of the children, and my children have suffered because of my career. And that's not fair. I've been torn and haven't been able to function fully in either arena."

Events would prove that, as the decade began—torn or not, disenchanted as she said she was about filmmaking after *They Might Be Giants*—Woodward was still intent on working as an actress in films.

☆ **11** ☆

☆

Paul Newman was announced as the star of many upcoming projects, including *Hillman*, *Where the Dark Streets Go*, and *Jim Kane*. Only *Jim Kane*, retitled *Pocket Money*, was produced with Newman. Lee Marvin was signed to co-star in this First Artists production, Stuart Rosenberg would direct, Strother Martin would have a key role, and filming would take place in the Southwest.

Newman and Marvin did not become buddies (when asked the title of the film, Marvin replied, "Paul Newman"). The two actors had disparate attitudes about filmmaking and dealing with the cast and crew. On this picture it was Marvin who was buddy-buddy with the grips, the crew, the stuntmen, while Newman, though friendly, was perceived as standing somewhat apart. He spent most of his free time in his trailer, reading and listening to classical music or sweating it out in his portable sauna.

One of the reasons he seemed different to the people working on this film may have been that a major change had taken place in his personal life. Newman himself later revealed that it was around this time that he had given up drinking hard liquor. He did, however, continue to drink beer, and indeed, his penchant for drinking beer and his association with Coors—and later Budweiser—became legend. It was reported that he drank as much as a case of beer a day, and whenever anyone spoke of him, invariably there was a mention of "a beer in his hand." (His friend Congressman McCloskey clocked him at "one every eight minutes, at least.") He was known, in these pre-pop-top days, to carry a church key (that is, a can opener) around his neck. But he had obviously realized the extent of his problem with alcohol and resolved to limit himself to beer and wine and to give up harder spirits.

Newman has said that people who do things to excess don't like themselves very much and are self-destructive. On assessment, he must have decided he did not want to die. His belief is that people with addictive personalities—no matter what they happen to be addicted to—are not convinced to stop by other people, but do so—if they're fortunate enough—when they themselves take control. He said, "I just decided to stop," and he was able to.

Newman was still projecting a macho, beer-drinking image at that time, and little was thought—and less said—about any problems with alcohol the actor had faced. However, Newman's own drinking certainly made it difficult for him to talk to Scott about the boy's problems with alcohol.

During shooting of *Pocket Money* the train transporting Joanne and the girls from Los Angeles to New York passed through Santa Fe, New Mexico. The cast and crew had gathered to wave as the train passed by. Joanne still disliked flying and would take the train whenever her schedule permitted.

She was more disillusioned than ever with living in Los Angeles, especially after the city had experienced a severe earthquake in the winter of 1971. "Between the smog and the last earthquake, I finally made up my mind," she said. "The earthquake was really the last straw. I thought how perfectly absurd it is to have a beautiful home and have to drive weekends to the beach so my child, who is allergic to the smog, can breathe, and on top of it almost be victimized by an earthquake. I've even been known to break out in spots from the smog."

Joanne convinced Paul that they should sell their Beverly

Hills home and move the children and all the children's animals back to Connecticut for good. When the school year was over, that's exactly what they did.

Joanne's film had been released and had not been a commercial success. "I feel that if Paul had directed George C. Scott and me in *They Might Be Giants*, the picture might have been a great one instead of a good one."

Joanne had retained her interest in ballet, both in New York and on the Coast, and she continued her ballet lessons with David Leshine in Los Angeles. At the time her interest in dancing certainly equaled that of her husband's in auto racing. Joanne even tried to point out to Paul that perhaps *he* should try it, since ballet was the most athletic sport of all, one in which every muscle was utilized. Newman was not interested.

Another of her ideas also fell on deaf ears. Joanne had been impressed when she saw Henry Fonda doing needlepoint to relax on the set of *Notion* (she, of course, was a needlepoint addict and had been doing it since she was a girl), and suggested to Paul that he take it up as a hobby. Paul laughed. (One can imagine a photo of Butch Cassidy doing needlepoint—it certainly would have been circulated to every newspaper in the world.)

Paul observed, "For two people with almost nothing in common, we have an uncommonly good marriage."

Joanne's reply to that oft-quoted remark was that she wished he'd never said it—but she admitted he was right. Except, she pointed out, that while they didn't necessarily *do* what the other did, they were interested in *what* the other did.

Paul was a good tennis player, so Joanne took lessons because she wanted to play *with* him. Ultimately, however, she realized she had no interest in the game and so resumed her piano lessons. Paul liked to ski with his children, and Joanne would accompany them when they went to the ski resorts in California or in Vermont. She was only there for companionship, however: "I'm undoubtedly the only person who rides the ski lift down. I don't know how to ski, and I'm not about to break a leg trying to learn."

While Paul and the kids were skiing, Joanne spent the time

reading, doing needlepoint, playing her guitar, exercising, or answering her mail, but she went along because, then, the family was together.

A Joanne Woodward self-portrait during this time: "Schizophrenic, manic-depressive, disciplined, undisciplined or discipline hardly won, lazy, emotional, compulsive, theatrical and prone to play roles."

Of course, no one accepted her self-description because the role she always chose to play on the set and in public was that of the warm, gracious southern lady. Her family, however, knew her moods and temperament, and the next film role Joanne Woodward would tackle—that of Beatrice Hunsdorfer—would, unfortunately, force her to explore in depth some of the darker sides of her personality. Beatrice is the overpowering, manipulative, heartless mother in Paul Zindel's *The Effect of Gamma Rays on Man-in-the-Moon Marigolds.*

There was another commitment to be handled before that film, however. Joanne was asked to narrate a TV documentary, "The Eagle and the Hawk." Nell also took a part in it, as a "friend of the birds." The Newman children loved animals, and there was a menagerie at the family's homes on both coasts.

Woodward went to England that fall, without Paul, since *WUSA* was opening there, and the Newmans still felt committed to publicize the project. Paul wanted to be able to shove rave European notices down the American critics' throats (the Europeans did not like it any more than the Americans had). During this period Newman was very anti-critics.

However, just a few years later, both Paul and Joanne reversed their opinions of *WUSA*. She said: "I don't think the film comes off, I never really liked it, and I only did it because he was in it and we could go to New Orleans. Which is often my reason for doing things." She did think, though, that it was "one of the best performances Paul ever gave, and highly underrated."

Newman returned the compliment: "I think it's one of Joanne's best performances. She's very sexy, very vulnerable." And he also said: "We made a lot of mistakes with the picture, but I think the film had much greater potential. But politically

—it should never have been a political picture. But when you're an actor in a picture, you sometimes don't see where the whole thing is going. That's my fault. I should have."

On her return to New York Joanne signed with David Susskind for a television project, one with the old gang. Fred Coe was directing Tad Mosel's Pulitzer Prize–winning play *All the Way Home* for NBC; and Pat Hingle, Eileen Heckart, and Richard Kiley were also in the cast. They rehearsed in New York but, because of union costs, went to Toronto to do the taping. The show was broadcast on December 1, 1971.

*Sometimes a Great Notion* hit the theaters and was not well received by the public. It did not offer the "Paul Newman" fans expected. In the big scene (the one for which Newman had bought the book) in which Richard Jaeckel's character is caught in a log jam, Paul's character tries desperately to save him. As Jaeckel points out, "There was no way the audience felt that Newman wasn't going to pull this jerk out from under the log. How could he miss? There's Paul Newman. There's only a few inches of water, and the tide's gone out, see? And when the guy finally does *die*, just like that, and it's finally over, people just couldn't believe it!"

Universal, which had not supported the picture with much of an advertising or publicity campaign, withdrew it from release after a short time, then changed the title to *Never Give an Inch* and released it again. And again the picture died. However, it had been released in time for the Academy Award nominations that year, and Richard Jaeckel received a well-deserved nomination in the Best Supporting Actor category.

Jaeckel recalls: "I called Paul. I said, 'Paul, what do I do?' He said, 'Make a lot of speeches.'" Jaeckel feels that Newman was understandably disappointed that his own efforts were not recognized. Although Jaeckel did not win the Oscar (Ben Johnson did for *The Last Picture Show*), the nomination nonetheless revitalized his career.

The film had proved also that Newman was not a one-shot director. The acting in the film was exceptionally fine, including Newman's, and Henry Fonda's death scene ranks with the best work the actor had ever done. In fact, Fonda thought it was *the* best work he had done to date in a career that had spanned over thirty-five years.

*Pocket Money* was released next, with a striking ad campaign spotlighting Newman and Marvin. Star billing had presented a problem that was ultimately resolved in a kind of compromise: Newman's name came first, on the left; Marvin's name, on the right, was on the top. In any case, the public did not respond to the film, and that made three Newman films in a row that had flopped.

His current production for First Artists, however, had the earmarks of a hit. *The Life and Times of Judge Roy Bean* was being directed by John Huston, who would also play a role in the film. Jacqueline Bissett was the leading lady, and Ava Gardner would be playing a cameo (unfortunately, her scenes were not with Newman). A newcomer, Victoria Principal, was in the cast, as were Tab Hunter and Anthony Zerbe. One of the industry's important new screenwriters, John Milius, had written the script. Location filming was scheduled for Arizona.

Newman liked working with Huston; they had what Newman termed "instant understanding." The actor found much to admire in his director: "Obviously, John's a man with a functioning ego, but that ego never intrudes upon his work. I don't know what things he's egotistical about, but I do know that it has nothing to do with pride of authorship or pride of initiation. All he cares about is getting a trigger—something that triggers off a good idea. He doesn't care whether it comes from himself or from the actors or from the script girl. So there is that marvelous kind of exchange that goes on."

When filming was completed, Newman headed east to continue his own directorial career—they were finally ready to begin shooting on *Marigolds*. They had wanted to film it on Staten Island, the locale of the script, but were faced with too many union problems, so they decided on Bridgeport, Connecticut, instead.

This location meant they would be close to their home in Westport, a situation that might be perceived as an advantage but ultimately proved otherwise. As Joanne later revealed, after a strenuous day on the set she was not able to go home to an empty apartment and unwind, but went home instead to a houseful of kids who were all, in her words, "rightfully demanding." She conceded it was detrimental both to them and to herself.

There were two weeks of rehearsal, then interiors were shot in the abandoned parsonage of a church in Bridgeport, the perfect setting for the dilapidated house required by the story.

Alvin Sargent's script of Zindel's play had not lightened the heavy material. Even Joanne, used to playing character parts, had never played a woman so frumpy. Her hair was dyed a mousy brown and in many scenes was wound in curlers. She has described how she found the sloppy clothing Beatrice wears: "I was supposed to be one of the frowziest hags in town. All the clothes were my mother's, because she's a pack rat and never throws anything away, so I went through her closet and dragged out a lot of old junk and dyed it an icky color and wore it."

Beatrice, an embittered widow, is a nasty character, who lashes out at her daughters and at life itself. In one scene she even kills her daughter's pet rabbit. Joanne was deeply affected by the role: "I was so depressed and suicidal during that film I couldn't stand it. I hated the way I looked, I hated that character, what she did to her children."

Later she said, "When Paul was directing me in *Gamma Rays*, I came close to sheer insanity. The role had an effect on me both during the shooting and afterwards. At home, I was a monster, and Paul and I avoided each other as much as possible. There was something ugly about the character of Beatrice that got to me. Such putrefaction inside. I understood her all too well. You know, if you're rejected and you reject yourself, then the goodness gets swallowed up by the ugliness."

Those on the scene were surprised at the intensity of the fights the Newmans had on the set. This time the director and his star were not clicking on how the character should be played. During production Newman said: "The only one who's uptight sometimes is Joanne. She thinks she's not funny enough or sad enough, and that some of the scenes elude her.

But she's got a lot of guts. She doesn't just sit back and let the character come to her."

The unrelenting search for her character caused Woodward to suffer tremendous angst. Her relationship with her own children during this period was strained to the limit. "My family thought that if I didn't get through *Marigolds* they were all going to have to move away," she later said. "I was awful to myself. I hated myself. That was the psychosis. That is the one picture I wish I hadn't done . . . it had a terrible effect on me. I was so ugly that I revealed to myself an ugliness that I didn't know I had."

Paul's direction was not the problem. "Paul is the easiest person in the world. We had big fights, but we have big fights at home, too. I never have to explain myself to him like I do with directors I don't know."

As far as Newman was concerned, if there were any problems in the husband/director–wife/actress situation, they were not on the set, but at home.

Newman was directing not only his wife but, once again, their daughter Nell, who was playing the younger daughter in the story. The character was a girl very much like Nell herself —a quiet girl, interested in nature. Her father said: "It's easy to direct her. . . . Her quality not as a performer, but as a person, carries her through. Put her face on camera, and let her twitch away, and you've got a scene."

Roberta Wallach, daughter of Anne Jackson and Eli Wallach, was playing the older daughter, the one who will undoubtedly turn into her mother. It was a demanding role for the teenage Miss Wallach, and she recalls that the Newmans were very parental with her but never condescending. As for the director: "Paul let you work. Let you find your own way to do it."

Occasionally the specter of Paul's status as the screen's leading sex symbol intruded on his new career as auteur/director. A large group of spectators gathered when they were filming outdoors one day, and suddenly at one point, a loud, collective *gasp* went up from the crowd—"it was frightening," remembered a member of the cast—it seemed that Newman had taken off his shirt. "I wouldn't want to have been Paul Newman at that moment without security men for protection," recalled the observer, who added, "We all realized that this was how the poor man had to live—what an awful predicament."

Newman was used to it, and much more. Virtually nothing seemed to faze him. One day Paul Zindel visited the set and brought a guest. "He was supposed to be a living god, in his late teens," relates Zindel, who had met the outrageously dressed character at a party. The young man, whose New England commune regarded him as God, had appealed to Zindel's sense of the bizarre. On the *Marigolds* set, Newman, Zindel and "god" had lunch. The young man, who had been dying to meet Paul Newman, related that in a past life he had been Ulysses S. Grant and Newman had been Robert E. Lee. "At the end of the whole thing," recalls Zindel, "Paul, all the while calmly eating his lunch, simply looked up and said, 'Well, I'm afraid I'm a little more traditional than that.'" Afterward, Newman had nothing negative to say to Zindel. Paul had viewed the visitor "strictly like one more looney who'd come out of the woodwork."

During filming, all the Newman children were on the set at one time or another. "Susan is the strong one," observed one of their friends. Others noted: "It wasn't difficult to see that young Scott had serious problems." When Scott was around, it was often a tense time for all concerned. Like other children from privileged backgrounds, the younger Newmans believed that whatever happened to them, Dad could take care of it. The truth, of course, was that Dad usually *could* take care of it. But, inevitably, when a parent either cannot solve a problem or decides that he *should not* solve it, then both parent and child realize that the youngster has not been prepared to deal with problem solving. This apparently was the case for Scott Newman.

Susan Newman, much to her father's displeasure, has discussed her upbringing and the inconsistent attitudes about money and power that she and her siblings were exposed to. In her opinion, her father was just as confused about all the fame and money as the kids were. Unlike the three younger girls,

Susan, Stephanie, and Scott were acutely aware of the disparity between their father's life-style and their own, because they spent a great deal of time with their mother. While Jacqueline (who had recently had another daughter, Kathleen) lived comfortably, she certainly did not live on the level that the Newmans did.

Susan has told of the time when, after her high school graduation, she flew to Europe; the trip was a gift from her father. Her other classmates were doing the same thing. A few months later, however, when she wanted to make a trip from Los Angeles to Connecticut to visit the family, she was told it was too extravagant! Her contention has been that her father and stepmother were often confused about priorities, and thus she and her siblings were confused about priorities.

Newman himself has recognized this confusion: "I was very inconsistent with them. I was all over the place, too loving one minute, too distant the next. One day they were flying on the Concorde, and the next day they were expected to do their own laundry. It was very hard for them to get a balance. . . . Maybe I could have behaved consistently with the kids if I had felt consistently good about myself."

And Joanne, discussing her stepchildren, conceded, "Unfortunately, I think that I experimented on them to their detriment, and maybe to the betterment of *my* children." She said they were all friends, though they had been through "rough" times: "I mean Scott and I didn't speak for several years. He was going through difficult times, and I resented the fact that he wasn't standing on his own feet and was using Paul. That made me angry, for Paul."

Susan, too, was a big problem for Paul, and for Joanne as well. At one point the teenager, who was five feet eight inches, felt she was overweight at one hundred and fifty pounds and decided to go on a fast. After thirty-eight days of not eating, she had lost forty pounds, but she had become very ill as well. Other concerns arose when through her late teens Susan was involved with an older man in what became a years-long love affair. Both Jacqueline and Paul were deeply worried about her.

As Joanne observed, "The age from sixteen to nineteen is a very hard period."

Susan has always been the maverick in the family. She has been outspoken and has often embarrassed her parents and her stepmother. For example, Susan revealed for public consumption that losing her virginity was difficult because she kept asking herself, "Do they want to lay me for myself or because I'm Paul Newman's daughter?"

The day Joanne at long last completed work in *Marigolds* she drove to New York to spend the evening *alone* at their apartment, while Paul stayed with the family in Connecticut. Beatrice had become a terrible problem, and she was happy to exorcise the character that had so obsessed her for the last few months. In the middle of the night, she found herself screaming—"like a mad creature. I couldn't get rid of it. It was like some terrible, demonic possession."

She was so hysterical that she called Paul at four in the morning and told him she thought she was going crazy. He raced to Manhattan, and when he arrived at the apartment, Joanne burst into tears. In summing up the whole *Marigolds* experience, she later said: "That picture left scars. . . . That kind of thing has never happened to me in any other film."

No sooner had she completed *Marigolds*, however, than she took on another depressing project, *Death of a Snow Queen*. Joanne said she was only doing it because Stewart Stern had written it for her. Her character, a middle-aged matron, comes to grips with the unpleasant realities of her life: the death of her mother, her son's homosexuality, her nonrelationship with her daughter, and her inability to love, or allow herself to be loved by, her husband of twenty-five years.

Few were happy with the title *Death of a Snow Queen*. One wag commented that it sounded like either the biography of Sonja Henie or the story of an avalanche on Fire Island. The film would undergo many title changes before release.

Paul, too, was about to begin a new film, one that had been in the works for months. Paul had known that George Roy Hill and Robert Redford were planning to make a film together, *The*

*Great Waldo Pepper*. It had been postponed for a while, however, and, in the meantime, Hill was considering another script, *The Sting*. The screenplay was a period piece dealing with two con men, and Redford was set to play one. The other role, however, was written strictly for a character actor of the Charles Durning type. Needless to say, neither Hill nor Redford had thought of Newman for the part. But after Paul read the script, he surprised his buddies by telling them he would take the part. The three men met and hashed it over. As Hill finally argued: "What the hell are we thinking about? The part can be played as a riverboat gambler. This isn't a classic. We enjoy working together, so let's just do it."

The producers, all five of them—Zanuck-Brown, Tony Bill, and Michael and Julia Phillips—were thrilled to have Newman aboard. Redford and Newman would receive the same salary—around half a million dollars apiece—but Newman would receive a percentage of the gross, and top billing.

Nineteen seventy-two was an election year, and the Newmans were again involved, this time campaigning for George McGovern. Again, the obvious question arose: Would Newman himself ever run for office?

"Impossible to do it," he replied. "Campaigning is intolerable medieval torture. And for presidential candidates, in addition to being dangerous, it's humiliating." Newman said again that it would be "arrogant" of him to run for office. It appeared that arrogance was the greatest sin of all to Paul Newman. He explained, "To be able to use power with grace is an enviable trait."

Meanwhile at Universal Studios production began on *The Sting*. Somewhat overshadowed by the Newman-Redford combination, though he received equal billing, was Robert Shaw, the brilliant actor and writer who was cast as the heavy. There was no Katharine Ross–like leading lady in this venture: Eileen Brennan had a small, but memorable, role. Dimitra Arliss's character also figured importantly in the story, but she was not on-screen for long.

As with *Butch Cassidy*, Newman, Redford, and Hill enjoyed a camaraderie and rapport, and there was, of course, the pleasure of their "hustles," as the men called practical jokes. The Porsche story has been related many times: Redford had seen a wrecked Porsche lying alongside the road. He bought the wreck and had it delivered to Newman as a present. Newman then decided to return the favor. He had the Porsche compacted, found a way to get into Redford's house without the burglar alarm going off, and left the block of steel with a note: "Although he appreciated it, Mr. Newman is returning this gift to you very simply because he cannot get the motherfucker started." Redford had the last laugh, however, because neither he, his wife, or the children would ever admit that they had seen the compacted car.

One aspect of Redford's personality continued to annoy Paul. As always, Newman prided himself on his punctuality; as before, Redford was often late. Newman gave him a framed needlepoint that read: "Punctuality is the courtesy of kings."

Paul Newman became involved next in a spy thriller, *The MacIntosh Man*. Robert Wise recalls that Newman sent him the script and wanted him to direct, but he turned it down. Several other top directors also turned the project down. John Huston was available, however, and since the men had enjoyed their previous collaboration, the deal was made. The film was shot in Ireland, Huston's adopted land.

On the set of *MacIntosh Man* one of Paul's hustles was not particularly appreciated, and even he later conceded that it might have given Huston a heart attack. Paul planned a stunt with a particular crew member who was known for his quick temper. Paul suggested to the crew member that they pretend to be arguing on the terrace, some sixty feet off the ground, then continue the argument inside the apartment out of view of the crew. They did this. Then all of a sudden Paul's body came flying out the window and plummeted sixty feet to the ground, landing behind a fence where no one could see it. Everyone was frozen with horror; then a few seconds later Paul appeared on the balcony and waved. Of course the men had thrown a dummy overboard, but the joke was perceived as malicious, not humorous. After this Newman was more careful about the types of practical jokes he played.

The previous Newman-Huston effort, *The Life and Times of Judge Roy Bean*, was now released and proved to be a disappointment. There were some wonderful scenes in it, but the film as a whole did not work, and it failed to reach a large audience.

In late 1972 *Marigolds* was almost ready to be screened for the critics. Newman invited Paul Zindel to attend a screening of a rough cut, before the music was added. "I thought that was generous," recalls Zindel. "My agent and I went and Paul was there and we saw the movie. I remember my reaction to it—I really was hoping it would be a big smash and make a great deal of money, but it seemed slow to me. Very slow."

Zindel felt that Joanne "was playing too far away from herself." As he explains: "She thought the challenge was to play nasty and to play mean, and she hadn't found in that performance the combination of humor and what was natural to her. She shouldn't have had to play as far away from herself as she thought she had to. I found her a bit one-noted and a bit forced at that time."

Zindel very candidly admits that in those days he would "shoot my mouth off just terribly" if something bothered him. He paraphrases one of his comments to the press at that time: "Nepotism was terrible and the idea of using the daughter was an unforgivable thing and . . . they should've used a real actress."

With comments like this Zindel, in his words, "burned so many bridges it was unbelievable." But he had hated the movie. "Why I hated it was because there was a record in my mind that could only play the words in one sequence with no other interruptions—that was the only way I could hear the play. When the movie did my words, which was very rarely, I liked it. When it did foreign words, it threw me, so I realized I knew it wasn't their fault, it was just the phenomenon of going from play to film."

After the initial screening, as Zindel walked out he said to his agent, "This is not going to make any money, it's too dull." The playwright's prediction proved to be correct.

A fascinating footnote: Zindel changed his opinion of the picture. As he explains: "About two or three years later it was sold to TV and I saw it on TV with commercials. It was *wonderful* with commercials. I found Joanne's performance, pushed down from the large screen to the small screen, became less strenuous, less transparent. The daughter was fine. I found that by cutting it up for commercials they had to show you where the peaks of the film were. The ending for it I thought was very good. So I loved it with all those commercials—beer commercials, McDonald's—I thought they added considerably to the film. It showed the rhythm of it. And so . . . in hindsight now, having come the full cycle and knowing more about what was going on, I would say they had done a very nice job with the piece. It was very sensitively done and very carefully thought out." Today Zindel says of Newman's direction, "I am more impressed by that now than at the time."

Newman felt his wife was brilliant in the picture. He subsequently stated, "I think Joanne is incredible. I'd like to get a bunch of film critics together, and run a reel of *WUSA*, a reel of *Rachel, Rachel*, and a reel of *Marigolds*—just back-to-back, all three of them. Because the lady is absolutely unrecognizable from one of those films to another, either in terms of physical mannerisms or basic quality. There's something of witchcraft in there."

Stewart Stern summed it up: "Paul has a sense of real adoration for what Joanne can do. He's constantly trying to provide a setting where the world can see what he sees in her."

Reviews for *Marigolds* started to appear early in the new year, 1973. The critics were not enthusiastic, to say the least, about Joanne's portrayal, and Newman was angered by the harshness of their criticism.

Meanwhile Joanne's schedule was, as usual, full of activity. She was shooting another film, going to classes, raising her family. "It's a madhouse," she said. "Our oldest daughter—she's fourteen—is an ornithologist and is training a hawk in her bedroom. There are papers all over the place because we have an undetermined number of pigeons, too." The household at the time included her two younger daughters, her two stepdaughters, four cats, two dogs, and two horses. There had once been a chicken, too, Dorothy, who thought she was a dog. "It makes for a very messy house," Joanne remarked. But anyone on intimate terms with the Newmans knew that Joanne did not really run a messy house, all things considered.

She agreed to be chairperson for a Planned Parenthood benefit scheduled for late in the year. Mrs. Alvin Ruml and Mrs. Thomas Grahame were organizing the volunteers for the event, which boasted the kind of all-star cast certain to make all the TV news shows and newspapers. Joanne's friends Shirley MacLaine, Eli Wallach and Anne Jackson, and Anthony Perkins said they would be there, as did Richard Benjamin and Paula Prentiss, Stacy Keach, Debbie Reynolds, Bobby Short, Marilyn Horne, George Grizzard, John Gavin, Judy Collins, Hazel Scott, and Ruth Warrick. Dustin Hoffman, Tony Perkins, John Gavin, and Newman were going to serve as bartenders for the evening. The event would be held at the American Shakespeare Theater in Stratford, Connecticut.

Joanne was vocal about Planned Parenthood. "I believe every woman should have a right to say how many children she wants. I'd like to write a biography of Margaret Sanger." Woodward's strong feelings on birth control sprang from her own experience. "The concept of going into parenthood with conscious thought was not something people of my generation did. We just had babies. That was what you were supposed to do, and you did it."

Her involvement in outside activities was limited by the demands of her acting career. She had begun shooting *Death of a Snow Queen* in the fall of 1972, and filming resumed after the holidays. *Snow Queen* was a difficult project, not only because the story was so unrelentingly down, but because Woodward's involvement in the role she was playing was again so intense that her doomed character's outlook virtually became her own.

Paul Zindel had long before removed himself from the *Mrs. Beneker* project, which had supposedly been shelved. In Zindel's opinion, "The thrust of *Mrs. Beneker* was used to embody that script [*Death of a Snow Queen*]. Now everything was disguised. I'm sure they said it came from something else. . . . As far as I'm concerned it's really basically the same story. I'm sure they didn't pay for rights or anything else like that. They simply waited a couple of years and recycled the thrust and energies of *Mrs. Beneker* into that. But I don't know the exact process of what they did. It was basically the same story, the same character, as far as I'm concerned."

Woodward has described the matron she plays as one "who makes the awful discovery of how brief life really is, too brief even to correct one's worst mistakes, and even worse, too brief really to ever change." She said during filming, "It's very depressing, and just between you and me, I've just about had it with being depressed."

Making a film was hard work, no matter how one tried to distract oneself. After submerging herself all day in the dismal life she was portraying in this film, Woodward found it easier—and definitely best for the mental health of all concerned—to go home to the empty New York apartment. If she went home to her family, *all* would suffer. The kids would naturally make demands on Mama that she would hardly be in a state of mind to respond to coolly and fairly.

Toward the end of filming, nerves were frayed. Everyone was tired. "When I get to the point where I burst into tears, I know I'm suicidal," Woodward said. One day she was really ticked off because she had carefully planned for a particular scene, and when she got to the set, she discovered that the writer and director had cut the dialogue dramatically. She felt they should have called her about the cuts. She let the director, Gil Cates, know how she felt: "We'd better finish this picture by Friday because I'm going off to Switzerland, period, after that."

"There's no doubt because I'm going off to Florida," retorted Cates.

Joanne immediately regretted her words and said to a writer, Jerry Tallmer, who was on the set, "I know what he's feeling, but he should know what I'm feeling, too, godammit. I guess I'll have to send flowers now. *Oy-oy-oy.*" Tallmer noted, "Cates spoke a few mollifying words and departed," and Joanne spoke about going home and getting drunk. "The trouble is," she said, "you can't get drunk on sherry."

Even when making a film, Joanne read voraciously. She was

completing a new biography of Isadora Duncan. Her husband had given her Simone de Beauvoir's latest tome, and Woodward was proud that she had just finished *all* of Anthony Trollope: "Literally for two years that's all I read, except for an occasional lapse into Agatha Christie."

When filming wrapped, Joanne intended to resume classes at Sarah Lawrence, at the college's Center for Continuing Education. She saw this as an act of "great indulgence." As she explained: "I never had the opportunity before. Now I'm creating the opportunity. Learning should be continuous anyway."

Newman was continuing with his budding career in racing. That year he raced a Datsun 510 in B Sedan, qualifying for the national championships and finishing ninth at the Road Atlanta runoffs.

Paul later acknowledged that he knew the 510 was hardly a glamorous vehicle, but at that juncture he felt it was the appropriate choice. He didn't want to take on more than he could handle, and remembering that it had taken him months of studying and observing at the Actors Studio before the results were apparent in his acting, he was taking the same approach to racing, learning it at a speed that was right for him. It didn't concern him at all if other people had greater immediate expectations for him.

At the box office Newman's film career seemed to have hit a snag with *The Life and Times of Judge Roy Bean*, which was not proving to have much popularity. He had two pictures due for release, however, *The MacIntosh Man* and *The Sting*, and was set to star in *The Towering Inferno*, a multimillion-dollar "disaster" epic to co-star Steve McQueen, Faye Dunaway, William Holden, Jennifer Jones, Fred Astaire, and Robert Wagner. The producer-director on this next one was Irwin Allen, whose *Poseidon Adventure* had broken box-office records all over the world. The film was a bread-and-butter project in that Paul Newman would earn millions for a sure-fire success. Scott Newman was subsequently hired to play a fireman and do stunt work.

Scott was living on his own in Hollywood and taking acting classes. Those who knew him at this time described him as intense, but they noted that he had an artistic sensitivity and loved beauty. Though arrogant and defensive, he did have a sense of humor and a winning smile.

Despite his family's wealth, Scott preferred to borrow money from his friends rather than his father. Whether he needed the money for liquor, drugs, or the rent, it certainly was easier to ask nonfamily members who would not question his motives, but would simply say yes or no.

Around this time Scott met Kathy Cronkite, daughter of Walter Cronkite, at an acting class they were both attending. She later said that a mutual friend confided that Scott felt a "special bond" with her, because she, too, was the child of a superstar. But interestingly, she cannot recall ever talking to Scott about their respective fathers.

As an actress, Ms. Cronkite found that it was not easy working with an actor as irresponsible as Scott Newman. No one in the class wanted to work with him at this point because he would not show up for rehearsals and often would not even show up on the day a scene was scheduled to be presented in class. But Kathy Cronkite worked well with young Newman, and was happy to work with him again. She has noted, however, that he was ambivalent about the acting class and possibly about the profession in general.

In any event, the small role in *Inferno* would be good experience for Scott, and he loved stunt work.

Paul Newman, in addition to signing for *Inferno*, was working on another package. *The Drowning Pool* would be another of Ross Macdonald's Lew Archer detective stories; Archer would again be called Harper.

Jack Garfein recalls: "My agent submitted me [as director] for the film and the producer wasn't interested because I hadn't done a film in a long time, so my agent got in touch with Paul, and Paul got in touch with the producer and said, 'Absolutely, I want Jack to direct.' My agent had said to Paul that it would be very important for me—it would kick off my film career again.

"Then a director Paul had worked with who had gone through some personal problem went to Paul and said, 'I'm desperate. I need this movie,' and Paul called my agent, Mike Levy, and said, 'Look, this guy came to me, he's desperate. He has no out, so I'm giving him this film.' "

Garfein admires Paul's compassion and his loyalty to people. "I always talk about the humanity and integrity of Paul Newman. His word is his word. There is no bullshit. He's very direct—it's remarkable that under all that pressure and all that chicanery and all that's going on around him he managed to keep that."

*The Drowning Pool* had a meaty but secondary role for Joanne, who understood with characteristic clear-sightedness that she and her husband had different statuses in the industry. "He's the big movie star," she has said, "and I'm a character actress. Probably things would be more difficult if it were the other way around."

She did not mind being Mrs. Paul Newman, having "passed through that identity crisis," but, according to Joanne, the couple were definitely not "content." She claimed their relationship was fraught with anxieties. "We could get a divorce next year," she said. "But we're still married. We like each other a lot. We have great respect for each other. We've known each other a long time and we feel very comfortable together. We don't believe in being together all the time." While for an ordinary couple that might mean spending an occasional evening apart, for the Newmans it meant spending about half the year together. Joanne felt the separations helped rather than harmed their marriage. In her opinion, togetherness had been "blown out of all reasonable proportions": "Why," she asked, "should husband and wife impinge on each other day after day?"

Additionally, as both Paul and Joanne enjoyed pointing out, they had practically nothing in common (*except*, of course, their family and their careers). But, as a friend of Paul and Joanne's explained, with the Newmans it wasn't what they said that counted but what they did. And they were continuing to lead pretty traditional lives. Many wealthy couples spend a great deal of time apart, pursuing separate careers and interests without sacrificing their marriage. Keeping *the family* together was paramount. The Newmans were, in effect, giving each other plenty of breathing room.

Many Hollywood observers felt that in reality Joanne's "identity" *was* submerged, and that if she and Paul ever got divorced, the cause would be "loss of ego." She herself admitted that she often felt like running through the halls shouting "I'm me, me. I don't know what my name is, but I'm me."

At this period in her married life she may have expressed this sentiment, but her actions have always indicated that Joanne Woodward had—and has—a very strong sense of identity. She illustrated her concept of Newman and Woodward as "the movie star and the character actress" with an amusing anecdote: She and her husband were walking down the street and they passed two girls. "One of them said, 'Oooh,' and the other one said, 'Ah.' The usual. Then one or the other of them said, 'Is that *her*?' "

"Her," as with most couples, was the one that kept their personal lives perking and their family life functioning. John Foreman noted: "Joanne has creative people stashed on both coasts and in Europe, no matter where she may be. Neither rain, sleet, nor snow stops her from her appointed rounds of all that is beautiful and artistic."

Paul and Joanne had bought another house in California, this time in Beverly Hills. Woodward had Louisiana magnolias planted on the front lawn (after uprooting all the palm trees). Still, the couple said they preferred Connecticut.

Using one of the Newmans' favorite adjectives, Paul said, "Joanne and I are very whimsical about things like where we live." And he explained: "There are desert people, mountain people, beach people, woods people. Joanne and I are seasons people. We love the weather change."

In Connecticut Joanne's childhood idol, Bette Davis, was a neighbor. "We've never seen her," Joanne said. "She phoned one day to thank Paul for something she read in the local paper, and he said, 'Come over and see us sometime,' and she said, 'Why?' I've loved her for that ever since."

Politically, these were the Nixon years, and there was an uproar when it was revealed that the president had an "enemies list," which included some of the top names in show business—including Paul Newman. Woodward's reaction: "Ridiculous when you realize that Paul is on it and Shirley MacLaine isn't. Shirley must be furious." Paul's reaction: "Send G. Gordon Liddy to pick up my award."

In the wake of the assassinations of the Kennedys and Martin Luther King, many celebrities in the late sixties and early seventies, especially those espousing political causes, suddenly realized they could be targets for kidnappings or assassinations. Ironically it was JFK who had observed, "If someone really wants to kill the President of the United States, no security in the world can prevent it." And movie stars hardly had the kind of security surrounding a top political figure.

The Newmans did not withdraw from public view, nor did they soft-pedal their often controversial positions. However, the Newman children were often keenly aware of the possible dangers. There was a period when Paul and Joanne did not want the children to be photographed because they feared kidnapping attempts. However, occasionally they would change their minds and be photographed with the children for a magazine cover.

Susan Newman was going through her hippie period, and with her friends she went to the ghettos of Los Angeles to work with the underprivileged. But as she has said, "Those people hated my guts." They knew she was Paul Newman's daughter, and resented her patronage. As they saw it, she would come to do a little cleaning up and then return to her luxurious life-style. And Susan, of course, was frustrated because her intentions were pure.

To Susan's frustration and chagrin, her social consciousness and her political consciousness were inevitably tied in with her famous father's. Once again she was struck by the fact that no matter what she did, it would be assumed she was doing it because it was what her father would do. It was particularly vexing to her that people thought she lived the same no-need-to-worry-about-money life-style of her father and stepmother.

Susan had not gone to college, and around this time Joanne brought her to New York, where the girl decided on an acting career. She took acting workshops and worked at Circle in the Square. She took classes in acting, dance, and speech, but again she found that people were not accepting her as herself but as Paul Newman's daughter.

When introduced as Susan Newman, she was surprised that people would ask, "Paul's daughter?" After all, Newman is a common name. It's not like Fonda or Vanderbilt. Like Scott, Susan at times changed her name. She called herself Susan Kendall when trying out for acting jobs. However, she has stated that people *still* knew who she was!

Although Nell (and later Melissa) acted with their mother, Susan is the only Newman daughter who has really professed a desire to enter the profession, and she has been candid in admitting that she cannot really say whether this was a voluntary decision or an inevitable choice because of her background.

Some people advised her not to become an actress. They spoke about inevitable comparisons, and pointed out that because of her father and stepmother, Susan's frame of reference was, of course, somewhat distorted. She was bound to be disappointed, so remote were her chances of equaling her parents' success.

Paul Newman did not try to dissuade his children from entering the acting profession, but neither did he seem—as did Lucille Ball or Judy Garland—to be taking his children by the hand and leading them into their careers.

# ☆ 12 ☆

Paul's movie *The MacIntosh Man* had previewed poorly and ultimately did not perform well at the box office. *The Sting* had also received a tepid reception when it was shown, minus musical score and optical effects, to members of the publicity department at Universal's home office in New York. Viewers found the pace of the rough cut slow and the plot blatantly contrived.

While Universal was in postproduction on *The Sting*, Joanne was gearing up for the launching of her film, now retitled *Summer Wishes, Winter Dreams*. At initial screenings reaction to her performance was very strong—almost as enthusiastic as the response to *Rachel, Rachel*. It was clear she would have the artistic success all had intended, although the commercial prospects for the film appeared no better than those for *Rachel*.

Producer Ray Stark, one of Hollywood's leading power brokers, knew the value of publicity and was determined to bring *Summer Wishes, Winter Dreams* the attention it deserved. This was one of Stark's "prestige" pictures, produced not to rake in the dollars but to receive honors—although Stark and Joanne would have loved to earn both.

Showing the picture at film festivals and timing the film's release for the end of the year guaranteed that Woodward's performance would not be overlooked or forgotten by the critics when it came to the all-important nominations for annual awards. And in the marketplace, since no one could be certain how the public would respond, hopes for *Summer Wishes, Winter Dreams* were high.

Woodward agreed to give interviews to publicize the picture —a task she disliked doing and felt she was not particularly good at. Interviews inevitably meant talking about her personal life, and she was bound to talk herself into a spot—and did. Richard Natale of *Women's Wear Daily* questioned her on the subject that everyone *really* wanted to know about—the Newmans' sex life. He mentioned some of the rumors about the couple that had circulated over the years. Joanne answered, "It's all true," and, according to Natale, "laughed wildly." Joanne continued: "It is a marriage of convenience and we are sex maniacs and everything in between. I think it makes it so much more interesting. The children, too—Nell, Lissie and Clea—all nymphomaniacs. And don't forget the chicken and the skunk." One assumes Natale was sorry he asked.

When Joanne was interviewed by the *Daily News* reporter Harry Haun, Paul had just been involved in an auto-racing accident in which no one had been hurt. Haun, a soft-spoken, highly intelligent southerner like Joanne, asked Woodward why she didn't just stop her husband from racing. She bristled at the question. How, she asked, could she stop him, since he was an adult man with a mind and a will of his own? Haun printed their conversation and was later informed by a mutual friend that Joanne wasn't at all pleased by his reportage.

Woodward's reaction to Paul's racing was then, and has continued to be, a topic of controversy. Both have given varied reports about how they deal with her feelings toward his racing. Obviously Joanne realized that Paul had made up his mind to race, and there was nothing she (or anyone) could do about it. (In later years she claimed she had never objected to Paul's involvement in the hazardous sport, but there is ample evidence from people who spoke with her directly that she did.)

Newman had started the 1973 racing season with great anticipation, although he had limited time to devote to the sport

owing to film commitments. If his last few films had not presented much of a stretch for Newman the actor, then the current assignment, *Towering Inferno*, was even less of a challenge.
Indeed, the only acting training necessary for this picture was
from the school of common sense, which is to say, he had only
to make sure that he jumped out of the way when the special-
effects crew set off explosives. Of course, everybody knew that
making believable characters out of one-dimensional roles was
perhaps the most difficult task an actor could face, and Newman, McQueen, Holden, Astaire, and company had their jobs
cut out for them in *Inferno*.

The changing nature of the movie business was evident in
the cast list for this film. Holden had been the number-one
male star of the mid-to-late fifties when Paul Newman was on
the way up; Jennifer Jones had been one of the industry's major
leading ladies (she and Holden had co-starred in one of the
biggest hits of the 1950s, *Love Is a Many Splendored Thing*); Fred
Astaire was a legendary star of the thirties and forties. By now,
however, Holden, Jones, and Astaire were merely supporting
actors for a picture top-lining McQueen and Newman. On-
screen, McQueen got first billing, with his name on the left and
Newman's name on the right, slightly higher. According to
Neile McQueen, Steve's former wife, getting billing over Newman was the highlight of Steve's career. McQueen had never
forgotten being an extra in *Somebody Up There Likes Me*, and
back then had vowed one day to be a bigger star than Paul
Newman.

Newman and McQueen had little in common. Paul was, and
is, essentially a supporter of feminist causes. McQueen was a
misogynist—in fact, it was known that he often beat his wives
and lovers.

McQueen, according to members of his family, did not really
like Paul; he was envious of Newman's background, which was
understandable, considering McQueen's very tough childhood
and his reform-school past.

Jack Garfein, McQueen's old pal, opines: "I can see Steve
being envious because he knew people really like Newman and
didn't like him. There's no greater envy than that. It's like

siblings, when you know parents like the other one. I'm sure Steve could sense the crew and people around liked Paul." No one, however, could quibble with the screen presence of either man; they were both very powerful actors.

There was quite a bit of publicity surrounding Scott Newman's appearance in the picture. Stills of Scott in his fireman uniform were circulated worldwide. The youngster had good looks and sufficient talent and there was no doubt that Scott could go far in show business if that was where his energies were focused.

Because of the grueling production schedule of the film, Paul was forced to curtail his racing—he missed virtually the entire season—even though his film contract permitted him to take weekends off to race. He assured his racing buddies that from this point on he would arrange his schedule so that every season he would be free to race from spring through fall.

Meanwhile, the attitude toward *The Sting* had altered dramatically in the months since that initial rough-cut screening in New York. The addition of Marvin Hamlisch's score, which was a starkly simple adaptation of Scott Joplin's music, made a spectacular difference in the film's impact, as did further trimming of several scenes and the addition of beautiful opticals connecting the various episodes of the story. Suddenly everything jelled, so much so that toward the end of the year the picture was previewed with sensational success and opened to blockbuster business.

Paul was named the number-seven box-office draw in the country for 1973. Early in 1974 Joanne won the coveted New York Film Critics Award for her performance in *Summer Wishes, Winter Dreams*. It was fascinating to observe her slipping into the role of movie star when the occasion called for it. Ray Stark and his wife, Fran, who were famous for their lavish soirees for Hollywood's "A" set, hosted an elegant party in Joanne's honor. She was beautiful to look at and beautifully mannered, and all agreed the lady had the one commodity that Hollywood couldn't fake: class.

A great advantage that Joanne and Paul have is that they can travel in and be accepted by either the jet-set chic or the racing and beer-bar circuit. The gifts they exchanged might be something toney—like jewelry or art—or it might be something funky. For example, for Joanne's forty-fourth birthday he gave her a motorcycle.

It was fascinating that in an America where youth and success seemed interlinked, both Newmans, in middle age, were still reaching professional highs. When the Oscar nominations were announced, Joanne was again in the race for best actress. The competition this time out was Glenda Jackson (*A Touch of Class*), Ellen Burstyn (*The Exorcist*), Marsha Mason (*Cinderella Liberty*), and Barbra Streisand (*The Way We Were*). It was a toss-up that year as to who would be the winner. There was no odds-on favorite; and in Joanne's case, the New York Film Critics Circle Award certainly did not hurt her chances of picking up a second Oscar.

At the Oscar presentations that year Paul and Joanne were in attendance. They generally never went to the Oscar ceremonies unless one or the other was nominated, but this year was special. Not only was Joanne up for the award, but so were several of the Newmans' pals. Sylvia Sidney, who had done a superb job playing Joanne's mother in *Summer Wishes, Winter Dreams*, was nominated for best supporting actress.

*The Sting* was nominated for Oscars in virtually every major category, but there was one stunning exception: Newman was not up for best actor, while Robert Redford was. Apparently, Paul's independence had not won him many supporters among his peers, despite what they said or did on other occasions to prove their admiration. But *The Sting* was up for best picture, and George Roy Hill was a nominee for best director.

Sylvia Sidney lost to Tatum O'Neal (*Paper Moon*). Redford lost to Jack Lemmon (*Save the Tiger*). Then the award for best actress was announced—Joanne had lost to Glenda Jackson. George Roy Hill did win, however, and *The Sting* was named best picture.

The awards snub aside, *The Sting* was not one of Newman's more satisfying performances. As far as he was concerned, the picture "was very long on plot and very short on character." The interrelationship between the two leads was not what held the movie together. What mattered, he said, "was that the audience saw a whole new con-man style of life. That's the thing that sold that picture."

Nonetheless, the film outgrossed *Butch Cassidy* by a considerable margin, earning over $69 million in the United States alone this first time in release and inspiring a reissue of *Butch* which itself went on to gross over $13 million during the year.

Although she had lost the Oscar, Joanne's career was moving along at full throttle. It was announced that she would return to the stage, appearing in an upcoming Lincoln Center stage production of August Strindberg's *Dance of Death*. Apparently, however, she was not ready to return to the classics; shortly after she agreed to appear, she backed out.

In any case, Newman and Woodward were hotter than ever among filmmakers and fans. They agreed to appear at a film symposium conducted by the critic Judith Crist in Tarrytown, New York. The couple were refreshingly candid and honest at the question-and-answer session. It was obvious that Woodward had no greater fan than Newman, and it was also obvious from her comments that no one was more aware than Joanne that she and her husband were, indeed, "the character actress and the movie star," with the "actress" part of her constantly at odds with her commitment to husband and family.

"A lot of mornings I can hardly make myself get out from under the covers and try to be me," she remarked during this period of her life. "I've had times when I figured the best thing Paul could do with me is to take me out in back and shoot me like a crippled horse. That's how 'fulfilled' and 'complete' *I* am."

There was no such conflict within Newman—thanks to Joanne, he knew his wife and family were *there* for him. Stewart Stern observed: "Joanne's love for him is as total as his for her. She's a source of reassurance and nourishment for him. They find constant comfort in one another."

Newman's problem was not work versus family but which projects to choose. Newman the actor was in demand everywhere. But the fact was that Newman really had nothing to prove to himself as far as his acting talent was concerned. For

him, part of the lure of racing autos was the challenge of tackling "something new where you're not even sure about your
own talent." This was exactly the lure ballet had held for Joanne, but she had realized that while racing and other interests
could be adopted late in life, ballet could not. Having given up
her vague hopes of performing as a ballet dancer, she remained
intensely interested in the art, and turned her energies to spon-
soring dance companies.

Paul meanwhile accelerated his racing activities. "Joanne has
mixed emotions about Paul's racing," stated one of her friends,
"but she understands that he loves racing just as she loves the
ballet. She does come to a lot of the races and she seems to
enjoy herself."

Newman was not a risk-taking thrill seeker on the track. He
was a steady driver, not one who fought for position. "He's a
conservative driver," observed a sportscaster friend. "He won't
stick his neck out any further than he thinks he should. But if
there's a rabbit to catch out there, he goes for it—with caution."

From the beginning Newman was well liked by the men he
encountered in the racing world. Winning the respect and admiration of the tough competitive characters peopling the
world of auto racing was quite an accomplishment. Brock Yates
recalled meeting Newman at Bonneville around this time
when Chinetti Motors was attempting to break records with a
couple of Ferraris. Newman was driving with pros like Milt
Mintner and the late Graham Hill. According to Yates, "[Paul
was] antsy about looking like a balloon-footed tyro in contrast
to his brilliant professional associates. It gave me the first opportunity to observe him up close, and he revealed himself as a
man of intelligence, depth, and compassion. Away from the
public and the shallow-running Hollywood pilot fish that are
usually in parasitic proximity, Newman may qualify as the
most normal superstar of them all."

Few of his racing buddies will talk about Paul and his relationship with other drivers, mechanics, and track buddies, and
this in itself is surely one reason why Newman loves the sport
—he is not a star to these men but one of the guys. Those close

to Newman confirm that he likes this time spent with the guys in the unpretentious bars and motels near the racetracks. Brock Yates tells a story about Newman at Bonnie and Brent's Hideaway Lounge, which Yates describes as being on the dusty perimeters of Wendover, Utah: "Newman was generally ignored by the locals and was able to act himself. He had a marvelous time, engaging in animated games of eight-ball (good form with the cue and a fair eye but far below hustler status) and numerous chug-a-lug contests. His close buddy, a wild, barrel-shaped rugmaker from Providence named Tommy Chiccone, shamelessly claimed chug-a-lug victory by pouring most of his beer down his shirtfront. It was a funny, semidrunken night with a collection of good and diverse people, one of whom momentarily seemed happier being just another guy leaning against a bar in a nowhere saloon than one of the mightiest stars in show business."

Inevitably there have been occasions when the worlds of superstar Paul Newman and race car driver P. L. Newman clashed. One incident occurred at the Bonneville Speedway with the Ferrari North American racing team. It seemed the Ferrari company had made a deal to be featured on a *CBS Sports Spectacular*, but there had been a huge misunderstanding. The CBS cameras and reporters were there in force, and CBS was under the impression it would be a program spotlighting Paul Newman. The star had had no idea that the entire special was being planned around him; he had not been consulted and he had no intention of cooperating. Paul joined his buddies at Bonnie and Brent's and was determined to stay in the bar and play pool until the situation was resolved.

Publicist Warren Cowan was summoned and one of CBS's retired presidents, Ed Sachs, was on hand to represent the network. The men went into Newman's motor home to confer. Finally Newman was convinced to give a brief interview—about two minutes—and the CBS unit producer, Bud Morgan, was to have his crew film the race, but they were not to focus on Paul Newman. The story vividly illustrates Paul Newman's style: He will not be exploited, but he is not unreasonable and is open to negotiation to resolve seemingly impossible situations.

During this period in their marriage Woodward was forever being told "What woman wouldn't trade places with you?" Well, it wasn't easy living with Sam Superstar, Joanne would counter, using one of her pet names for Paul. She had done it successfully for sixteen years, however, and apparently knew the rules. She said she was a complainer and not a "grin and bear it" person, but the fact is that she *worked* at keeping the relationship healthy. She cared deeply about her children's happiness and her *friendship* with her husband. She said it was "damn hard" living with him because it was difficult relating to a superstar who, she explained, had nothing to do with Paul Newman. What public and press saw was a larger-than-life image that *they*, not Newman, had created. It was an awful thing to live with. His wife, of course, knew he was a human being, not a god. That was one of the reasons Newman loved her. But sometimes even those close to him would forget "who he really is and what he's really like."

The children were often bewildered, unable to separate the man from the star. Was this father an ordinary person or someone who deserved special treatment? He certainly received special treatment from the media and from fans, and even from many in his profession. An incident involving Susan Newman illustrates the problem. Once she drove with her father from New York City to Connecticut in one of his Volkswagens with a Porsche engine. Paul was speeding along the highway, and his daughter was clutching her seat. Suddenly the lights from a police car were flashing behind them. Paul pulled over quietly, then sat and waited for the policeman. The cop was yelling as he approached the car.

Susan was terrified. She thought the policeman would actually search the car. But she also knew who her father was, and she was waiting to see if he was going to identify himself. He did not. Then, Susan realized that, of course, he didn't have to —in a few moments the cop would be reading Paul Newman's driver's license.

When the cop saw the license, it took him about a minute to

put the face and the name together; then his mood changed abruptly. His voice lowered, and he stammered something to the effect, "Oh, Mr. Newman, well. Why didn't you say something? I'm sorry. I mean, listen . . ." Paul was then admonished for driving a bit fast, and it was suggested that maybe he should be a little more cautious in the future. There would be no speeding ticket.

Incidents like this had a powerful effect on Susan and her siblings. In fact, Susan has said of this particular moment, "[It] really pissed me off." She realized that her father had power, and even though he was a qualified race driver and a responsible citizen, he could get away with such behavior because of his status as a star.

What must also have added to Susan's frustration was the realization that it was *his* power, and that that power did not extend to his children.

Joanne Woodward, as mother and stepmother, had to contend with all the tensions fame thrust on the family. Some of their friends thought Joanne tended to downplay her contributions to the couple's successful relationship and their family life. Gore Vidal found this quality of modesty in Joanne "refreshing in a world where most people go the opposite way."

Joanne admitted her husband was selfish, but selfish in a *positive* way—he was a man capable of satisfying his own ego; therefore he did not require ego massage.

Joanne was still fighting the tug-of-war between Woodward the dedicated actress and Joanne Newman the mother. She had misgivings about her performance as a mother, rating herself 6.5 on a scale of 10 (her daughters' rating of her, she allowed, might be considerably lower). She felt guilty about neglecting her family for her career, and still tried hard to leave a character on the set so that she could come home and be the mother she wanted to be to her kids.

Years ago she had received advice from a friend which at the time she considered shocking: "Whatever is good for you is also good for your children." Now this concept made sense to her. She saw that the girls were doing well, even though, in Joanne's judgment, she was not giving them the devotion and attention she once thought they had to have. At least with Jo-anne the children were spared one of the more unpleasant as-pects of celebrity: the aggressive fan. When with their father, they would find themselves being shoved aside by admirers eager to get a close look at "superstar Paul Newman."

Joanne and Paul were trying very hard to give their daugh-ters whatever it took to survive and flourish. Joanne observed it takes "a huge amount of ego strength to be the child of celebri-ties, especially if one of them is a sex symbol."

It was of course impossible for the children to pretend that they were not "different." For them the question would always be: Are you accepted as yourself or as the child of famous par-ents? The Newman girls often commented on this with such dinner-table chatter as, "By the way, so-and-so found out who we are!" And then they would joke, "Who are we?"

Scott was especially affected by the disadvantages—and ad-vantages—of reflected fame. He was torn by the suspicion that people liked him or wanted to know him only because of "who he was." Yet, according to a person close to him, he would often be heard to say, "Don't you know who my father is?"

Scott was twenty-four now. He and his father saw each other occasionally, as they shared an interest in racing; sometimes Paul and his son went to the track together. Scott continued performing stunt work and sporadically tried out for acting jobs. Many of his friends, also struggling actors, found they had to drop the friendship because they could not cope with Scott's drug taking, drinking, and what some have described as young Newman's weird therapies.

Through the years Scott had tried different nutrition pro-grams and would often jump from one currently popular ther-apy to another. He tried yoga, astral projection, and several pop psychology remedies. Most who knew him say they could not tell whether Scott was seeking answers or escape. Most disturbing to his family and friends was Scott's belligerent be-havior when he was under the influence of whatever substance. Incidents arising from the situation had been kept quiet, but when Scott was arrested on assault-and-battery charges and for disturbing the peace, the news could not be suppressed.

Nor could Paul Newman, as a parent, work any miracles: "You go into the kitchen and you get about three ice cubes and you chill a beer mug and you sit there and think a while. Listen, there's not much you can do except offer what support you feel is required."

The support that seemed to be called for, and that Newman could well afford, was psychiatric help. From this point on there would be two psychologists on call twenty-four hours a day to try to help Scott.

A year after the arrest Paul Newman complained about press coverage on Scott. "The incident with him was blown all out of proportion," Newman stated. "The accusation is always on the first page and the retraction on page nineteen."

Insiders claim that it was extremely difficult for Paul to communicate with Scott at this point. Certainly a father whose past included a similar incident with the police and his own bouts with alcohol was in no position to be judgmental. There were clear indications, however, that Joanne's attitude was quite different—she felt Scott should be more responsible for himself and stop being an emotional drain on his father.

Meanwhile Paul Newman's interest in political matters was intense as ever. "You don't stop being a citizen just because you have a SAG [Screen Actors Guild] card," he observed. "You also don't immobilize yourself because you're afraid that you carry more weight than some people think your credentials will allow."

Newman had no qualms about voicing his opinion concerning an older actor who had successfully entered the political arena, but he stated that while he didn't like Ronald Reagan, he felt an actor, just as anyone else, was entitled to run for public office or to endorse a candidate.

The inevitable comparisons between the opposing political viewpoints of Newman and Reagan (who had recently finished his second term as governor of California and was about to make the big push in his presidential bid) elicited the usual plea to Newman from his political cohorts and admirers: why didn't he run for office? "Well, I would be pretty far to the left of Ronald Reagan for a starter," he replied. "But I don't think I have the patience for politics; I would be able to run for one term—so it wouldn't be as though I were changing a career because politics would be a very short-lived career for me. There would be no way I could survive. I mean, they'd never elect me anyway because my platform would be too outrageous to begin with."

Even if the climate was right for him to run, he simply knew his limitations: "I've been asked to run for office and I've declined on the basis that I think I can make my presence felt as well as an actor and can have as large a platform as I could if I were actively working as a politician."

Furthermore, Joanne's sensibilities were on Newman's mind: "If Joanne suddenly found herself in a position where she had to throw one of those fancy Washington bashes she would—well, that'd be the end of the relationship. She'd say, 'Well, you're on your own, kid.'"

Newman was a board member of the Center for the Study of Democratic Institutions. He was active in a new citizens' group, the Seaside Environmental Alliance, or SEA, and had personally gathered signatures for petitions to keep the California coast free of oil and other pollutants.

However, the only races citizen Newman was interested in entering were those on the auto track, and even though he raced under the name P. L. Newman, there was no such thing as anonymity for the movie star. At the 1974 Labor Day race at New Hampshire's Bayar Motor Sports Park, an amateur event, there were spectators who had come just to see Newman. In fact, guards had to protect him from a crowd of autograph seekers. What the fans saw was a gum-chewing, crude-talking, nail-biting, gray-haired man nervously rubbing his hands together before the start of the race.

In the race Paul was running a close second, and although members of his crew were shouting for him to overtake the leader, Newman stuck to his game plan—sure but steady. Then the number-one car was suddenly engulfed in smoke and was out of the race; Newman was in the lead—and he held it. He won. In his euphoria he consented to something he rarely did: an on-the-spot interview for television.

The following day P. L. Newman was driving a Ford Escort at Lime Rock Park in Connecticut, in a professional meet. There were ten thousand people on hand, including Joanne, her daughters, and Susan (now twenty-one). It was apparent that the Newman girls were there merely to lend moral support, since others in attendance noted that they were not interested in the race, even though Paul was in the lead. But then the thing most feared in racing suddenly occurred: There was a crash. A deer had wandered onto the track and had been hit by one of the cars. Almost immediately four other cars crashed into the disabled vehicle. One auto skidded off the track and hit a tree. Two others collided.

Newman was not involved in the accident, but the whole thing was upsetting for his family. They rushed to the pit and got there just as Paul was pulling in.

Officials cleared the track, and the race was set to restart. Susan, in the spirit of the moment, helped her dad's mechanics push his Escort back into place. It seemed Paul had a good chance of winning, but on the sixty-sixth, and final, lap his car momentarily spun off the track. The car in second place, a Porsche, sped by, and Newman placed second.

After the race P. L. Newman momentarily became the Paul Newman the fans expected to see. He changed his shirt in the pit, an act he knew from experience would engender wild squeals from some in the audience.

P. L. Newman's prize money was $325.

He was being paid considerably more to re-create the role of Lew Harper in *The Drowning Pool*. "I simply adore that character," Newman observed, "because it will accommodate any kind of actor's invention. He can do the most outrageous things. It's great to go to work, because you know you're going to have a lot of fun that day."

Woodward played an over-the-hill southern belle who hires Harper. The leading lady and Newman's love interest in the film was played by Gail Strickland. Richard Jaeckel had a good part, that of a sheriff of a small southern town, and Anthony Franciosa was "the bad guy."

Jaeckel recalls working on location: "We went down to Lafayette, Louisiana, and did a lot of driving and fooling around, and, as far as the parts were concerned, we did a lot of chases . . . and it was fun. And it was a reminiscence of an earlier association. And everybody else picked up on it, because I like to think that we still have great affection for each other."

Joanne was back home in Connecticut and attending classes at Sarah Lawrence. The previous semester one of her history courses had required a term paper, and when her professor returned it with the written comment "good thinking," Joanne was thrilled. "That was something that really made me feel good. No Oscar can begin to compare."

It was apparent to all that Joanne was going through a period in which her film career was less important to her. She was not retiring, however: she and Paul had agreed to host their first TV special together. It was a documentary, *The Wild Places*, and in it they would be the guides for a tour of the American wilderness. The show's real star was nature, magnificently photographed.

The special aired in December on NBC. That same month *The Towering Inferno* was previewed successfully. Now, one year after *The Sting*, Paul Newman had another blockbuster in the nation's theaters, and he had risen to the rank of number-three box-office attraction.

The self-described "aging juvenile" turned fifty in January 1975. "I am lurching toward fifty," he had said, "with all the eager anticipation of a kid having a woman for the first time."

Paul Newman at fifty was still undeniably a sex symbol, whether he appreciated the appellation or not, and he was not making any pathetic attempts to look thirty—he was letting his hair go gray, and on him it looked good.

Newman was very much an object of desire as far as the nation's youth was concerned. Joanne said he received passionate love letters from teenagers—some as young as thirteen. Such teenage crushes, of course, are nothing to cause concern; attention from older fans could be more problematic. Joanne has said she has never had occasion to worry about someone that age having a serious "crush" on Paul because she had never been aware of that happening; no woman had thrown herself at Paul while she was watching: "What goes on while I'm not watching, I don't know."

As to whether she worried about Paul's possible infidelities when he was off on movie locations, she claimed that she dismissed rumors and never speculated about what might be happening. She felt secure. Of course Joanne realized that virtually all women flirted with Paul—from waitresses to publicists, from script girls to leading ladies. She knew she wasn't getting any younger, but was aware that Newman's female costars most definitely were. Joanne coped; it was part-and-parcel of being Mrs. Paul Newman. But while she wasn't young, she also didn't feel old, and she worked at staying as youthful as possible.

One of the publicists who worked with the Newmans once queried Joanne about her obsession with keeping her body in shape. Joanne retorted, "Look at these kids!" (meaning her daughters and their friends, who were constantly about the house). Woodward was determined to keep her body youthful, although, like Paul, she does not try to look or dress younger than her age and thus looks spectacular for her age.

While Joanne had momentarily put her career on hold, Newman forged ahead with his. It was announced he would star in the eagerly awaited film version of the best-selling novel *Ragtime*. It was also announced that he would be one of the stars of *A Bridge Too Far*, William Goldman's much-publicized million-dollar script version of another bestselling book, this one a World War II epic. Joseph E. Levine was producing the picture with an all-star cast, a genre of filmmaking Darryl F. Zanuck had elevated to popularity ten years earlier with his production of *The Longest Day*. Newman did not appear in either film.

Newman was aware he saw the cream of the crop as far as material was concerned. Top agents, producers, et al. sent him scripts which he found "uniformly bad." His standards were very high, however, and he pointed out that any film dealing with a *serious* topic—the only kind of film he wanted to make—had to be virtually flawless, because a poor film about an important subject was harmful to the subject. (And probably would lose a lot of money as well.)

Newman expressed interest in a property that dealt with homosexuality. *The Front Runner* is a novel about an athletic coach who falls in love with one of his students. Newman wanted to play the coach, and he reportedly approached Redford about the role of the student. The blond actor's response was purported to be along the lines of "Paul, are you crazy?!"

Newman noted that in England actors aren't concerned whether they play gays, straights, fascists, anarchists—it's the *part* that counts, how it's written and if it's interesting. But he had no illusions about the American scene. He suspected the public would not accept him in the role of a homosexual, and he furthermore feared that they would perceive something fake about the characterization. It was a "no win" situation.

Newman's feelings about homosexuality are what one would expect: "Well, if people can find serenity and peace and comfort among each other, I'm certainly not interested in what their sexual proclivities or their sexual interests are." And he has always been a supporter of gay rights, "and not a closet supporter, either." He has said that from the time he was a youngster he has never understood attacks on homosexuals. He feels that there are numerous qualities that make up a human being and that people should concentrate on all the positive aspects. Decency, ethics, and morals have nothing to do with sexual orientation, he states; that a person has sex only with someone of the opposite sex does not make the person a better human being.

Because of all the problems inherent in the project *The Front Runner* was put on the back burner. (To date, the film has not been made.) Finding a vehicle that struck all the right chords was a problem Newman shared with virtually *all* of his superstar peers. Newman's demands were even more difficult to fulfill—he sought material of real literary merit, and he was obviously not finding what he wanted. "Most young writers have no craft," bemoaned Newman. "There's a visceral rather than an intellectual process. What do these kids know about Aristophanes and Euripides, or Marlowe, Schiller, G. B. Shaw or even James Agee?"

Newman observed, " 'Entertainment' films are fine, as long as they're not all you do."

Yes, even Paul Newman had trouble putting deals together. One of his daughters has said that when her father could not get his way professionally, it was a great revelation to her. If he, with his unique fame and power, could still not do what he wanted to do, then who could?

On one front things were working out. All the elements were finally coming together for Newman's company to film Arthur Kopit's *Indians*, which was being retitled *Buffalo Bill and the Indians*.

Meanwhile Paul's racing career was gaining not only momentum but validity. He won the northeast division title in the same Datsun 510 that Bob Sharp had driven to the 1972 Sports Car Club of America national title. Newman finished sixth in the SCCA runoffs, and he proceeded to form his own auto racing team, P. L. Newman Racing. If anyone had perceived Paul Newman as a dilettante racer, the actor was, in his slow-but-sure fashion, forcing them to change their opinion.

Paul tried to balance his interest in racing and his commitment to his career with family matters. At home in Connecticut the Newman children were continuing to be a source of fascination, interest, and concern for their parents. Most parents hope that by the time their kids reach their teenage years, their career interests will be clarified somewhat, but with the Newmans, as with most families, it was impossible to know what the future held in store for the children. Joanne said all six kids were different and as much of a mystery to her now as they had been when they were younger. Communication was sometimes difficult—a universal complaint. But at least Joanne talked to her children—"a lot more than my parents ever talked to me," she noted.

According to Joanne, the Newman kids (particularly her three daughters) did not have too much to rebel about, all things considered. They had led a very atypical and interesting existence. Joanne reasoned that *no* child had parents who were home *all* the time and who were all-knowing and secure and capable of solving any problem. She felt that there were certain things kids needed to work out for themselves, and she wanted to be sure she gave her kids the leeway and support to do this. If they needed outside help, she would see that they got it.

Scott Newman was still battling with his problems, but he seemed to have made some progress in getting his life together. He delivered a very effective performance in an episode of *Marcus Welby, M.D.*, the hit TV series produced by MCA. He had also done some stunt work and appeared in a small role in *The Great Waldo Pepper*, the George Roy Hill film starring Robert Redford. Scott also guested on Merv Griffin's TV talk show, and the handsome youngster came off as a very likable guy. Certainly he had as much to offer as any of his peers currently working in the business.

While Paul did let his son know how pleased he was at the way he had handled himself on the Griffin show, their relationship remained mercurial. Paul later admitted, "We were like rubber bands, one minute close, the next separated by an enormous and unaccountable distance." For the moment, however, things were finally looking up for Scott—or so it seemed.

Susan, using the professional name Susan Kendall Newman, had made her debut as an actress Off-Broadway in *We Interrupt This Program*. Paul was very proud of her but had no comment on the play, which quickly closed.

Woodward's work schedule had slowed down, and she felt she was becoming "an appendage" to Paul. As a result, she was growing more adamant about separating her own identity from that of her husband. It was difficult being married to a superstar, very tough on her, she said, and as she was getting older (she was now forty-five) she liked to be known as Miss Woodward. She was "Mrs. Newman" only when dealing with matters pertaining to her children's affairs.

Paul understood how she felt and was unhappy when Joanne was unhappy. "Paul is one of the few genuinely kind people I know," she said. "Most people pretend to be kind, but he really is."

Home life for the family continued to be comfortable but

consistently inconsistent. In later years, the Newman children would comment that in their daily lives their parents often went from one extreme to the other to accommodate changes in their social or political consciousness. For example, ecology was a major concern. The energy crisis of the early seventies prompted the Newmans to dispose of all unnecessary electrical appliances, like the can opener, and Joanne, in an effort to conserve gas, drove a Honda (her Mazda was an acknowledged luxury).

During this period the family ate a lot of organic food. The cleaning lady observed that they ate just like "poor folks." Sacks of oats sat in the kitchen, giving it the appearance of a small-town general store.

All the Newmans enjoyed their freedom to live wherever and however they liked, and had the luxury of being able to indulge their preferences. Privacy was much easier to maintain in Connecticut, but California had its appeal. Newman liked the changing seasons on the East Coast, and New York City continued to excite him, but he enjoyed having the mobility to move back and forth as he chose.

Paul's exercise regimen was not too different from a man of thirty-five (or younger). He ran daily, sometimes as many as several miles. He once joked that he ran because Joanne put him on a rope at the end of a car. He said his insurance value appealed to her, because she would undoubtedly outlive him and would like to collect as soon as possible. He added dryly that Joanne also made sure that after jogging Paul jumped into the ice cold river, "on the theory it will start my heart or stop it, one way or the other."

Paul described Joanne in those years as "awfully self-effacing." She also seemed to denigrate her own talent, apparently feeling that when something came easily to her, it must therefore mean that the result was no good.

Certainly ballet dancing didn't come easily to her. Newman noted that she had gone on point in middle-age and would be the oldest ballerina to try *Swan Lake*.

Woodward had become deeply involved—financially as well as creatively—in ballet. She backed *Dancers*, an experimental dance group in Manhattan, and served as Chairman of the company's board of directors. Dennis Wayne was the creative force in this venture. Many dance critics considered his choreography less than inspired, but there was no disagreement on his personal magnetism. "He is a very virile, attractive man—and straight," states a knowledgeable source. "Women are very drawn to him and he has quite a way with women."

## 13

For the first time in years the Newmans, when out in public together, began revealing aspects of their relationship that heretofore had been kept private. For example, the couple had a fight one evening in Sardi's, the famous New York restaurant frequented by show people.

There was another incident when the Newmans attended the gala world premiere of *The Great Waldo Pepper*. The evening had been a klieg-light event in the old Hollywood tradition of red-carpet film openings. The picture premiered at New York's Rivoli Theater, and two busloads of stars attended, including Newman and Woodward, Redford, Dustin Hoffman (currently working with Redford on *All the President's Men*), and other personalities.

Outside the theater there was pandemonium, with policemen joining arms to hold back the throngs as the stars arrived. When Newman appeared, the mob surged forward with such force that photographers and publicists at the doors leading into the theater lobby feared being pushed through the thick plate-glass doors. Injuries were barely avoided as the stars were inched through the throng without mishap.

At the postpremiere party at the Rainbow Room, atop the

seventy-story RCA Building in Rockefeller Center, there was, as part of the festivities, an auction. Joanne, wearing her blond hair cropped short and a very trendy suede outfit with calf-high matching boots, looked gorgeous. During the auction she made a winning bid on something that Paul apparently did not like, and Paul was angry. They had words and everybody present knew it. The tension between them seemed to last for the rest of the evening.

Some of their friends subsequently downplayed the incident. Other celebrity watchers said the couple's PR representatives would be issuing a statement regarding Newman and Woodward's marriage (they did not).

In fact, the publicity minds behind the Newmans took a different tack. Suddenly Paul and Joanne as a duo were available to selected members of the media. Stories about their lives together—with headlines like "They Rarely Let Interviewers Penetrate Their Privacy"—soon began to appear. Paul and Joanne, the public was being told, were like any couple who had been married for almost twenty years. As she put it, "It is very difficult to live with somebody for a long time and like him all the time."

He said that in their relationship they had had "some pretty bad hassles," adding that it would be "pretty goddamn dull" if their life together had been hassle-free. Newman did not want an unchanging relationship, he said. Change meant growth. He realized Joanne had not had an easy time of it: "It has been difficult for her, having my three older children, but she certainly has held her end up. God, she is marvelous."

He said he *missed* her when he was away from her. Their relationship was, he explained, based on respect and tolerance. He was aware that most relationships fell apart because one partner usually grew emotionally, and often professionally, faster than the other. With Newman and Woodward, Paul claimed, the process was more or less equal—her talent had not been buried in the kitchen while he went from triumph to triumph in a galaxy of beautiful people. They had grown together.

Newman continued to talk about his luck, which he felt had

played a major role in his life. Now, at fifty, he said he was having the time of his life, and anything else that happened would be gravy.

The message to the public was clear: The couple, while obviously extraordinary people, had ordinary problems, and their love and respect for each other was what made the marriage work.

*The Drowning Pool* had previewed none too successfully in June. Joanne was excellent in a showy but small role, playing one of Harper's former lovers who hires him to solve a murder. She, in turn, is murdered.

The picture, however, was going to be sold not as a Newman-Woodward movie but as a Paul Newman action picture. Unfortunately, it was ten years since *Harper*, and somehow the character was less attractive this time out. In addition, the plot was convoluted, and the picture simply did not hang together as the initial *Harper* had. The box-office outlook was not good beyond the solid advances theater owners had forked over.

That fall, with the racing season over, Newman embarked on one of his most challenging assignments; he was to play the title role in *Buffalo Bill and the Indians*. His agents and business associates could not have been happy that their prime client was tackling a character role in which his famous face would be camouflaged under a white wig and beard, all in the interest of realism: the actor would be made up to resemble the legendary Buffalo Bill. And the image-shattering theme of the film—demythifying American heroes—was not the stuff of *Butch Cassidy* and *Towering Inferno*, escapist fare that was packing the movie theaters across the country.

Robert Altman, who was directing *Buffalo Bill*, was an innovator and creative risk taker whose unorthodox approach to moviemaking—allowing his actors total freedom to improvise and invent—made him a favorite with stars, character actors, and "ordinary" actors, but not with film companies. Altman had had only one big commercial hit, *M\*A\*S\*H*, but there had been many a succès d'estime. Newman and Altman became pals as well as business partners during this time.

Actually, the star and the director were a highly promising combination. But Newman's fantasy of the perfect movie wouldn't necessarily appeal to anyone else. He said he'd love to work on an idea with a writer, then work with a great, imaginative director, sign the *right* costars (right in type, not necessarily name value), rehearse for a month—then pull the plug, never shooting the movie, and never showing it to an audience.

Newman and Altman certainly wanted people to come and see *Buffalo Bill*. They sought the diva Beverly Sills, then at the pinnacle of her stardom, to play the role of the opera singer. She came close to signing—"Who wouldn't want to be in a picture with Paul Newman?!" she exclaimed on *The Tonight Show*—but she didn't sign. Evelyn Lear got the role.

Newman had been working on this project for a long time, and it had assumed great importance for him. "*Buffalo Bill* has a clout people won't realize until they start thinking about the film three days later," stated Newman. "What it does is shoot down all those legendary people. That includes Buffalo Bill and me and Redford and Muhammad Ali and Churchill and Stalin and Roosevelt. There's simply no way that any human being could be anything like what legend makers try to convince the public he is. This picture is an adult fairy tale that accommodates almost any kind of actor's invention. But you have to be careful that the invention has the size of the character."

Altman was calling the film his "contribution" to the bicentennial. Certainly key movie critics throughout the country were eagerly awaiting the picture.

Paul's working with Robert Altman naturally prompted questions about whether there were other directors with whom he was interested in collaborating. Newman was direct: "I have no urge to work with any specific directors or actors. I only have a very real desire to find a script that's genuinely distinguished." He seemed to disagree with the popular auteur theory, according to which the director *is* the film. He felt if the characters were good enough, *they* could carry the film. If the story was compelling enough, *it* could carry the film. In Newman's opinion there were at this time two truly original filmmakers on the scene—Stanley Kubrick and John Cassavetes.

"That doesn't necessarily mean that they're good," stated Newman, "but they're original."

One currently hot director wanted Newman for a cameo, and as a lark Paul filmed a short sequence for Mel Brooks's latest comedy, *Silent Movie*. Other stars who did cameos for Brooks in this film were Mrs. Brooks (Anne Bancroft), Liza Minnelli, Burt Reynolds, and James Caan.

It had been touted that Newman had turned down many films because of their violence. Violence on-screen—a sad reflection of the times—"bored" Newman, and for that reason he was not interested in working with Sam Peckinpah, whose pictures had stretched the limits of cinema violence.

However, for someone interested in working with distinguished scripts and avoiding on-screen violence, Newman's next project was certainly questionable. *Slap Shot* may have seemed a worthwhile script to some, but there was no doubt that physical violence was integral to the story. In fact, not only would a great deal of physical violence be shown, but Newman's character, a small-time hockey coach, spurs his teammates to violence. In fairness, however, the film is perhaps most accurately viewed as a satirical statement on the *demand* for violence in sports.

Despite the violence, Newman found the script very original. This was a movie he loved, and, too, he took great pride in the fact that during filming "it got to the point on the ice where you couldn't tell the skaters from the actors."

For the role Newman had to be a *good* ice skater. He said, "Isn't the movie business great? I've learned how to drive a race car [*Winning*], ride a horse [*The Left-Handed Gun*], play the trombone [*Paris Blues*], box [*Somebody Up There Likes Me*], shoot billiards [*The Hustler*], and play ice hockey."

Not only had Paul Newman learned all these new activities, but with car racing and ice hockey he was tackling sports that most men his age were content to watch on television while sipping their afternoon beers.

For *Slap Shot* Paul and one of his co-stars, Melinda Dillon, filmed a seminude scene in bed. The shooting of such scenes, according to professional actors, is actually a very mechanical experience, often nerve-wracking and anything but genuinely passionate and erotic. Dillon has recalled that during the shooting of this scene, Paul was "full of jokes" and put her completely at ease. The experience was, she said "a breeze."

The film was being shot on location in Johnstown, Pennsylvania. Paul learned that Susan, in New York, was very discouraged about the fact that her career was going nowhere, and was in a deep depression, so he phoned her. She later revealed that he had initially offered her a small acting role, but it evolved instead into a fourteen-week "girl Friday" assignment, requiring Susan to do a bit of everything. She was pleased, however, to spend so much time with her father; they had seen little of each other over the previous two years.

Important, too, was the presence of the "cave man" extras— the real hockey players who were cast in the film. Susan was captivated by these men who were so different from her friends from the dancing and theater worlds in New York. "I fell in love with several of those guys," she said.

When *Slap Shot* finished shooting, Susan went back to Hollywood to pursue her acting career. She later did dinner theater on the Coast, appearing in a play in which she played a porno star. Her costume posed a real challenge for the naturally modest Susan; she was not required to appear nude, but did have to walk around on stage in a revealing bra, panties, and boots. Since Susan considered herself a modest person, she said that taking the role represented a very strong psychological challenge for her. This was not experimental workshop theater in New York but commercial dinner theater, and as Ms. Newman later recalled, many of the men after a few drinks would be making comments about her body. She, very naturally, had used another name and could take solace in the fact that although many had come to see a pretty girl running around half-naked, at least nobody came to see her just because they knew she was Paul Newman's daughter.

Meanwhile Woodward was at a crossroads in her career— and she made a decision: She would return to her roots—television. The stories that could provide her with the kinds of roles she longed to play were *only* being done on television. "Like it or not, I *must* act," said Joanne. "If I don't I'm going to be impossible—a displaced person. If that happens, my family will suffer as much as I do." Acting, she acknowledged, was for her an innate behavior: "I wouldn't know how *not* to act. It's like being born with a deformity: you not only learn how to live with it, you wouldn't know how to live without it."

In addition, she was motivated by making money—not for herself but for the Dancers group. Some sources state that practically all her earnings from acting had gone to Dancers from 1975 on.

Ironically, Joanne's return to dramatic television would be in a vehicle very reminiscent of *The Three Faces of Eve*, only this time Joanne would be playing not the multipersonality role, but the psychiatrist. And the title role—Sybil, a character with sixteen personalities—would launch the actress Sally Field (*The Flying Nun*) just as Eve had done for Woodward nineteen years earlier.

While Joanne was getting back to work, Paul was eager to finish his film commitments and to focus his attentions on the racing season. Nineteen seventy-six would mark his last year as an amateur driver, and it proved to be an impressive finale for him. After five years on the amateur circuit he won the President's Cup, which is the Sports Car Club of America's foremost trophy for amateur drivers.

Paul was giving himself an entire year away from filmmaking, to devote his energies to racing. Also, it was a presidential election year, and Paul was campaigning for candidates in whom he believed. Naturally, he supported Jimmy Carter for president, and on a more local level he campaigned for Ramsey Clark, who was running for the United States Senate seat in New York State. Paul was aware that his involvement with political candidates could often lead to criticism. One magazine ran the headline "Ramsey Clark Finds A Gimmick—Paul Newman." Paul and Joanne, however, have always been philosophical. Exposure to criticism would never deter them from espousing a cause: being involved is better than not being involved.

Joanne's career was on the upswing. Her return to television was a resounding success. *Sybil*, a four-hour movie, which aired on two successive nights in November on NBC, had been written by Stewart Stern. Its graphic depiction of the horrors experienced by the title character made the once-shocking exploits of the schizoid woman in *The Three Faces of Eve* seem almost mild. "As Dr. Wilbur, Woodward underlines professionalism with compassion. . . . [she] brings a glowing authority to her role," wrote Judith Crist in *TV Guide*.

The film, directed by Daniel Petrie, was much talked about in the weeks and months after it aired. Woodward had been impressed by Sally Field and was very generous in her praise of the actress both to the press and in private. In fact, it was virtually unheard of for one actress to laud another's work in such an unselfish and genuine manner.

In December Joanne was the narrator of a ballet version of Louisa May Alcott's *Little Women*, also on NBC. Her friend Edward Villella was featured in a principal role.

The following month the Newmans were in Hollywood where Gore Vidal hosted a party for Paul's fifty-second birthday.

*Slap Shot*, then in preparation for release, was receiving a lot of industry attention—the film featured a lot of X-rated language. There had been no attempts by Newman or Hill to soften either the story or Newman's character and physical appearance.

"I think Paul is bored with acting," noted Hill. "It's too bad. He has the capacity to become a great actor. When he's hitting on all twelve cylinders he is a joy to watch. He'll never be as great a race driver as he could be an actor. But being a celebrity is a process of dying, and that has been the hardest thing for Paul to cope with."

Though insiders knew Paul was bored with acting, Newman, the consummate pro, did not let his boredom show on-screen. In fact, his portrayal of Reggie Dunlop in *Slap Shot* was probably the best work he had done in years. The role was decidedly "out of character" for the star of *Towering Inferno* and *The Sting*, for Dunlop was a distinctly unlikable lowlife.

Susan Newman's small acting part in *Slap Shot* was just that; she was an extra. It was a start, however. Robert Altman cast her in his upcoming production of *A Wedding*, to be shot that summer in Waukegan, Illinois. Susan was one of several children of stars in the cast, which included Desi Arnaz, Jr., Geraldine Chaplin, and Mia Farrow.

Most of Susan's scenes were with the veteran actor Vittorio Gassman, and Susan had no illusions about the fact that in the editing, if it was a choice between her or Gassman, he would be favored.

Paul Newman had no great wisdom to offer in advising Susan on her acting career. All he told her was, "Learn how to relax when you're not on." Obviously he saw Susan in a different light than did other producer-directors; he thought of her as a Grace Kelly type. Those who know her have described Susan as cool, aloof, and smart. Some say she is cynical, but then again this is undoubtedly one of her defense mechanisms as the child of a superstar.

To launch *Slap Shot* that spring, Paul Newman agreed to do something he disliked—to meet the press en masse at a special luncheon at Manhattan's lavish Tavern on the Green restaurant. Out-of-town press were flown in, and key New York reporters were present as well. All were treated to an elaborate luncheon, after which Newman, accompanied by roving publicists, sat down at each table and chatted with reporters.

While Universal's publicity department coordinated the proceedings—and picked up the tab—individual, *very* select interviews had been set up by Newman's PR firm, Rogers and Cowan. Those speaking with Newman one-on-one were screened in advance—not on the basis of specific questions, but for their friendly disposition toward Newman and the nature of what they had written about him in the past. It was a very subtle, but very effective, form of press management.

Newman, as usual, handled himself with dignity and aplomb, appearing friendly but definitely reserved. While he was handsome as ever, there was, surprisingly, something fragile about his appearance. Those who expected a tough, larger-than-life exterior were disappointed.

*Slap Shot* previewed well and was expected to be a commercial success, although how big a success remained to be seen. Without "repeat business" a picture would not, in current terms, be a hit. *Buffalo Bill* had opened and bombed, becoming the lowest-grossing Paul Newman film to date.

Newman's success on the racetrack, however, was increasing. He had made his professional driving debut at Daytona, and the results had been excellent. His partners in the venture were Elliott Forbes-Robinson and Milt Mintner, both old pros; the car he was driving was owned by Clint Eastwood. During the twenty-four-hour endurance race, Newman's speed at times hit 180 mph. His final standing was fifth, only fifty laps behind the first-place winner; fifty-seven vehicles had started the race, only twenty-four finished; Newman's total driving time had been around six and a half hours; he'd raced at night for the first time. "I'd never driven at night before," he noted afterward. "I'd never driven a car with this much horsepower [he had driven a Ferrari] and I'd never been involved in a race more than three or four hours long. Would I like to do it again? You bet your life." He entered the twelve-hour endurance race on the schedule at Sebring in March and drove a Porsche.

Driver Milt Mintner voiced an opinion about Paul Newman the competitor: "There's just no Hollywood air about him. And he's smart. You tell him about a driving mistake and it's the last time he'll make it."

Forbes-Robinson, too, had found Newman to be such a regular guy that he forgot he was a star. "I'd say let's go to this place, and he'd answer, 'Man, I can't—too many people,'" Forbes-Robinson has recalled. "He's very dedicated. I don't think there are many people who could start driving competitively at the age Paul did and be doing anywhere near as well."

Meanwhile a new cause had grabbed Joanne's interest—the National Society for Autistic Children (NSAC). "I hesitated when they asked me," said Woodward, "because I'd long since decided that I would never be an honorary anything. I don't believe in lending your name to a letterhead unless you are willing to get involved in the work. But I couldn't turn this down. Can you imagine having a baby that seems normal, and then slowly discovering it can't relate to you or anything else in its environment; that it can't eat properly or even enjoy playing?"

Joanne became NSAC's honorary national chairperson, but she also became *involved*: "I got involved because I really admired the devotion of these parents. They could have put their children in an institution. But these people didn't opt for that. They are all really working to create a world for their boys and girls. Their special kind of love, the kind that just won't stop, is what brought me here in the first place."

There was a film project in the making that Joanne wanted very much to do, Arthur Laurents's *The Turning Point*. The story was about the world of ballet and focused on two women, an aging prima ballerina and her former best friend, a dancer who gave up a career to marry and raise children. This was a real "woman's picture" in the Bette Davis–Miriam Hopkins tradition, with the added fillip of ballet as the backdrop.

The actress Joan Fontaine says that Joanne brought the *Turning Point* package to Alan Ladd, Jr., then head of production at 20th Century-Fox. Ladd loved the script, but, according to Fontaine, said to Joanne: "I don't want to work with you. I don't like you."

Whether this tale is fact or fancy, the film was made without Woodward. Anne Bancroft and Shirley MacLaine were cast in the leads, and both women received Oscar nominations. Mikhail Baryshnikov made a dazzling debut, and in general the picture was highly praised and a success at the box office. One must assume that not securing a lead in *The Turning Point* was a major disappointment for Joanne.

She was announced for another big-screen venture that had possibilities, one that would team her with the currently hot male sex symbol Burt Reynolds. Reynolds was going to star in and direct *The End*, a comedy about a man who is dying. Since filming was not to begin until late summer, Joanne had plenty of time to fly to London to star in a TV film with her childhood idol, Laurence Olivier. The vehicle was William Inge's *Come Back, Little Sheba*; the 1949 Broadway production of this famous play had won for Shirley Booth the Tony award for best actress. (Booth later won the Oscar for best actress when she re-created the role in the 1952 film version.) The TV production boasted a fascinating cast, with Olivier, now seventy, playing the role of the alcoholic husband. Carrie Fisher, eager to do serious work after *Star Wars*, would play the young lodger who disrupts the lives of the characters played by Olivier and Wood-ward.

When, during shooting, Joanne told Olivier about the time, back in 1939, when she leapt into his limousine during the Atlanta premiere of *Gone With the Wind*, to Joanne's chagrin, the actor claimed to remember the incident *vividly*.

During filming Paul joined Joanne in London. The British press speculated that he would do a racing film—if not, he would devote the entire year to actually racing. The American press speculated that since Joanne was taking an apartment in London, the Newmans had obviously decided to live apart. The official story: She would remain in England while Paul returned to the States to "baby-sit." For this year, at least, Jo-anne was the one doing location work and Paul would have to take more responsibility in managing the family.

For the moment daughter Susan's acting career was ongoing. Eighteen-year-old Nell was a student and experiencing the usual adolescent rebelliousness. Sixteen-year-old Melissa was going to have a try at acting and take a small role in Mom's upcoming new made-for-television movie, playing, appropri-ately, Joanne's daughter. Only Stephanie and Clea appeared to have no interest at all in even trying the acting profession. Both girls were interested in horses and riding, and Stephanie was also interested in photography.

Stephanie and Susan, of course, had more to cope with than the other girls because their mother's life-style could in no way compare with their father's, and Jacqueline was sensitive to the fact that she could not compete in any financial way with Paul or Joanne as far as providing the kids with luxuries was con-cerned. Once, when Joanne and Paul presented Susan with a fur coat as a gift—something Susan thought "extravagant for them"—the girl was fearful that her mother's feelings would be hurt. She knew her mother well. At first she avoided telling

Jacqueline about the gift—she dreaded the confrontation that might ensue. When she eventually told her mother what Paul and Joanne's gift had been, mother and daughter had a scene in which there were tears and recriminations. Once again Susan felt she had been put in the middle of things.

Susan and Stephanie had obviously found methods of dealing with their two families—father, stepmother, and half-sisters on one side; mother and younger half-sister on the other—which meant they would avoid playing their parents off against each other and would try to keep the emotional traumas to a minimum. The story with Scott was somewhat different.

Although he had been living on his own for several years, he was still a concern to both his families. His acting career had stalled, so he had changed his name to see if he could start a career without the Newman connection. For the past few months Scott had been working as a nightclub singer under the name William Scott, and was talking with the record artist and songwriter Don McClean about recording an album. Family and friends were very worried, however, about his life-style, including his skydiving and other hazardous hobbies. Obviously, he was actively courting disaster.

His father no longer had any influence over the young man. Paul later revealed that both of them had backed away from communicating with each other. Of course, as one of Scott's close friends later said, the pressures on Scott as the only son and the oldest child certainly must have been different from the pressures on the girls.

And even concerning his daughters, Paul Newman later admitted that he had been a good father only "in flashes," and that there were times when they were apprehensive about even approaching him because of his mood.

Paul coped with the family and balancing his varied interests while Joanne finished her commitment in London. Although some reports stated that she was remaining in England for a year, in reality she returned to the States that summer, staying at a bungalow in the Beverly Hills Hotel while filming *The End*. In the film she plays Burt Reynolds's ex-wife—a woman of middle age who has finally decided to concentrate on her own life and future; no longer would she be consumed by her former husband's neuroses. Although Woodward's part in the movie received a great deal of publicity, in effect it was a small character role.

Susan was in Hollywood, back from her location shooting on *A Wedding*. While she read for several key roles, she was still torn by the fear that people might use her only because she was Paul Newman's daughter. She had read for Steven Spielberg, who was producing a film about Beatlemania, *I Wanna Hold Your Hand*. He was supposedly looking for six unknowns—three females, three males.

Susan discovered she had lost out not to an unknown but to Debbie Reynolds and Eddie Fisher's daughter, Carrie. Then a few days before shooting started, Susan was called back in; Carrie Fisher was out and she was in. Although she took the part, Susan was suspicious that they had merely wanted the child of a star in the film. According to her, when, a week into shooting, the director, Bob Zemekis, casually asked, "Susan, are you Paul Newman's daughter?" she was delighted. She had gotten the part as an actress and not as a daughter.

After telling her father about landing the job, he wanted to know how many points she was getting. She was crestfallen, and told him she was glad to get the salary she got. She's never forgotten this incident—it made her realize that her father had lost touch with the reality of the ordinary actor, who was happy to get a job, let alone demand percentage points of the film's gross!

While Susan and Joanne were in California working, Newman was racing at various meets across the country. At a race in Garrettsville, Ohio, he was involved in an accident when a car driven by Robert Dyson flipped over and landed on Paul's Datsun 510, crushing the roof. Of course he had on a safety harness and crash helmet, and escaped with only bruises on his shoulders and neck, but again, it was a stark reminder that regardless of his statements to the contrary, Newman was courting danger by pursuing racing. Accidents such as these did not deter him, however.

According to reliable accounts, his wife's reactions to these crises in his driving career were what one would expect—first concern, then anger, and finally resignation. In any event, at this time Joanne had a great deal of work to distract her. Like Newman, Joanne often integrated personal interests into the parts she played. She had joined millions of Americans in the then-current passion for jogging, and would use this interest to help create a memorable role.

When she completed her part in *The End*, she immediately headed for Boston to do the TV film *See How She Runs*. Produced by old pal George Englund, from a script by Marvin A. Gluck, the telefilm concerns a divorced mother who earns her living as a schoolteacher but is seeking greater fulfillment. When she takes up jogging, it provides the necessary arena for her to prove that she can be successful at finishing something— ultimately she enters and completes the Boston Marathon. The film, which includes a vivid re-creation of the marathon, contains all the elements Joanne searched for in a script—perhaps most important, its relevance to burning issues in her own life —and she made the most of them.

*Slap Shot* had been the Paul Newman picture for the year, and although controversial from an artistic point of view, it had done respectable business and in the industry, at least, was viewed as a moderate hit.

*Come Back, Little Sheba* was aired on NBC on New Year's Eve, not exactly a time slot to garner big ratings. Reviews were mixed, with the prime recipient of negative response being the material itself. The play had not aged well—it seemed more a vehicle for two actors rather than a poignant, timeless statement about the human condition.

*See How She Runs*, however, was a stunning success, and Woodward's memorable performance won her an Emmy for best actress. In the television world she was *hot*. Unfortunately, for big screen work she needed a similar hit. While *The Turning Point* would have given an important jolt to her movie career, *The End* did nothing for it.

Susan's career was about to be launched—or so all assumed at the time—with the opening of *I Wanna Hold Your Hand*. Although Susan has said that she did not think her father wanted her to be an actress, she also noted that he would not do anything to hurt her career and he would help her when he could. He certainly helped her now by agreeing to try to launch her in a big way. He posed with Susan for major magazine covers, and shots of him visiting her on the set of *I Wanna Hold Your Hand* were used to publicize the movie. Susan was given the big publicity push, but it did not help the movie. It simply did not interest the public. Susan had said that this film was "either going to make [her] a credible actress or not." And credible she was, though after the picture's failure her acting career faded.

Paul meanwhile had embarked on a second co-production with Robert Altman, *Quintet*, which was being shot that winter in Montreal. Paul liked working with Altman, a director who shared his raucous and raunchy sense of humor. The Altman-Newman film projects, however, did not reflect the men's camaraderie. Again they had chosen offbeat material, this time an unrelentingly bleak futuristic story about an ice-age world. Newman's character is an emotionless detective, and some saw homosexual overtones in the script. It seemed to producers that you could only interest Newman in a part at this point if he was not typecast.

Actor Paul Newman was offered a new role by President Jimmy Carter. The men had met, and Carter liked Newman, apparently responding to the actor's genuine concern about what was happening in the world, the nuclear threat in particular (though, to Newman's consternation, the president was most interested in the intimate details of filmmaking, not in discussing world issues or even auto racing). Carter appointed Newman a public delegate to a special session on disarmament at the United Nations. Senator George McGovern was another of the president's public delegates to the conference.

The conservative columnist William F. Buckley dragged both men over the coals in print, declaring that neither man knew anything about nuclear disarmament: Perhaps, Buckley wrote, the Georgians in the White House "are thinking that after a hundred conferences with the Soviet delegate, Mr. Newman will have so confused the Soviet Union that it will unwittingly dismantle its entire intercontinental missile system; or, more likely, that the Soviet Union will determine that the farce at the United Nations isn't worth one more conference with Paul Newman."

But Paul was not a fool. He knew his strengths and weaknesses and very concisely analyzed his contribution to this (and any other) cause. On television's *Today* show, when asked why he had been selected as a delegate, he answered: "If ten or twenty or sixty or a hundred or a thousand or two thousand more people are watching this show for the wrong reason [to see Paul Newman], and if I can get their attention and make them do their homework about where this country's standards are, then I simply will have served a function, won't I?"

Many people have confirmed that although Paul may not be able or willing to discuss the details of a particular social or political issue, he knows what he believes in and what he is willing to lend support to, and he has never underestimated—or, to his credit, misused—his value as an influential force.

These were especially busy times for both Paul and Joanne, who seemed to be traveling constantly. Though they might buy, sell, or rent houses or even stay in hotels in California, their haven remained their house in Connecticut surrounded by its eleven acres of woods. And they enjoyed their magnificent two-bedroom co-op, with picture-postcard views, on Manhattan's East Side.

The New York apartment's ambience was comfortable but formal—quietly *expensive*—not, in any way, bohemian or avantgarde. There was ample art and top-quality antiques, and the apartment was filled with plants and greenery. Joanne's genteel touches abounded—any visitor felt at once that this was a home its owners *cared* about and maintained meticulously. One of the walk-in closets had been converted into a sauna for Paul. He would stay in the sauna, which Joanne said was his "haven," sometimes for as long as an hour, reading *The New York Times.* Sitting in a sauna reading a newspaper was something that "would drive [her] up the wall," but if it made him happy she was all for it.

During the school year the Newmans tried to stay in California so that the girls' educations would have some continuity. To keep even busier, Joanne had become involved in the American Film Institute, for which she was writing, directing, and editing a short film called *Lover*.

Her friend George Englund was producing a movie for television, *A Christmas to Remember*, starring Jason Robards and Eva Marie Saint, for which Joanne did a cameo role.

Joanne was still chairman of the board of Dancers, the ballet company, but her desire to act inspired her to return to even deeper professional roots: she did summer stock in Massachusetts. It was at this time that she was forced to confront a situation regarding her mother's health. Mrs. Carter's mental state had been deteriorating for years, and at first Woodward had ignored it, attributing her mother's erratic behavior to temperament. Joanne had not been willing to face what might be happening, but this summer, when her aunt brought her mother to see Joanne perform in summer stock, Woodward had finally to face the fact that her mother's memory had completely lapsed, and that something had to be done. It was diagnosed that Mrs. Carter had Alzheimer's disease, a condition about which little was known at the time. Quite naturally it presented a major concern for Joanne; it was a problem for which there was no easy resolution.

The entire Newman family was going through difficult emotional times. Joanne said during this period that since she was a woman who liked to act "morning, noon and night," when she was not working it was a problem for her family. If she was not acting onstage or on-screen, they had to suffer because she was giving "brilliant performances at home."

## 14

Paul returned to Kenyon College in the fall of 1978, to direct a student production of *C. C. Pyle and the Bunyon Derby*, Michael Cristofer's play about a con man in the nineteen twenties.

Five years earlier, Paul had committed himself to direct a play for Kenyon when his alma mater had asked him for a contribution toward the $2 million theater it was planning to build.

"I'll direct the first production for nothing," Newman had promised, and now he was making good on his promise.

Newman arrived at Kenyon with a minimum of luggage—primarily his portable sauna. He was staying at the on-campus home of the spinster Kate Allen. ("He's a bit disorderly but nice," observed Ms. Allen, obviously referring to the cases of beer Newman stored on the premises, and also to the fact that he never made his bed—but always apologized for not doing so.)

Apparently one *can* go home again—that is, if one is Paul Newman. Dorothy, a local barmaid who had been at the job since Newman's college days in the late 1940s, laughed with him about the good old days. She vividly recalled Paul's being tossed off the football team after a drinking and brawling incident.

"I always thought he might make it," quipped one of Newman's former drama professors, "if only he could learn some self-discipline."

Local residents who had hoped the returning Paul Newman would be only too happy to allow them to exploit him for their own purposes soon discovered what so many in show business and in racing had already learned: nothing doing. The local Beekeepers Association didn't land Newman for their luncheon, despite an offer of payment: a hive of bees. A lady who had a house for sale, and who figured that a picture of Paul Newman standing in front of the house would increase its salability quotient, found that she would have to sell the house without Newman's aid.

But with the students, Newman was not at all remote or aloof. He would often jump onto the stage to block out a move or direct an actor, and the students responded to him immediately. Nick Bakay, who was a sophomore at the time, noted, "I didn't expect him to be so low-key in such a nice way."

A spirit of camaraderie prevailed among the young company and its senior associate. When one day Newman wore a Band-Aid to cover a blister on his lip, the entire company subsequently showed up wearing similarly placed Band-Aids.

"You mean you all have the clap too?" joked Newman.

It was a Sunday, a few days before Thanksgiving. Back in Los Angeles, Scott Newman was in desperate need of help. Drugs and alcohol continued to be an overwhelming and crippling influence in his life. He had recently had a motorcycle accident and was in a great deal of physical pain. Since his arrest he had of course been given access to psychologists who were on call day and night. There were periods when he eschewed help and other periods when he called for it. He was in a bad way as the holidays approached. He was staying at the Ramada Inn in West Los Angeles. He was drinking heavily and popping pills, and he needed someone to talk to.

One of the people young Newman had been seeing was Dr.

Robert Scott. Another was Mark Weinstein, a clinical psychologist. Scott Steinberg, a young associate of Dr. Weinstein's, was often assigned to stay with Scott Newman when he was going through a period of extreme stress or depression.

This particular Sunday had been a tough day for Scott Newman. All afternoon he had been downing liquor in an attempt to dull the pain in his shoulder and in his ribs. He watched pro football on television at a buddy's apartment. The pain persisted, and his friend gave him some Valium. Scott took five tablets, and an hour later three more.

He obviously also knew that he would need psychological help to get through the night. He called Dr. Weinstein. The psychologist saw young Newman and spoke to him for over an hour; he gave him some Darvon for his shoulder pain. Since Scott and his buddy were returning to the apartment, Weinstein sent young Steinberg with them. Later that night Steinberg took Scott to the Ramada Inn.

Unbeknownst to Steinberg, when Scott went into the bathroom, he downed some Quaaludes (a heavy barbiturate) and sniffed cocaine.

Although Steinberg was there to keep an eye on Newman, he obviously had no way of knowing how much alcohol young Newman had consumed or how many drugs he had taken. Newman began to feel sleepy and retired for the night.

Sometime after midnight Steinberg noticed that Scott was having trouble breathing. Steinberg phoned for help. Paramedics arrived and tried to revive Scott Newman. They rushed him to the hospital, but it was too late. At 1:07 A.M. Monday, November 20, Scott Newman was pronounced dead. An autopsy would follow, but it was presumed that he died of an accidental mixing of drugs and alcohol.

Paul Newman received the devastating news in Ohio. The dreaded call had come.

The next day the news was spread across the country via the media. All reports contained the word "accident"; but the public understood what had been left unsaid: *overdose*. Although there was no evidence of suicide, it was painfully clear from the boy's behavior over the years that he had been suicidal.

Even the headline of the *New York Times*'s obituary smacked of sensationalism: "Paul Newman's Son . . . Dies of a Drug Overdose." The AP story reported that young Newman "was found in a room at the Ramada Inn in West Los Angeles," but omitted mention of Scott Steinberg. In other accounts the police lieutenant Tim Wapeto was quoted as saying that the death was "apparently accidental."

One story noted that young Newman "had been trying to break into the big time for the past several years."

The fine hand of Rogers and Cowan was evident in the obituaries that discussed the relationship of father and son. One account of the tragedy contained the following: "Friends said the son and father were on good terms but seldom saw each other because of Paul Newman's busy schedule, not only in movies but also in car racing." Dr. Robert Scott was quoted in the article: "There was no competition between Scott and his father. They adored one another."

Years later Paul Newman would speak publicly about his son. His own relationship with Scott in the years before the boy's death had been bad, Newman acknowledged; and he hadn't known what to do about it: "I had lost the ability to help him."

To the surprise of some, Paul remained at Kenyon. Of course he knew that everyone had heard the news of his son's death.

"Paul walked in totally choked up," recalled one of the drama students, Clair Bass. " 'I don't know what to say,' he began. 'But what I need right now—I need the show, I need all of you. I need the rowdiness.' "

Later that evening some of the young women from the group, eager to do something to ease Newman's grief, put on clown costumes and went to see Paul at Kate Allen's house. It was late at night. Newman came to the door in his nightshirt. They gave him their offerings: a bottle of whiskey and a case of beer.

Newman smiled. He downed a snort of the Jack Daniel's: "It's the first time I've touched hard stuff in eight years." A student recalled: "A tear ran down his face. He said, 'I'd invite you in, but . . .' He stuck out his cheek and we each gave him a kiss. It was heavy, but we didn't know what else to do."

He spoke quietly, then he said good night.

Scott Newman's burial was a strictly private affair—so private, in fact, that several of Scott's friends, including the actor Alan Goorwitz and Burton Kittay, held their own service to commemorate Scott's passing. Goorwitz and Mimi Leder, another friend, took out a memorial ad in one of the trade papers.

At the memorial, held on November 24 at the Actors Studio West, there was sobbing and crying. His friends knew that Scott had been a daredevil, that he was self-destructive. They knew about his drinking and his drug taking. But still, he was only twenty-eight.

People shared their memories of Scott. They discussed his problems with his father; their difficult relationship; the burden of his father's fame. They discussed Scott's talent and irresponsibility, his alcoholism and drug abuse.

They shared the horrible sense of loss. They all recalled their pal's charm and wonderful smile. How he could get around you even after aggravating or annoying you. How he was always out of money and looking for a loan. And how he was constantly seeking answers to the big questions in life. They all wanted to believe that their friend's death had been truly accidental.

Some people who knew Scott and the other Newman children have speculated that Scott alone had a certain sensitivity, and indeed that sensitivity may actually have been responsible for his inability to cope. There is a resilience about the others, a survival instinct that Scott Newman did not possess.

Joanne could not explain why Scott was least able to cope. Scott undoubtedly had an addictive nature, and he was unable to separate his own identity from his father's. Perhaps being a male is more of a burden than being a female, when one's father is famous.

Scott's mother, Jacqueline, made no public comment at the time of her son's death, or subsequently. She had nothing to say to the press about Scott, or Paul, or their life together.

Paul and his former wife had now experienced one of the

most horrible tragedies life can deliver. As the old axiom states, "the worst curse is to outlive your own children."

Back at Kenyon Newman finished his commitment. The students had really impressed him, not only as people but as actors: "They act with a built-in naturalism. The only explanation I can think of is that they've been exposed to so much on the idiot box."

In Washington, D.C., on December 7—Pearl Harbor Day— there was a one-day conference on nuclear war. Despite the recent tragedy of Scott's death, Paul felt obligated to attend. He was so committed to educating the public about the nuclear threat that he had even footed the bill for the conference— $25,000.

The multimillionaire Stewart Mott also attended, as did members of the Unitarian Universalist Association. The liberal establishment was present in force, and Newman himself was present the whole time, sitting with other panelists on the podium. The hot television lights did not discourage Newman from remaining front and center, and he was virtually the only one among the three hundred plus persons in attendance that wisely kept his comments to a minimum.

The purpose of the conference, according to its literature, was to educate the public about "the problem of nuclear war in concrete, realistic terms . . . not in generalized abstractions with little meaning." Co-chairing the meeting were Gene R. La Roque and Richard J. Barnet. Richard Falk of Princeton, the psychiatrist Jerome D. Frank, the author Harrison Salisbury, the Harvard Nobelist George Wald, the journalist I. F. Stone, Homer Jacks of the World Conference on Religion and Peace, the Iowa senator John Culver, and the administration's civil defense chief Bardyl Tirana were other prominent participants.

Media coverage of the event was impressive, and public reaction was gratifying. Paul Newman had shown that he could influence, and encourage, public discussion of issues he regarded as critical. People *liked* and *respected* him, no matter what.

The conference and his work at Kenyon were certainly potent momentary distractions for Newman.

"The *pain* of that son's death—can you imagine what that must do?" reflects a friend of the Newmans. "It's *such* a blow that no matter how you externalize those things, . . . it's got to take years, years."

"I will not *should* on myself today," the ever-supportive Joanne embroidered on the sampler she was making for her husband—the burden of his guilt was heavy indeed.

# BOOK III

## 15

Paul Newman *really* immersed himself in the world of racing after the death of his only son. Up to this time Newman had "resisted previous impulses to try the more dangerous forms of racing," according to his racing pal Sam Posey. Now Newman made a decision: he would enter two famous, and hazardous, endurance races, at Daytona and at Le Mans.

Through the years Newman had been involved in minor accidents, though none were publicized. On one occasion his brakes had failed. He was going 140 mph at the time but managed to find an escape route that slowed the vehicle down to 60 mph. He then slammed against the wall and, in his words "pretzeled the car."

In another mishap he and a second driver were on a dirt track near New Orleans. The car hit a rut. Neither man had his seat belt on as the car skidded on two wheels. Luckily they were not thrown out when the auto went over onto its right side. The windshield, made of a special glass that breaks into powder on impact, shattered, and Paul and his companion climbed out. He had escaped harm this time, but Paul was no fool; he had reflected earnestly and intently on the possibilities of injury.

At Daytona Newman's Porsche had a breakdown early in the race, and Newman had to drop out.

In France for the Le Mans competition he was stalked by paparazzi, anxious for photographs and any kind of news item. Even though he was living on the three-hundred-acre estate of the marquis de Vesins, Newman's 7 A.M. jog along a deserted road was interrupted by the sudden appearance of photographers. They seemed to swarm around him like locusts, their cameras clicking away furiously. It was the kind of attention Newman loathed.

For the race, he was teamed with the owner of the Porsche, Dick Barbour, and the crack German driving pro Rolf Stommelen. It rained, which made the driving even more hazardous, and there were close calls. Newman's driving skill prevailed, however, and he finished a spectacular second. He was thrilled. After seven years, things were finally coming together. He *felt* it. That season alone he won over fourteen races.

Back in the States, at the tracks where he had first started racing, he seemed delighted to pose for pictures for his fans. The change in attitude did not last long, however. When a matron asked him to pose holding her poodle, he drew the line: "That's it. . . . All I am is a piece of meat—just a piece of meat on the circuit."

Newman was in fact having quite an impact on the sport of racing. The youth cult was finished, claimed Sam Posey, who pointed out that Paul was so fit and trim that putting *on* weight was an ordeal for the actor. Posey speculated that the time Paul spent in the sauna was his secret.

Posey also noted: "Newman has something that drivers can only be born with—a soft touch. He can get the most out of a car without hurting it, which is necessary in long-distance driving."

"If Paul had come into motor racing earlier," said Dick Barbour, "he might never have been an actor."

Jim Haynes, proprietor of the Lime Rock track in Connecticut, said that Newman would have been a world champion if he had started racing twenty years earlier.

Newman's mother was rather less approving of her son's

racing interest. He was, after all, no "spring chicken," and she was concerned about his welfare. He was planning, nonetheless, to return to Le Mans the following year.

Throughout most of his racing career Newman has been associated with two sponsors. One is Budweiser beer. As he once explained the choice: "Michelob, Budweiser, and Coors seemed good to me. None had forced fermentation or forced carbonation and I liked the beer. I went with Budweiser and I've stayed with them happily."

The other sponsor is the Nissan Motor Company. Newman has even done commercials for Nissan, for the Japanese market, though he has never done ads for the U.S. market except for public service announcements (for safety belts and for the Library Association).

While Paul was pursuing his racing interests, Joanne of course was pursuing her career. Woodward filmed a powerful television movie, *Streets of L.A.*, which reunited her with the creative people who had put together *See How She Runs:* the producer George Englund and the writer Marvin A. Gluck. The new project was a drama with social significance; in it Woodward portrays a real estate agent whose car is vandalized by an illegal alien. The story explores vital issues and makes the kind of social commentary that appeals to Woodward.

She and Paul narrated *Angel Death,* a TV documentary on the dangers and horrors of the drug known as angel dust. The producer was David Begelman. The movie company executive had been convicted of embezzlement; his sentence, a lenient one, called for community service, and producing this film was part of his community service.

At the box office Newman's film career was in the doldrums. *Quintet* had bombed. His current film project seemed a surefire hit; it was another Irwin Allen disaster epic. Allen had signed Newman, Jacqueline Bissett, and William Holden for *The Day the World Ended.* The stellar supporting cast included Valentina Cortese, Burgess Meredith, Ernest Borgnine, James Franciscus, and Red Buttons. The script was by two top-level screenwriters: Carl Foreman and Stirling Silliphant.

It was strictly a no-message movie highlighting special effects, and Newman received $2 million for his efforts. Clearly, he was at this point making movies strictly for the money.

But there is certainly no business like show business. The columnist Liz Smith observed that even though Newman hadn't had a box-office hit since *Towering Inferno*, he was going to get $3 million for a film project called *Madonna Red*.

"You might ask how a guy can command $3 million for a movie when he is on a losing streak," wrote the knowledgeable Liz. "Well, there just aren't enough superstars to go around—that's how."

*People* magazine named Paul America's leading male movie star (Redford came in second).

The deal for *Madonna Red* fell through, but there were plenty of offers to choose from. One part Newman turned down was the lead in Bob Fosse's semiautobiographical *All That Jazz*.

On a personal level, the Newmans were living through a stormy period. They had learned that another one of their children was having a drug problem. This time it was Nell. "She never got to the addict stage," Joanne later revealed, but it was a dreadful time for all concerned.

Around this time Susan, frustrated and angry about her brother's death, talked about problems in the Newman family. Paul and Joanne did not live in the real world—though she was quick to point out that this wasn't a bad thing, it was just not real. And she and her sisters lived a life that was "draining" and "painful."

That Paul and Joanne's marriage survived the crucial time following Scott's death is a testament to their fortitude and determination. "Some men would rev their sports car up and drive it off something," says a friend of the Newmans.

But the Newmans had each other, and Paul and Joanne had their work. Also, the Newmans would soon share with the world the establishment of the Scott Newman Foundation. Although Paul didn't talk about it at first, Joanne did. She said it might sound banal but the family didn't want Scott's life to have been in vain. His life, she stated, did not appear to have had much point and "we wanted—even after the fact—to make it have a point."

The public has been led to believe that the Newman family created this foundation, but this is not the case. Warren Cowan explains that the foundation was started by a group of the couple's close friends and business associates—Cowan himself, Stewart Stern, John Foreman, David Begelman, Irving Axelrad, Edward Traubner, and David Chasman.

Soon after the foundation was established, Joanne volunteered to serve on the board. Then Susan became involved, and finally Paul began to underwrite the antidrug films that the foundation wanted to produce.

There was no doubt that once the Newman family became involved they were the driving force behind the organization. Susan Newman became a spokesperson for the Scott Newman Foundation. In diplomatic language she issued the official statement regarding the family's involvement: "In the aftermath of Scott's death, the Newman family attempted to assess what it could do most constructively to abolish this type of tragedy for other American families. We decided that our collective skills in the communications field would provide us with a solid area of expertise."

At the beginning Joanne was the most vocal about the objectives of the foundation. She emphasized that reaching kids at a very young age and educating them on the harmful effects of drugs on the mind and body, might very well be the answer. She asserted that if Scott had been alerted to the dangers early on, things might have turned out differently. In Joanne's view, most other so-called solutions—such as putting teenagers in jail —were equivalent to shutting the barn door after the horse had escaped. She sadly noted, "What finally happened to Scott could have happened a lot of other times much earlier; we knew it and we had to live with it."

Nell, it appeared, had rebounded from her experimentation with drugs and was going to reenter the world of show business, this time behind the camera. Her dad was about to embark on a film project, *Fort Apache, The Bronx*, and Nell was to be a production assistant.

Nell, who had a certain screen presence, had not pursued an acting career. Acting, Joanne has said, was never romantic for

Nell; it had no appeal. Nell didn't want to work with anyone except her father.

Susan was also to work with her father in an upcoming project. Joanne Woodward had become good friends with Michael Cristofer; she had worked with him, as had Paul. Cristofer's Pulitzer Prize–winning play *The Shadow Box* had yet to be made into a movie, perhaps, some said, because the subject matter was too depressing. But its social significance was unquestioned: the work was about cancer patients in a hospice and how they confront death.

It had all been Joanne's idea—to do the property for television and to have Susan produce. Susan and her partner, Jill Marti, would produce for Paul Newman's company, and Joanne cleverly suggested that Susan ask her father to direct.

He agreed, and with the package Susan was able to finalize a deal with ABC.

*The Shadow Box* would be a no-frills production—with neither special dressing rooms nor star perquisites. The project was being deficit-financed, which meant that if costs exceeded the budget, the extra costs would be absorbed by Paul Newman. Susan was *determined* that the picture not go over budget, no matter what. As it was, Paul was not getting even a fraction of his normal salary—Susan jokingly remarked that he would probably "blow his salary on new spark plugs for his race car." Shooting for *Shadow Box* was set for the summer of 1980. Paul would have to interrupt his racing season to direct.

The Irwin Allen movie had not yet opened, but insiders knew the final picture was a major disappointment. Warner Bros. was already considering changing the title, a sure sign of impending doom. Meanwhile Paul approached his role in *Fort Apache* with some enthusiasm. He had obviously used a far more discerning eye in selecting this vehicle. Here was a story combining a social message with hard-hitting drama. *Fort Apache, The Bronx* dealt with the conflicts facing policemen assigned to one of the toughest sections of New York City.

The film's director was Daniel Petrie, who had worked with Joanne in *Sybil*. Petrie noted, "I was lucky to get Paul in a more dedicated mood than he was in, say, doing *The Towering In-*

*ferno.*" Petrie was particularly impressed by Newman's professionalism and dedication. To prepare for the role of a cop, Newman sought the advice of two former policemen, Thomas Mulhearn and Pete Tessitore; it was their experiences on duty at the tough 41st Precinct—known as Fort Apache—that formed the basis for the film.

Reports were that Paul was getting close to $3 million and fifteen percent of the profits from producer David Susskind. Susskind, a former agent with MCA, was vocal, in private, about the "outrageous salary and percentage demands from today's stars." He also said, "At least with Paul Newman you know there won't be production delays."

Newman wanted John Travolta for the role of the younger policeman. The deal did not materialize, and newcomer Ken Wahl got the part.

Newman had been all over the world in his lifetime—but The Bronx was something new. "The Bronx is a revelation," he said. "To realize that you live on its doorstep and never realize what's going on inside your own city came as something of a shock to me. I think what I learned about the police is what a difficult thing it is for them not to become anesthetized to human suffering, to blood, to everything."

Newman was vitalized by *Fort Apache.* It had something important to say in an era when escapist movies like *Star Wars* and *Close Encounters of the Third Kind* were bringing in the biggest crowds. "As people get fed more and more movies that are baby food, I think it's important to hit them emotionally with a battle-ax," said Newman.

During the filming of *Fort Apache* in the South Bronx controversy erupted when local Puerto Ricans protested the film's portrayal of area residents; the drug addicts and wackos that peopled the fictional Fort Apache were, the protesters said, not at all representative of the vast majority of people living in the area.

To address the allegations, the film company set up a press conference, and then all hell broke loose. The *New York Post* reported the story in what Newman considered a biased, unprofessional, and sensational manner: "The *Post* took quotes out of context and made the conference sound like a racist thing. They said it was broken up when protesters stormed the hill, when, in fact, there was only one protester outside. They printed a caption under a photograph of me that was a complete fabrication. The caption read 'Paul Newman wards off protesters,' when the situation didn't exist."

From then on, Newman missed no opportunity to publicly deride the *Post* and its colorful multimillionaire publisher Rupert Murdoch. Paul Newman became the first star to take on not a particular newspaper columnist or feature writer—many stars had done that over the years. No, Paul Newman went a step further: He took on an entire newspaper.

*The Village Voice* (also owned by Murdoch) was on Newman's hit list as well. *Voice* reporter Richard Goldstein has said: "Newman yelled at me, accusing me of misquoting him, when I hadn't even quoted him at all in the original article. He embarrassed me to the point where I left before the end of the *Fort Apache* press conference."

Newman was not one to let today's newspaper headline become tomorrow's trash-basket liner if the issues meant something to him. "The picture is not what the protesters say it is. Listen, it's a tough film. It's tough on blacks, tough on Puerto Ricans, tough on cops. But if you are going to do a picture about policemen, you can't have as part of the fabric Easter-egg hunts and wedding ceremonies."

He said on another occasion: "Sure, there are Puerto Rican bankers in the South Bronx. But it's a cop film, and you can't have a Puerto Rican banker coming up to the desk sergeant and saying, 'I'm a Puerto Rican banker, and I'd like to give you a loan on your home in Hunts Point.' The film is tough, but it's toughest on the cops."

The director, Daniel Petrie, has said, "I had no intention of making a movie that is anti-black or anti–Puerto Rican."

Rogers and Cowan, however, was there, as always, behind the scenes, to keep the Newman publicity barge afloat and moving smoothly through the waters of controversy, despite incidents like these. Newman "speaking out" was actually in keeping with his image—people respected him for it, and since

Paul Newman was larger than life to most people, it was appropriate that he chose as an adversary an entire newspaper.

*The Day the World Ended*, now retitled *When Time Ran Out*, opened and was the box-office disaster all had feared. Newman needed a hit movie, and all concerned were hoping that *Fort Apache* would prove to be that hit.

But right now Newman was back on the racing circuit. As a present to Nell for her twenty-first birthday, Paul and Joanne sent her to the Road Atlanta Race School. Even Woodward said that she was going to go to race school to get over her fear of driving fast.

This season Paul was involved in several more accidents, one of them major. First, on Memorial Day there was a three-car crash in Lime Rock's GTU car race. Twenty-five thousand fans watched with horror as Newman's car was involved in a series of rear-end collisions when the front brakes on his vehicle locked. There were anxious moments, then Newman finally emerged, unscathed, from his Datsun ZX, which was removed from the race.

There was another accident at Brainerd, Minnesota, but then came what Sam Posey has characterized as "the first major crash of Paul's career." It happened at the Golden State Raceway in Sonoma, California. Posey was in the car behind Paul's, and when he rounded a curve an unexpected sight awaited him: Paul's car had flipped and was lying on its roof. As Posey slammed on his brakes, he saw Newman, a bloody gash on his forehead, scramble out the car window.

The smashup apparently did not affect Newman, however, for a few days later he was back racing professionally and at the top of his form. He joined Joanne in Dallas, where she was completing another made-for-television movie of social significance, *Crisis at Central High*. Then they both joined Susan in California to begin *The Shadow Box*.

Because of the "get it done fast" mentality prevailing in TV land—a condition dictated by the economics of the industry—it was not a medium that usually attracted directors of Paul Newman's stature. But the ABC network had made important concessions. They agreed to give *The Shadow Box* company two weeks of rehearsal and twenty-one days of shooting. The high appeal of a Newman-Woodward package apparently made a difference. The two-hour movie was budgeted at $1.9 million.

A top-drawer cast had been assembled: Christopher Plummer, Valerie Harper, James Broderick, Melinda Dillon, and Sylvia Sidney. After interiors were filmed in Hollywood, location filming would continue at a Salvation Army camp in the Santa Monica mountains, which would double as the hospice in the story.

For Susan, *The Shadow Box* was a mixed blessing. Professionally she had taken great pains to remain independent of her superstar relations, and now, here she was affiliated in an important way with *The Shadow Box*. Susan was, it would seem, in a no-win position. If things went smoothly, people would say: "Of course it went well. Paul and Joanne are known for their professionalism and knowledge of production." And if things didn't go well: "What did you expect? Susan is a neophyte producer—they should have gone with an experienced pro." Either way, the charge of nepotism was sure to rear its ugly head.

Few people realize how unglamorous and ulcer-causing a producer's lot really is. Worrying over details was the name of the game, and the details were endless. For example, keeping Paul's supply of beer on hand was one of the producer's responsibilities—no minor concern if the star opened the fridge and no beer was there.

Susan wanted to promote the film in the trade papers, via an ad campaign, and Paul at first agreed. In any other instance he would have vetoed such a suggestion at once, so strong was his loathing for self-promotion of any sort.

Susan was under tremendous pressure, working with her stepmother and the man whom, at home, she called Dad; and having to navigate the "testy" waters of a complex working relationship. Much to her credit, Susan weathered it all beautifully. To Joanne she was "my daughter, the producer," and Jill Marti spoke admiringly of the Newmans' strong *sense* of family.

Paul, of course, stated that he knew Susan was a big asset because she would never do anything that was not in her father's best interests. "She watches everything like a hawk," he said.

The writer Aljean Harmetz saw Paul Newman during the filming of *The Shadow Box*. "Amazingly," she wrote at the time, "he has retained, at fifty-five, an extraordinary beauty." He seemingly did everything he could to disguise or play down his good looks—by wearing what would, on anyone else, look like thrift-shop attire; but, Harmetz observed, it did not work. As with Katharine Hepburn, Paul Newman's non-sense of fashion was in fact fashion making a statement!

Newman has explained why he decided to direct *The Shadow Box*: "It's distinguished theater, and as a director I like to deal with material that has some emotional link with the characters in it. The play says that we should use our time, not wait until tomorrow or until we are facing death, but use it *today*." And time, he acknowledged, was for him an ever-present concern: "You get my age and you can't avoid thinking about time. When I was twenty, it used to take a year for a year to go by. Now a year goes by in two and a half months."

Woodward, of course, relished working again with her husband. "When Paul and I are working together, that becomes our primary relationship. He's one of the best directors I've ever worked with, and in that relationship I'm the actress and he's the director." There was no doubt, however, about how she viewed their private lives: "I'm his wife and he's my husband all at the same time. We simply can't put that away." (Those who worked on this project say the Newmans definitely did not take the day's professional problems home with them. Newman himself said that, unfortunately for him, the only role Joanne had ever brought home with her over the years was the harridan from *Gamma Rays*.)

In *Shadow Box* Joanne had initially considered playing one of the "plain"-looking leads, but her husband and stepdaughter persuaded her to do the flamboyant, ultrachic wife of the writer (played by Christopher Plummer), a role that would be a great stretch for her. Paul knew she could play that part, and one night she finally saw that he was right: "We sat in the

Jacuzzi drinking wine. Paul was cueing me, and the whole bizarre atmosphere lent itself to the craziness of the role."

Despite her initial insecurity, once rehearsals began, Joanne became confident. Then one aspect of the script began troubling her: she didn't think she was performing it effectively. Newman felt she was playing it exactly right. But focusing in on what she thought she wasn't getting right "spread like an infection until she was convinced she wasn't doing the rest of it very well either," recalled Newman. But Newman left her alone—feeling she would, as always, work her way out of it and be the best one in the film.

Interestingly, there was absolutely no feeling on the part of any of the other actors that the director was favoring his wife over any of them.

Melinda Dillon loved working with Newman again. "He's a wonderful director," she said. "In the weeks it took to make *The Shadow Box* there wasn't a moment of waiting. We were always rehearsing. It was like being back at the Actors Studio. . . . He *is* a Method actor, and that's not a dirty word. He develops his character, his and everybody else's—who they are, how they got there, what is going to happen to them."

Dillon saw the experience as a positive one for Newman the artist. "He's fought that star thing so hard," she observed, "that he's remaining alive and growing better and better. It shouldn't be so surprising."

By now the public's perception of the Newmans had undergone a subtle change, and Joanne was aware of it: "As we've gotten older, we tend to be regarded rather like elder statesmen. And it's nice. I really like that." Paul, for his part, was decidedly less enthusiastic about their new status, particularly if it meant "taking walks in the woods and going fishing"—anathema to a man who was forever strapping himself into racing machines.

It was racing that kept him youthful: "The racing has helped. It's a visible confirmation that my reflexes are good, that my eyes are still working. As a driver I seem to be getting older and *faster*. That's not the way it usually works."

Paul enjoyed quite a season on the track during 1980: he

placed second at Sears Point and third at Road Atlanta, won two races at Lime Rock and at Riverside, and was second in the SCCA runoffs for the national championship. He was considering racing a new 700-horsepower car. The press now referred to him as "the daredevil screen star." Joanne was often by his side at the events, sometimes wearing a wide-brimmed hat pulled down over her hair, always wearing sunglasses. She would be with him on the track just before the start of a race and then after it was over.

She bluntly denied that Paul's racing terrified her and that she wanted him to quit. She said that she attended every race she could and that she loved it, noting she screamed and yelled and cursed like any other spectator and rode on every victory lap. She asserted she saw no reason to be fearful. Paul was an adult and chose to race and Joanne said she never would ask him to quit—which, she supposed, was what people expected her to do; it fit their image of her as the perfect wife. She also stated that contrary to myth, Paul often accompanied her to the ballet and loved it—admittedly not as much as she did, nor did she appreciate racing to the extent that he did. Degree, however, was not the issue; her point, explicitly made, was that they *shared*.

Paul Newman and Joanne Woodward, actors, continued their respective dual careers. They bought the film rights to their friend Hotch's novel, *King of the Hill*. To date, the film has not been made. Often projects are in development stages for months, even years, and never materialize. Stars like Paul and Joanne are often said to be considering certain roles. For example, it was said that the Newmans would do a biographical film on the life of the political columnist Walter Lippmann. Paul was reportedly interested in playing Ronald Woods, the naturalist, in Carl Foreman's proposed film. There was a project in the works for Paul to play Papa Hemingway (Hotchner, of course, is one of the leading Hemingway biographers).

Then again stars are mentioned for many roles that in fact go to other stars. For example, Paul was sought for *Rollover*, to play opposite Jane Fonda. Kris Kristofferson ultimately played the part. Newman turned down the leads in *Romancing the Stone* and *Missing*.

The point is that stars like Paul and Joanne and their agents and lawyers are constantly dealing with possibilities. It is a time-consuming and exhausting process.

What's more, now that the family was committed to the Scott Newman Foundation, they would give more of their time to publicity. They realized that if the foundation was going to have the impact it warranted, they would have to go public with more than the harsh fact that Paul Newman's son was a drug addict.

Paul was still silent, but Joanne held nothing back. She spoke about Nell's problems with drugs. Woodward said drugs had messed up the girl's schooling and private life to a serious extent, and it would take her a while to catch up.

Joanne was very aware that such revelations were "jarring" to their image—in the public mind they were, after all, one of America's perfect families. She felt the public did not even want to know such things about them. All the same, Woodward regretted not having talked about all of it sooner, because people could only help one another by learning from one another.

Even though her daughters were close in age, Joanne was amazed at the difference in their values. Nell was a "free spirit," and there had been problems; Lissy, now eighteen, was also a free spirit—but without Nell's problems. Clea, now fifteen, was an A student, a very proper and traditional young woman.

At the age of fifty, Woodward was no longer fighting the fact that actors' families were *not* like everyone else's. She acknowledged that no matter how she tried to make things "normal," it was always tough on the kids. Almost all kids want to blend in; they certainly did not want to stand out because of who their relatives are. And the Newman kids had sometimes preferred being at their friends' houses because their friends' families were more like *people*.

Joanne attended est meetings. She later revealed that she was trying to resolve several issues in her life. One, she felt guilty about being a creative dilettante; and two, she had to admit that if she lived in Paul Newman's shadow it was because she had chosen to do so.

Joanne's needlepoint samplers are a kind of diary of her life and Paul's; they record sentiments of specific periods in their relationship. One reads, "I will regulate my life, JWN," and displays a light bulb and an exploding cannon. They have referred to it as Paul's view of Joanne's character.

Joanne was no longer desperately trying to be the perfect wife and mother. She admitted that years of concentrated effort had almost broken up her marriage and destroyed her children.

She realized that being a good parent took talent, just as being an actress or a dancer took talent. She acknowledged that her attitudes about parenthood and career had at times engendered hostile reaction in some circles—sometimes in the form of anonymous, often frightening letters. The Newman daughters were aware of this—and hardly pleased about it. Joanne was all too aware that people regarded "Paul and Joanne" in a certain, very elevated way, and she was expected to live up to it.

Woodward certainly appreciated the power she and Paul had as fund-raisers for the causes in which they took an interest. Not all their causes dealt with life-and-death matters. Joanne loved old Victorian houses and worked to preserve them for future generations. The previous year she had planned on getting the public's assistance to save a house in Westport that would have made a great arts center. However, while she was in California, the mansion was torn down. One source said, "She blamed herself for not getting a campaign going in time."

Joanne was determined not to let that happen this year to the Wheeler House, a two-hundred-year-old landmark in downtown Westport. The Westport Historical Society was trying to raise $300,000 to buy the house, which would then become the society's headquarters and, at the same time, a museum.

Joanne informed the society that she and Paul would be delighted to host its annual summer patrons' party—Woodward would mingle with the crowd and Newman would tend bar. Furthermore, the Newmans would appear the next year and the year after that, until all the money was raised.

The Newmans' appearance resulted in, to quote one account, "a star-struck, sellout crowd." Within a couple of seasons the necessary money was raised. The couple who hated being movie stars were perfectly willing to play movie stars if, by so doing, some worthwhile cause or organization would benefit.

To promote *The Shadow Box*, which was expected to be a hard sell all the way, Paul Newman agreed to appear on selected TV talk shows, something he had not done in over five years. He was not particularly suited to such formats—glib, self-revealing, light chatter was not his forte in public. But business was business, and Rogers and Cowan arranged for two shows guaranteeing the widest national exposure: *The Mike Douglas Show* and a Barbara Walters special.

There was a condition: no questions about Scott Newman's drug involvement. Douglas, a favorite with the older audience, was hardly a tough interviewer. He asked Newman such questions as "What ever worries you?" and "How do you keep your tan?" To the former, Newman answered, "Two things make me sweat; live TV and the government." The answer to the latter: "Sitting in the sun and reading bad scripts." Newman said he was *very* pleased with the way *The Shadow Box* had turned out—it was, he said, "very close to my best work."

Douglas wanted to know how much beer Paul drank. Newman smiled and quipped, "I guess six or seven cases a day." And since Newman loved popcorn and junk food, how, Douglas wanted to know, did he stay so slim? Newman laughed. "It's genetic Russian roulette. Seriously, I run a lot, four miles a day. Then I put my face in ice water and that gets the blood out of your eyes and back in your brain."

Barbara Walters was of course more probing than Mike Douglas, but her attempts at piercing the Newman wall of privacy were not particularly successful. He did speak openly about his ability as an actor: he told Walters he was "a limited actor," and he had tried to do classical parts and had come away from them "whipped." Walters, however, wanted details about his private life: Was he a good father?, and the like. Newman, unlike most other Walters interviewees, made no effort to play the game Miss Walters's way, though he was always polite. Indeed, he made it clear that certain topics were none of her business. When, at the end of the interview, Walters noticed the noose hanging in Newman's office, she asked, "Who is it for?" "Visitors," he replied.

Much to Newman's dismay, *The Shadow Box* was going to be aired on December 28, without institutional sponsorship. ABC had not found a Hallmark, a Xerox, or an IBM to lend its prestige to this evening of theater on television. With spot commercials *Shadow Box* would appear to be just another movie of the week.

However, *The Shadow Box* received fine reviews, as did Joanne's other television film, *Crisis at Central High*.

*Crisis at Central High* told the powerful story of a famous, historic incident: the integration of a high school in Little Rock, Arkansas, by nine black youngsters in 1967. Joanne was portraying Elizabeth Huckaby, the vice principal of the school. (Ms. Huckaby's journals were the basis for the Richard Levinson–William Link script.) Under Lamont Johnson's expert direction, *Crisis at Central High* was television at its very best: informative, entertaining, highly dramatic, and deeply moving. Woodward's quietly dynamic portrayal of a woman of intelligence, principles, and determination was virtually flawless. She was acting, of course, but her technique was invisible. For the audience, she *was* the character, every moment. It was a performance of enormous effectiveness, thrilling in its simplicity.

"My acting teacher, Sandy Meisner, used to say it takes twenty years to make an actress or an actor," Woodward said. "You can't just learn to act. Acting becomes an innate thing, like playing the violin. Nell asked me how I prepared. I told her I didn't prepare consciously. I don't sit there and say 'Who am I? What am I doing? Why am I going into this scene? What is my action?' There was a time when I did; but now I don't do it consciously—in the same way I'm sure Yehudi Menuhin doesn't think, 'Where do I put my finger to get that note?' One doesn't abandon technique; your subconscious takes it on, you automatically come in with something."

Newman articulated his views on acting from a different perspective: "Sometimes I feel it's all here . . . the next day, that it's garbage. One minute you take all this stuff you've been through—all the experience, some of the pain, some of the laughter—and you put it all out on the floor for everyone to look at; the next minute, you say it's just a game. Even in a really emotional scene there is fifteen to twenty percent of you standing back like a camera. One side of you is always looking at the other and going 'Tsk, tsk, tsk.' It's a funny experience—you can't feel very stable about yourself."

*Fort Apache* had put Paul Newman's career back on track. The picture opened in February 1981 to critical acclaim and good box office. The critic William Wolf noted, as had many others, that Newman "proves in *Fort Apache* that he can still broaden his range."

Wolf also very accurately observed: "At this state in his career, he would be wise to avoid any more walk-throughs, or roles that further promote his familiar image. It's easier to say that than it is to find a challenging screenplay. But Newman needs more parts as meaty as Murphy [the cop in *Fort Apache*] if he's to make the most of his screen future and, to borrow his expression, come even closer to crawling out of his skin."

Newman was tackling another highly controversial big-screen property. In *Absence of Malice* he had found not only another good script—this one by Kurt Leudtke, a former reporter for the *Detroit Free Press*—but a powerful director, Sydney Pollack. Newman had become part of the project by default. Al Pacino had originally been cast as the male lead but had dropped out at the last minute.

Sally Field was playing the other leading character in this provocative, complicated drama about an ambitious newspaper reporter (Field) who is tricked into ferreting out information about a hard-shelled businessman (Newman) who is the son of a deceased Mafia figure. The police think Newman has information they need to unlock an explosive case. Field prints inaccurate information on Newman, fed to her by the police. The Newman character, tough and sophisticated, is nonetheless an innocent dupe—and when he and Field are attracted to each other and begin a romance, yet another complication enters the picture.

*Absence of Malice* poses the question, What is the proper role of a responsible press in a free society? It is this subtheme that attracted Newman's interest.

Newman explained; "I was savaged by some papers after *Fort Apache, The Bronx*. I was most offended by *The New York Post*. But journalists and newspapers protect each other, like doctors do. They won't name the paper that did these things. They'll only say, 'Mr. Newman has attacked a New York newspaper.'

"That's too bad, because if some papers are not accurate in their news stories, and report events that didn't occur, it damages the credibility of all papers, through guilt by association. It's unfortunate when responsible newspapers won't take the irresponsible ones to task. So I felt I'd like to do a picture about media abuse."

He said in effect that the point of the picture was not to indict the press but simply to alert them to possible abuses in their own field. (Of course, there is no record of comments Paul Newman made about the David Begelman scandal and abuses in his own industry, where motion picture executives and stars closed ranks and protected themselves against outside scrutiny.)

Newman on-screen, of course, gave no evidence of his often-expressed boredom with acting. As Sydney Pollack later observed: With this film there was "a greater degree of maturity in Paul. Maybe he's catching up with things that happened in his life. He's always been a sane actor with an enormous amount of intelligence and decency. You're seeing him now at the top of his form."

Paul, however, like Joanne, apparently could not feel totally comfortable in accepting a talent that came so easily to him. After all, it was no longer even necessary to spend days and nights in total solitude poring over a script. It wasn't necessary anymore to get drunk for an evening in order not to focus in on specific facets or a role that eluded him.

At the time of *Malice* Paul was involved, behind the scenes, in an antidrugs, antiliquor film project to be funded by the Scott Newman Foundation: *Say No*. The film was aimed at helping youngsters deal with peers who urge them to drink and take drugs.

The producer, Jane Warrenbrand, said: "Paul's very excited about this project. He's talking about turning it into a prime-time special for TV."

The immediate plans called for three animated films, directed by Peter Wallach (son of Eli Wallach and Anne Jackson), to be shown at schools. Talk was that these might be combined into a long film. Newman was eager to have Bill Cosby do the narration and to have Henry Winkler and John Travolta make appearances in the film.

After completing *Malice* Paul turned his attention to the racing season and a new enterprise. For years he and his Connecticut neighbor and pal A. E. Hotchner had been bottling Paul's personally prepared oil-and-vinegar salad dressing.

According to Hotchner's recollections, each year they would make more and more bottles of the dressing. The Newman kids wanted to take it back to school with them, friends of the Newmans and the Hotchners wanted bottles of it, and Paul had taken to giving it away as Christmas gifts. Hotchner has said that Newman decided they should go into the salad dressing business. However, it was an undertaking that was not so simple as they first thought. Many details would have to be worked out. For one thing, the dressing could not be made in Newman's basement. The Food and Drug Administration was strict about where and how foods for public consumption were prepared. The ingredients for the dressing would have to be changed somewhat so that the product would have a shelf life. It would be some time before the details were worked out and the product was ready to be marketed.

From the outset it was decided that any profits from this venture would go to charity. Newman considered it "tacky" to use his fame in a commercial way. Neither he nor Hotchner realized that they were embarking on what would prove to be a large-scale business enterprise.

The Newman estate in Connecticut, with eleven acres, an orchard, and a swimming pool, continued to be their key residence, although, at this time, Paul and Joanne had a house in Beverly Hills and of course an apartment in Manhattan. Now they bought an eighteenth-century farmhouse across the river from their main house. They decided to keep the big house for the girls and to refurbish the new farmhouse and the barn for themselves. The renovated barn would be used as a screening room and as a guest house.

Woodward, meanwhile, was ready for new professional challenges. She had directed a pilot episode of a proposed anthology series for television, *Sense of Humor*. This episode, "Come Along With Me," is the story of an eccentric widow who assumes a new identity in each town she visits. The idea was from one of Shirley Jackson's unpublished novels.

Woodward also helped to write the teleplay with June Feinfer and Morton Neal Miller. She cast her old friends Estelle Parsons, Sylvia Sidney, and Barbara Baxley in the leads. Of course, Joanne had already directed an episode of the TV anthology *Family*. Those in the industry thought she might be paving the way for her directorial debut on the big screen.

But her interest in theater seemed greater than her interest in directing film. That summer Nell was going to be an intern at the theater program at Kenyon College. The college had recently launched its summer theater festival. Woodward decided to accept Kenyon's invitation to perform there. She would play the lead in George Bernard Shaw's *Candida*. Michael Cristofer would direct.

Naturally Joanne used the opportunity to voice her strong opinions about the importance of regional theater. She was very concerned that President Ronald Reagan had drastically cut the federal government's support of such ventures. "And to think the President is an ex-actor!" she exclaimed. In choosing to return to the stage in a return regional production she was making an important point. The future of all theater, she believed, depended on regional theater, for that was where theater audiences of the future would originate.

*Candida* was an ideal character for Woodward. "I have always wanted to play Candida," she said. "Shaw was ahead of his time—he was making a statement about the power and importance of women way back in 1894. Candida is a strong, modern woman who rules her roost and makes life at home smoother for her handsome, successful, popular husband. I understand her."

There were bigger plans in the hopper than summer stock in Ohio. If everything worked out, Joanne would play the role on Broadway, returning to the world of big-time commercial theater for the first time in seventeen years.

During the spring and summer Paul's racing career remained steady. He drove in the top five positions and placed sixth at Sears Point, tenth at Road Atlanta, and twelfth at Lime Rock.

For years Caesars Palace in Las Vegas had been angling to be the site for a major auto race. The hotel had financed a new 2.2-mile track. Mario Andretti was heading Paul Newman's racing team, and Newman and Andretti held a press conference to announce that the Formula One Grand Prix would be renamed the Caesars Palace Grand Prix, and would take place in Las Vegas on October 17. Newman would be the chairman.

Their separate interests were keeping the Newmans apart. He was not at Joanne's Broadway opening of *Candida* that October at the Circle in the Square Theater. Paul had to be in Vegas, where the Grand Prix would be run a few days later.

There were no flowers or telegrams for Joanne at the theater either. But she later said that by her bedside that night she found a bottle of sherry and a note, which read: "Just in case."

Cynics did make a point of the fact that Paul and Joanne spent a *great* deal of time apart, and Newman countered, "When we're working separately, we visit each other a lot." He also noted that he had visited her in Ohio for two out of the five weeks she spent there.

While Joanne was on Broadway in *Candida*, Clea was competing in the National Horse Show at Madison Square Garden. For the third year in a row the girl had made it to the finals. Naturally her parents were there to see her.

By this time, because of Clea, Joanne herself had become a horsewoman. When she had taken up riding, she had told friends, "I like to test myself." Woodward's trainer out in California was Jean Torrey, who also taught Brooke Shields. (According to Torrey, "Film people take direction well.")

All the Newman women were interested in riding. Joanne had even bought herself a horse, Mama's Boy, and had learned to jump. Stephanie owned her own stable in Michigan. Woodward, too, had invested in a stable, in upstate New York, about twenty miles from their Westport home. Eventually the stable had been so extensively renovated that Paul, half jokingly, said he wanted to have an oil painting made showing beautiful people throwing money into a huge hole. It was obvious that this expensive hobby was a real-life money pit.

Joanne had even competed in horse shows herself. In the Santa Barbara Horse Show the previous year, Joanne had won six ribbons and Clea had achieved championship status.

But at the National Horse Show at Madison Square Garden this fall, halfway into the thirteen-jump course Clea's horse tripped over one of the three-and-a-half-foot fences. What's up, Doc?, her chestnut gelding, rolled over onto its sixteen-year-old owner-rider.

Joanne and Paul ran toward the ring, Paul in the lead. But by the time he reached Clea she was already sitting up. She had bruised her shoulder and her hip but was otherwise unhurt.

Her dad, used to mishaps in his own sport, realized that the worst was over. But the impact of the accident and what might have happened horrified Joanne. She had to be at the theater for a matinee that day, and when the other cast members learned what had happened, they suggested Woodward let her understudy go on.

But Joanne said, "I have never missed a performance and I'm not about to."

Joanne's appearance in *Candida* would ensure a decent run on Broadway, and there were already negotiations for her to do a film version for cable television. Susan Newman and partner Jill Marti would produce.

The Newmans have always been supportive of theater. When Paul's old pal Jack Garfein founded the Harold Clurman Theater on New York's Off-Off Broadway, Newman sent Garfein $20,000 for the project. To date, however, while Newman sends in a yearly $10,000 contribution to the venture, Garfein notes that Paul has yet to see a production at the Clurman.

*Absence of Malice* was ready to be screened for the press before the end of the year—a testament to the fact that total professionals could indeed deliver a first-rate finished product in a reasonable time if all were cooperative from start to finish. Production had taken under a year, and the film would be released in time to qualify for the Academy Awards.

This picture presented a massive PR problem because its target was the press. Tavern on the Green was again the site for a Paul Newman date with the press. Also in attendance were his co-stars Sally Field, Bob Balaban, Barry Primus, and Wilfred Brimley, the director, Sydney Pollack, and the screenwriter, Kurt Leudtke.

Arthur Bell of *The Village Voice* focused a sharp eye on Newman and company: "Not all the journalists were charmed. On being introduced to a *Post* staffer, Sally Field cooed, 'Wouldn't you rather say you're from someplace else?' Strange, since Field had granted her first New York interview to the *Post*'s Stephen Silverman, and they got along peachy keen. On meeting Diana Maychick of the *Post*'s drama section, Paul Newman snapped, 'I hate your paper,' then snubbed Maychick when she tried to engage him in a conversation about *Malice.*"

According to Bell, "Newman condescended, however, to move from table to table and discuss journalism with the journalists—not to mention ethics and the vicissitudes of being a major star in a world of false values. Just like the *Absence of Malice* screenplay, his slanted rhetoric went under the guise of contemporary social truths. Over veal and carrots, he played the guru with all the philosophically correct answers, and his performance didn't sit too well. Are we supposed to write attractive copy about one of the most bankable movie stars in the world when he obviously doesn't like us and is using the press to make him more bankable for his next project?"

On meeting Newman at the event, Bell wasted no time on

courtesies: "Why do you have such contempt for the press?" he asked.

According to Bell, "Newman's blues went thoughtful." And the actor replied, "Only some aspects. *The New York Post* being an example."

Bell asked Newman if his views on the press had been different before the infamous *Fort Apache* press conference. Newman answered no. And then Bell asked what others over the years had certainly wondered: "If publicity is water torture, why do you do it?"

"In the past," Newman replied, "I was willing to divest myself of the responsibilities of promotion work, but there are more middle-ground pictures made that could benefit from a push. I can't keep my attitudes consistent about interviews and selling pictures anymore. But let me say, if you want to feel boxed, go out and do a lot of concentrated interviews. The same questions are asked over and over. You either repeat, or invent new answers."

"Poor put-upon Newman," concluded Bell. "If only he were broke and a nobody."

*The New York Post* wasn't the only paper Newman had something negative to say about. On another occasion he commented: "Look . . . at what *The Washington Post* printed about Carter. They said 'We don't believe it, but if it's rumored in Washington, we have to print it'—and their retraction later on was pussyfooted: an undercover memo given to Carter instead of a front-page apology."

*The New York Times* came under Newman's scrutiny as well. "Even as early as the fifties, going on location all over the country, I remember discovering that papers like the *Atlanta Constitution*, the *Cleveland Plain Dealer*, the *Detroit Free Press*, the *St. Louis Post-Dispatch*, among others, were as good as *The New York Times*. When the first global meeting on disarmament since 1932 took place, the *Times* didn't pay too much attention to it." (Paul was referring to the conference that he attended as President Carter's citizen delegate.)

There were other opinions Newman would express about the press. "I would say that ninety percent of what people read about me in the newspapers is untrue. Ninety percent is garbage," he said. "[Reporters] are expected to come up with something sensational every night of the week to keep their readers' noses buried in the pages and, well, you tell me, if nothing's happening, what do you do? Well, in their case, they make it up."

Newman's opinion of television journalism wasn't too high either: "TV broadcasts in a sensational vein. Their news is for the lowest common denominator. If television can do that . . . well, we're in a lot of trouble."

Newman was back in Washington in December 1981, fighting for yet another cause. "The next big battle in Congress is going to be over decontrol of natural gas," stated Newman, an involved party. Paul had helped found a consumer interest group, Energy Action, which was merging with the Citizen Labor Energy Coalition to fight against deregulation of natural gas.

Newman, as usual, was outspoken. At a press conference he said the Alaska natural gas pipeline was "a scam" and made the robber barons of old "look like cheap stuff." He appeared tense, and jokingly repeated what he had often said: There were two things that made him sweat, live TV and government. "So, you're going to see me pretty nervous up here."

Newman handled things well, but one question did rouse his ire. Why, he was asked, was an actor involved with energy problems? His "snappy" response: "I'm here because I have five kids and I don't want to put on my tombstone that I wasn't part of my time. Okay?"

# ☆ 16

Robert Redford had been first choice for the role of Frank Galvin, a down-and-out attorney in the Zanuck-Brown production of *The Verdict* (Zanuck-Brown had also co-produced *The Sting*). There was behind-the-scenes politicking regarding who would direct. Redford wanted his pal Sydney Pollack. In addition, Redford had not wanted to play the gritty, hard-drinking, ambulance-chasing character as initially written by David Mamet, so there were rewrites.

But the producers and the writer knew that the character's seediness—from which he rebounds spectacularly—was essential to the story. Surely there was a superstar actor who would accept the challenge of this glamorless role. There was indeed: Paul Newman.

Newman later noted that some roles were difficult because of a poor script; others were difficult because the script was good and demanded an intense emotional commitment. He had responded to *The Verdict* because of its quality on all counts, and also because of the emotional demands of the role.

Sidney Lumet had been signed to direct. Lumet and Newman were longtime friends, having worked together in live television over a quarter of a century earlier. (Lumet had directed Joanne on-screen in *The Fugitive Kind*.) They had not worked together since then, however. Their reteaming certainly occurred at the right time. And they achieved an extraordinary result.

Lumet was an actor's director; but equally important, he was the kind of director Paul Newman responded best to. Lumet's credo: "Good acting is really self-revelation, and that's a very painful, complicated, and frightening process. And it takes time to get people free enough to do that."

Lumet knew that Newman was a *very* private person and loved that quality in him—he said he found it magical, and recognized that it was painful for Paul to act "because it requires of him the revelation of a lot of feelings he'd rather not go public with."

Lumet, a former actor himself, knew how to get his actors to reveal themselves. "That self-revelation process is done much better, and better nurtured, off the set, away from strangers and in a private atmosphere, where you can try things and not feel foolish," explained Lumet. "There isn't the pressure of the sun going down, or the 'Oh my God' of airplane noise or any of that. So it's a much more concentrated time than you ever get on the set, and therefore you can use the time much better—both for me and the actor. I think I spend more time in preproduction rehearsals with the cast than most directors."

With Paul, Lumet knew, "flattery will get you nowhere. . . . He doesn't want to hear what's good because, first of all, he knows, and second, if there's trouble he wants to know about it."

Newman would be doing a character role, and he was ready, indeed hungry for the challenge. The other actors were impressed with the no-holds-barred intensity with which Newman tackled the role. Co-stars recall one particular scene, for example, that called for Newman to appear winded and out of breath. No artifice was used. Newman ran around the soundstage until he was literally out of breath. Then he was ready to shoot the scene. He didn't care how he looked.

"Paul was 'sold' [to audiences] on his looks," observed Milo O'Shea. "Now there are some lines and wrinkles in his face,

giving him the character that perhaps he has been seeking."
Sophisticated makeup and lighting tricks could easily have
camouflaged that "character," but neither actor nor director
considered that route. All seemed to sense that this picture was
a very important one in the actor's career. He had complained
for years that in film after film he simply repeated himself in
performance, and now at last he would be asked to reach for
something fresh and vital.

The soul-searching, concentrated effort paid off. Newman's
performance has a visceral quality about it, something he had
never achieved before.

"He's found hidden depths that he hasn't plumbed before,"
noted Milo O'Shea. "He personally has been through a great
deal. Losing his only son was a terrible blow both to him and
Joanne. You can't push that off, not when you have a great
wound like that. It has had a great effect on his work and his
life. He really is feeling his way into a deeper part of himself, to
a layer that has never been exposed before."

The cast for *The Verdict* was top drawer. There was James
Mason, who had worked with Lumet on several occasions. This
film gave Mason, too, one of the best roles he'd played in recent
years—that of the high-priced establishment lawyer. Charlotte
Rampling, Jack Warden, Lindsay Crouse, Edward Binns, Julie
Bovasso, Roxanne Hart, Lewis J. Stadlen, and Wesley Addy
were also featured.

Rampling, like all actresses playing opposite Newman, had
to get beyond the image and the incredible impact Newman
had on all women. His physicality and magnetism could be
almost overwhelming. She discovered, however, that the person belied the image, that Newman was straightforward, simple, and without pretense. Rampling later noted that she felt as
though they were long-time friends, that she liked him immensely—a response she didn't often feel about actors she'd
worked with. She summed it up: "Paul is so attractive because
he's so *human.*"

During production the Oscar nominations were announced.
Paul was up for best actor for *Absence of Malice.* His competition: Warren Beatty for *Reds*, Dudley Moore for *Arthur*, and the

two veterans Henry Fonda for *On Golden Pond* and Burt Lancaster for *Atlantic City*.

*Absence of Malice* was nominated in two other major categories: best supporting actress (Melinda Dillon) and best screenplay (Kurt Leudtke). But the key nomination was Newman's. Emotions ran high as far as the voters were concerned, and the favorite appeared to be Henry Fonda. Fonda, like Newman, had never won an Academy Award, and it was widely known that he was in very poor health. *On Golden Pond* could well be his last hurrah.

Making movies, as Joanne herself has pointed out, can be physically hazardous to an actor. Lights or sandbags fall from catwalks onto the floor of the set without warning, and filming on location presents even more serious risks. That spring, cast and crew of *The Verdict* were shooting in a house in South Boston. A giant chandelier tore from its ceiling mounting and crashed onto a couch where Newman had been sitting just a moment earlier.

Newman, it was said, was lucky to be alive. "God was with us," said the producer, David Brown. "No one was hurt."

Production continued, with Newman showing himself to be the consummate professional. Brown rhapsodized about the virtues of his leading man: "Paul Newman sets the standard by which all superstars should be measured. . . . Working with him is like a month in the country! He has no temperamental outbursts, no nasty moods; he doesn't make special requests or travel with an entourage and bodyguards. He's just *there*, on time, impecabbly prepared. . . . His only demands are that he be supplied with popcorn—and some beer."

Production, as on all Lumet films, was on schedule. All were praying for Paul to win the Oscar; it was his fifth nomination, and he truly *deserved* to win.

Paul flew to Los Angeles for the March 29 ceremonies. *On Golden Pond* swept the awards and Henry Fonda was named best actor.

With the performance Newman had just completed in *The Verdict*, however, it seemed certain that he would receive yet another nomination. The award would probably be his in 1982.

Following the wrap-up on *The Verdict* Paul, Joanne, and their daughter Melissa took a trip to Europe. When they returned, Joanne went to Kenyon for the college's summer theater festival. This year she would do the lead in Noel Coward's frothy comedy *Hay Fever*.

Newman, of course, spent the summer pursuing his second career, racing. He had a terrific season on the track. There were three GT-I wins (at St. Louis; at Mallet, Oklahoma; and at Lime Rock). He placed second a total of six times, including a spectacular second in the SCCA national championship. He enjoyed the biggest win of his racing career to date in August at the Brainerd, Minnesota, SCCA Trans-Am.

He was happy to publicize the sport of auto racing—which, he said, "needs all the help it can get"—and he would answer any and all questions pertaining to it and his participation in it. He said he was still searching for a great film story on the subject. "You write the script and I'll do it," he told a group of sportswriters. To date, Newman had not found the right script on the subject.

There was very sad news for Paul in August—his mother died of cancer. That same month Newman's professional life took a turn with the launching of a new venture. The product was Newman's Own, a salad dressing made of oil and vinegar.

Of everything Paul Newman had ever done in his life, this endeavor was easily the most *fun*. He and his partner, A. E. Hotchner, had joined forces as businessmen-philanthropists, and as long as they called *all* the shots, with the financial rewards going to charity, Paul Newman would willingly attach his name to the product.

The evolution of the salad dressing business was complicated. Newman, Hotchner, and his wife, Ursula, had found a factory in Boston that could properly manufacture the product. Mrs. Hotchner was coordinating the venture, and plans were under way for a modest launching of Newman's Own salad dressing in New England.

The product was an overnight sensation, and the men didn't quite know how to proceed. A marketing company advised them to invest half a million dollars in test-marketing the dressing in key areas across the nation. Newman and Hotchner decided they wanted to proceed, but not on such a grand scale. Instead, with an investment of $40,000, they set up an office in Westport. They furnished it with a Ping-Pong table, assorted pieces of lawn furniture, and other odds and ends.

Advantage Food Marketing, a company in Port Washington, New York, took on the project and lined up scores of food brokers who would distribute the dressing to about eighty percent of the supermarket chains in the country.

At first the salad dressing was available only in the New York–New Jersey–Connecticut area and in a few stores in Boston, Washington, Baltimore, Minneapolis, and Chicago. But by Christmas distribution would be national.

A massive publicity campaign was in the making, and a key component would be a booklet entitled *A Pict-Oral History*, which recounted the "founding" of the company. Newman and Hotchner, outfitted in *Butch Cassidy*–style garb, posed for a series of gag photos ostensibly showing how they had formulated the dressing. The photographer, Stephen Colhoun, did a masterly job in capturing the mayhem—the pictures *are* funny. (Hotchner, based on these photos, could easily get work as a character actor any time he chose.)

Joanne scowled for the camera, on cue. Her shots were captioned: "The neighbors turn ugly." In fact, all the captions in the booklet reflected the spirit of fun surrounding the project. Hotchner calls himself a "renowned long-distance swimmer," and P. L. Newman is described as an "itinerant political activist."

(In fact, in another context Newman jokingly explained why he had gone into the salad dressing business: "I suddenly realized I needed a power base. . . . When Reagan became president I discovered I had been end-played and that the power base I formerly operated from no longer existed.")

Launching a new food product is not an easy task. General Foods, Kellogg's, and other major conglomerates spend tens of millions of dollars to get product recognition. With Paul Newman as namesake and spokesperson, Newman's Own salad dressing received recognition overnight.

The food writer Mimi Sheraton, then with *The New York Times*, interviewed Newman at his Fifth Avenue office. The headline of her piece summed it all up: "Newman's Salad Dressing: Oil, Vinegar and Ballyhoo." The article displayed humor on the part of both interviewer and interviewee.

"Some people have sexual dreams, but I dream about food," Newman said. "Then when I wake up I want to eat the food I dreamed about. That means I have to keep a big pantry, because you never know."

Paul Newman was having a good time with Newman's Own. "I guess I've had more fun doing this than anything else I've done in a long time," he told Sheraton. "But remember, it's really my way of telling Ronald Reagan that his salad days are over."

In all publicity for his new business venture the actor was quick to stress that any and all profits would go to charity—"tax-deductible charities and causes, some church-related, others for conservation and ecology and things like that." And, Newman pointed out, each year he and Hotchner would publicize, via newspaper ads, how and where the profits would be distributed.

Nineteen eighty-two was an election year, and Newman as usual spoke on issues and candidates he backed. This time around, however, the print media, remembering his negative comments during his promotion of *Absence of Malice*, now turned a cold shoulder upon their erstwhile critic. In October, when Newman called a press conference in Minneapolis to push a candidate for the U.S. Senate, Mark Dayton, very few reporters showed up. The TV press turned out, but the Minneapolis and St. Paul dailies did not.

Candidate Dayton had asked Newman to help him out. Dayton was hardly a struggling politician—he was a department store heir, and he was married to a Rockefeller. He had spent close to $10 million of his own money on his campaign, the most spent by any candidate that year. Dayton subsequently lost to David Durenburger by more than 150,000 votes.

Paul Newman had been following the anti-nuclear movement for years, and the California ballot that year included

Proposition 12, a nuclear freeze initiative. Newman agreed to debate Charlton Heston on the issue, on statewide television. Greg Jackson hosted the ABC show, *The Last Word*. Moses, of course, represented the pro-nuclear movement; and Cool Hand Luke, naturally, represented the anti-nuclear philosophy.

When queried on how he felt the debate had gone, Newman said: "I've done better, I've done worse. But in the final analysis it's better than not doing anything at all."

The nuclear freeze initiative subsequently passed. But it is interesting to note that in almost all cases, Newman's support of an issue or a candidate does not appear to influence the way people vote. Most of the liberal candidates he has backed over the years have lost.

That fall Newman attended but did not race in the Caesars Palace Grand Prix. Then it was on to California where the Newmans had invited a group of television stars to their home, for the purpose of discussing the Scott Newman Foundation.

Susan Newman addressed the group. The journalist Peter S. Greenberg recalls the event: "When Susan spoke to the group and mentioned that the evening would have been Scott's thirty-second birthday, Newman got up and moved to a remote seat near the pool. He sat there, with his head in his hands, until she finished speaking."

Greenberg spoke to Paul, who, he noted, was "still very un-comfortable talking about Scott's death": "When I reminded him of his reaction to Susan's talk, his voice grew quiet, he took pauses between sentences and tears came to his eyes."

Paul was about to embark on a new project, *Harry's Boy*, which he had co-written with an old pal, Ronald Buck, who was a lawyer, restaurateur, and builder in the Los Angeles area. The story concerned a father-and-son relationship, and natu-rally it was assumed that the true subject was Paul and Scott.

He said he definitely would make a film about Scott's death someday. But this wasn't it. If anything, he later said, this story was more about his relationship with his own father. In *Harry* Newman's character has a solid, traditional job (as a construc-tion worker). His son (played by Robbie Benson) wants to be-come a writer. The father loses his job, and in a confrontation with his son, the father tells him, "You can get a job, that's what you can get for me." The son replies heatedly, "I don't want to spend a whole lifetime working at something that pisses me off!"

Buck later said that the script for *Harry's Boy*, eventually retitled *Harry and Son*, was "rewritten twenty-five times in two and a half years." He added, "We were still writing on the eve of shooting." Buck was nonetheless impressed: Newman knew how to write dialogue and worked to produce a script that was "vastly improved."

As Buck explained: "[Newman's] credo is 'less is more,' in all aspects of life. He doesn't like spicy food or flashy clothes. He cut some funny lines out of the script, saying, 'Don't go for a laugh just for a laugh's sake.' Also, with emotion—he'd say, 'We've got too much emotion; when we really want to have emotion, people will be tired of it.'

"Paul has the ability to concentrate more intensely than anyone I have ever seen. . . . His breathing changes. That's what makes him a good screenwriter, and a great racing driver and a great star."

Though Scott was never mentioned, Buck was certain that for Paul the central characters were not creations of the imagination, rather they were drawn from life, from his own painful experience. In a key scene the father realizes that the son can physically best him. Buck recalled that Paul once told him, regarding Scott, "The kid's bigger than me, and I can't tell him what to do anymore."

Paul wanted to direct the film. Also, he wanted Gene Hackman for the role of the father. The studios were not interested: if Paul Newman was going to be involved, they wanted him on-screen.

Newman was angry. He later recalled: "I originally said I wouldn't act in the damn thing, but I was cornered. I had a real dilemma there—I didn't want to bring in someone else to direct, and I couldn't get the movie made with anyone else in the role."

With a director-star, he said, "something's got to suffer. You can't pay enough attention to the other actors when you're acting, and you can't do your role justice when you're directing."

Movie industry talk was focused on *The Verdict*. A. E. Hotchner went on record as saying that in *The Verdict* his pal had finally pulled together all his experiences and had refined them into a technique. Hotchner was very specific: "I feel that he's finally opened himself up as he used to on the stage, as in *Sweet Bird of Youth* . . . now he's not playing it as safe in his films. Somehow, Newman has found a blend of what the stage and movies require."

Newman himself acknowledged that he had crawled out of his skin to deliver this performance, and it had been a gratifying experience. This was a film about characterization, not a plot. Its success was largely dependent upon the effectiveness of the lead performance: if the lead performance was not on target, the picture would fail.

From a box-office point of view, Paul Newman playing an aging, tired loser, and an alcoholic to boot, was far from a sure thing. In the movie industry he would garner praise and undoubtedly another Academy nomination. But would the public pay to see Newman in a film where he was playing so dramatically against type? It was up to the publicity and promotion people to generate interest in the "new" Paul Newman.

A massive campaign was launched, and Newman's cooperation would be essential. And of course the campaign would not hurt his chances of finally winning an Academy Award. Although he loathes self-promotion, he went along with the campaign for this film. After all, it was apparent there was more to sell here than Paul Newman the star. There was his racing, his political interests, and his charitable works via his burgeoning salad dressing empire. There was also his position on drug abuse and his involvement in the Scott Newman Foundation.

Certain questions would inevitably come up regarding his private life and his personal feelings, but skillful PR management would ensure a measure of control.

Even before *The Verdict*'s release Paul Newman's blue eyes looked out from the cover of *Time* magazine, a publication that he had been known to criticize. But business is business, and there was a picture to be sold.

Other covers would follow, for publications that ran the gamut from the traditional to the countercultural. Newman was soon on the cover of *Rolling Stone*, a magazine that rarely did features on men who were old enough to be grandfathers (he would be fifty-eight the month the article appeared).

He had spoken at length to an interviewer for *Playboy*, though not about sex. The reaction to his last *Playboy* interview had taught him to avoid this topic.

*The Verdict* opened December 17, and the critical acclaim for Newman's performance virtually assured him an Oscar.

The tidal wave of publicity continued into the early months of 1983, and generated countless stories about Paul and Joanne's marriage. That it had endured was in itself extraordinary, the stories went; and no less remarkable was the fact that the couple had remained on good terms. And there were, of course, the intimate tidbits: His current nickname for her was Birdie ("I just like the way it sounds when I think about her"). He allowed that he was no prize to live with. To understand him, he said, was to understand his offbeat humor.

Paul Newman, the man now referred to as "one of the most envied men in America," and Joanne Woodward, who had maintained her own stardom and identity, celebrated their twenty-fifth wedding anniversary in January 1983. They held a small party for family and friends at their Connecticut home. There was no publicity: the event was not to be shared with the public. The couple again exchanged wedding vows and reaffirmed their commitment to each other.

In February, when the Oscar nominations were announced, *The Verdict* was a contender in virtually every major category: best picture, best director, best screenplay, best supporting actor (James Mason), and, of course, best actor. The competition was fierce. Newman was up against Dustin Hoffman *(Tootsie)*, Ben Kingsley *(Gandhi)*, Peter O'Toole *(My Favorite Year)*, and Jack Lemmon *(Missing)*. A win for Newman this year would really be meaningful; Hoffman and Kingsley had created two truly memorable and timeless characterizations. They, like

Paul, were campaigning for the Oscar. All, of course, would deny this vehemently, but it was obvious to the public and the press that the Oscar races were organized and run like national political campaigns.

When *Newsweek* dared to suggest that Paul was campaigning via his powerful PR agency, Rogers and Cowan, Warren Cowan wrote a letter to the magazine's editors denying the allegation.

The Oscar awards presentations were two months away. Paul resumed work on *Harry and Son*. A deal had been made with Orion Pictures, but Paul had to make a lot of concessions to get the project off the ground. He admitted that he was never objective about any of the films that were important to him, and that once a pet project was turned down by the moguls, it became more of a challenge for him to make it work. He had devoted a great deal of time and effort to this project. And he said, "I'm showing myself that it can be done, not them."

Woodward herself was cast in *Harry*. "Paul created my part," recalled Joanne. "Originally, there was no part—about three lines. It was a long location in Florida. . . . I just wanted to go, to do something. It was a tiny part."

Paul even asked her to direct him in one of the film's key scenes, his death scene—which she discusses with a certain self-effacement: "I was sitting behind the camera when Paul was acting in front. He was wonderful! Did I direct him? I *couldn't* direct Paul."

Two of the Newman daughters watched as Joanne directed Paul in several takes. During one take one of the girls became agitated, so real was her father's performance in the death scene. Even Joanne was moved to tears. It was obviously an emotional moment for all of them.

Paul was unhappy shooting this picture. He knew that as lead actor *and* director he could not do justice to either role. In his words, "I threw caution to the wind, and as far as the workload, I really regretted it. . . . Physically, it was just too much. You can't do your best work when you're beat. Between acting, directing and rewriting the script on the set, we were putting in fifteen-hour days, six days a week. That's just dumb."

Joanne and Paul took time off from the filming to fly to Los Angeles for the Oscar awards ceremonies. This time Ben Kingsley won the award for best actor.

Newman quipped, "I flew to the Coast only to prove I'm a good loser."

A disgruntled Newman fan, Ed Jones, from Ventura, California, published an ad in *Daily Variety* a few days later: "To the members of the Academy: I would surely like you to see *The Verdict* once more and tell me what Paul Newman has to do to win an Academy Award."

Newman returned to Florida and worked on the editing of *Harry and Son.* Perhaps not surprisingly, he caught himself in sequences where he was "watching the other actors instead of playing a character." Careful editing removed these lapses.

For the rest of the year Newman, as usual, devoted his time and energy to the racing circuit. In May his food company introduced Newman's Own Spaghetti Sauce. The label featured the drawing of Paul's face that was on the salad dressing bottle. This new product was inspired by Ursula Hotchner's recipe for spaghetti sauce. Paul likes to improvise while cooking, and using Ursula's sauce as a base, he created his own sauce. The group then decided to market it along with the salad dressing.

The dressing was already a national hit. In fact, that year a *New Yorker* cartoon showed a hostess offering her dinner guests "Bleu Cheese, Thousand Island, or Paul Newman?"

The spaghetti sauce, like the salad dressing, found an immediate market.

During the racing season Paul found time to return to Westport where for the third consecutive year he and Joanne hosted the Westport Historical Society's annual fund-raiser.

Newman's season on the track was respectable. He placed third at Summit Point, West Virginia, and third again at Riverside, California. At the SCCA national runoffs he set a new qualifying record. The season would be capped by the national title run, to be held in Brazelton, Georgia.

Woodward was there for that race. And for the first nine laps of the eighteen-lap race, Paul's Datsun was in the lead. Doug Bethke, driving a Corvette, was right behind Newman and eager, of course, to take the lead. When Paul slowed down, Bethke hit the back of Newman's car. There are differing versions of what happened.

Bethke says: "Suddenly he slowed more than I would have expected. . . . We'd gone through this corner three times the same way, with me right behind him. When the crash happened, I was sure we were both on full throttle. . . . I think he must have missed a shift or misjudged the corner."

That's when, according to Bethke, he "tapped" the Datsun: "I just touched his car. After that he got all crossed up—he was going sideways. I wasn't trying to hit him a second time. I was going to get around into the clear. I thought I was home free." Paul's car, now in a spin, then hit Bethke's car, and this second crash forced both cars off the track.

Onlookers, of course, relate different versions. Some say Paul slowed for traffic in front of him. Others imply that he hadn't slowed his vehicle smoothly enough.

In any event the crash, while not major by racetrack standards, was certainly upsetting. The front of Newman's car was smashed in, and the hood was pushed up over the windshield.

Joanne rushed to the pit, and arrived there shortly after Paul drove the car in. Naturally, photographers were there too. Newman and Woodward quickly escaped their surveillance, and no one overheard what the couple said to each other, but their exchange was intense.

Newman later claimed the crash had only been a minor incident. He voiced strong objections to the sensational coverage that appeared in some newspapers. Paul was angry that it was implied that the crash was his fault; that he was too old to be driving; that some drivers questioned his seriousness about the sport; and that his wife wanted him to quit (this last suggestion being perhaps the most upsetting to him).

In fact, years before the crash Newman's age had become an issue for observers of his racing career, and, yes, some had suggested that P. L. Newman was long in the tooth for this kind of sport.

There are reports that Paul told Joanne that he would quit the sport; this was his fourteenth year on the track. Supposedly she jumped for joy.

With the racing season over, the Newmans returned to their busy professional lives. In New York Paul and Hotchner met to discuss distribution of the profits from Newman's Own, which were running into the millions. Paul was discussing a new film project with Marty Ritt. Paul and Stewart Stern were contemplating writing a sequel to *Rachel, Rachel*.

In Los Angeles the Scott Newman Foundation would be honoring people in the film and television industries who contributed to public awareness of the drug problem in America. When Paul learned that Charlton Heston—an actor whose politics were right wing—was set to introduce him at the awards dinner, he voiced his displeasure. Heston was replaced by Donald Sutherland.

As usual the Newmans bounced back and forth between coasts. They had moved into a new Manhattan apartment, and once again Paul had a sauna installed. Joanne liked New York, where she was active with actors' workshop groups. Her responsibilities as a mother had diminished now that all the girls were on their own. With the exception of Susan, the Newman daughters have made a concerted and successful effort to keep their private lives private. They have asked their parents not to discuss them in interviews, not to give any information about where they live or what they do. They are often described as students. Melissa has an interest in art. Stephanie and Clea have an interest in horses. Nell dabbles in acting and continues to be interested in animals and ornithology. Along with Ursula Hotchner, Nell Newman even edited a cookbook, based on Newman's Own recipes.

The Newman daughters, of course, are as mobile as their famous parents. At different times they travel, work, or live with one parent or another. By now Susan had taken a very active role in the work of the Scott Newman Foundation. It was reported that she was negotiating, on behalf of her father, with the Max Factor Company for a Paul Newman line of toiletries. Proceeds would of course go to the Scott Newman Foundation. (To date the project has not materialized.)

Susan is the only one of Paul's children who has talked candidly about the problems of being the child of a superstar. Paul, though gentle in his public statements on her revelations, was undoubtedly displeased. Children who discussed their famous parents publicly, he felt, had limited perspective on their situation and could see things only in the context of their own adolescent problems.

However, as the years progressed, he, too, would admit publicly that he had created problems for his children. He would speak about his inconsistent attitudes toward them, especially about money and life-style.

With the exception of *Harry*, Joanne Woodward had done little film work in recent years. She now accepted a role in a TV movie, *Passions*. She would play a middle-aged wife who, after her husband (Richard Crenna) dies, finds out that he had a mistress (Lindsay Wagner) and an illegitimate son. *Passions* was pure soap opera *sans* social significance, *sans* challenge.

Paul and Joanne had rented a house in the Malibu Colony while Joanne worked on *Passions* that winter. *Harry and Son* had opened, and reaction was lukewarm to disastrous. Newman had not planned on doing publicity for the film, but when he saw that *Harry* might die at the box office, he changed his mind. He did two of the three network morning news programs and gave interviews to key newspaper and magazine reporters.

Newman believed in the film and what it had to say, and he was honest about why he was suddenly willing to publicize it: "You don't want to do something and have four people go to see it after you've spent one and a half years of your life on it. I think there's a very big audience that welcomes an emotional experience they can identify with. We have a lot of anesthetics in today's society, a lot of things that dull our lives. This picture is a chance to break through that."

To one questioner, he said: "There is a lot in it I could identify with as a parent." And to another: "Some of what's in

*Harry* comes from my own life, although I'm not exactly sure in what ways."

Through the years he would be questioned about the theme of the film and how it related to Scott's death. Newman's response never varied: "You can't fictionalize grief."

After publicizing *Harry*, Newman returned to the racing circuit. Obviously, over the winter he had had second thoughts about retiring. Woodward reportedly told him, "Do what you want, but I've finished my obligations." "A comfortable compromise," Paul called it.

He had a mediocre season on the track. However, he was driving a new car that year, a Nissan 300-SX turbo, and there were problems with it.

He took time off to campaign for Walter Mondale, and Joanne went to England for the British release of *Harry and Son*. The picture did indeed die at the box office in the States, but the project did spawn a lucrative by-product. On location in Florida, Paul had begun making popcorn for the cast and crew, as an afternoon refreshment. ("It was incredible how cranky those guys would get if they didn't get their popcorn exactly at four o'clock," he said.) And so it was that Newman's Own Old-Style Picture Show Popcorn came to be added to the line of Newman's Own food products.

By the end of 1984 the profits from the business were staggering. Paul and Hotchner gave out close to $2 million to charitable organizations.

Woodward embarked on a new television project—this one a movie of the week that had both social and personal significance. *Do You Remember Love?* is the story of a college professor and poet who, at the early age of fifty-one, becomes a victim of Alzheimer's disease.

For years Joanne's mother had been in a retirement home for Alzheimer's victims, and Joanne visited her frequently. As the years progressed, her mother's condition worsened. By this time, Joanne's mother was so severely disoriented that Woodward could only sit her on her lap and rock her like a baby.

Woodward would play the college professor in *Do You Remem-*

*ber Love?*, and certain elements of her characterization would come from her mother.

The director, Jeff Bleckner, observed: "I think Joanne was often quite depressed while doing the film. On our last day we shot in a real convalescent home with many victims of Alzheimer's Disease. Joanne got very quiet, and you could tell that it upset her. But she's a consummate professional and her work was never affected."

Paul seemed to put his own acting career on hold for a while. His philanthropic activities were often front-page news. Although his annual personal income was about $2.5 million, the profits from Newman's Own products, all donated to charity, were estimated at $4 million that year. And they would soon double and triple.

Paul Newman didn't have to make movies, or race cars, or donate money to charity to make the front pages. His mere existence was sometimes newsworthy. When Newman reaches a certain age, people are reminded of it. When he was forty, he was newsworthy. At fifty, he was newsworthy. Now, "Can It Be He's *Sixty*?" trumpeted one magazine headline.

While others might concern themselves with the limitations that age implies, Paul Newman was not one to do so. In fact, his career on the racing circuit, now that he had passed his sixtieth year, was described as his "finest season ever." He set many new track records in 1985.

He also found time to appear at congressional hearings on drug abuse that spring, and there were reports that Paul and Susan had met with members of the Kennedy family, to discuss forming a new foundation. This was shortly after young David Kennedy, one of the late Robert Kennedy's sons, had died from a drug overdose.

Early in the year the Scott Newman Foundation had affiliated itself with the prestigious Health Behavior Research Institute at the University of Southern California, thus creating the Scott Newman Center for Drug Abuse Prevention and Health Communications Research.

The center's goals were to create material for the media that would bring its anti-drug message to the country.

Susan Newman, as director of special projects, became deeply involved in the work of the center. For the rest of the year she would tour the country, making appearances before school groups, conventions, and commissions on alcohol abuse. She appeared on major television shows, including *Entertainment Tonight* and *The Phil Donahue Show*.

"Drug use is so socially acceptable—there's a hipness, a cachet," she said. "God forbid that you have a party in this town and you don't put out some good pot and some good coke."

Her outspokenness about the life-style in Hollywood made her *persona non grata* at "A"-list parties. However, she was proud of the work that she was now doing, even though the Scott Newman Center and other similar groups were not having a major impact: "We've been talking with major people in charge of the studios and television, and their support has not been forthcoming except at the most superficial level. They don't think there is a problem. We felt out the MPAA [Motion Picture Association of America], and we were met with tremendous resistance. The support just wasn't there."

Susan's mother had also come on board at the Scott Newman Center, but as Jacqueline McDonald. She was not identified as Scott's mother in any of the publicity material.

The Scott Newman Center proudly listed its board of directors and trustees, which include Betty Ford, the mayor of Los Angeles, Tom Bradley, the film executives Sherry Lansing and Michael Phillips, Dr. Art Ulene, Wallis Annenberg, Irving Axelrad, Norman Cousins, Fay Kanin, and Lynn Swann.

That year the Newman family and the Scott Newman Foundation also endowed the Scott Newman Chair in Pharmacy at USC.

In dedicating the Scott Newman Center, Paul spoke about the future of children, the future of the world, and the fight against substance abuse. He discussed harnessing the vast potential and resources of the entertainment industry, and the research work being done by the Health Behavior Research Institute. "It is," he said in conclusion, "my heartfelt hope that together we can begin to curb and eventually abolish this insidious killer of our best and our brightest—our children."

With *Do You Remember Love?* Joanne entered a new phase of her
career. The program had aired on CBS to immense critical acclaim and had gone on to garner a slew of Emmy nominations.
Woodward and the screenwriter, Vickie Patik, would be winners in their respective categories. Joanne was once again
hailed for her phenomenal acting, for her involvement, and for
her masterly touch with "message" entertainment.

She said around this time, "This is probably the last movie I
will ever do. I'm going into a new, quieter phase of my life."

Patrick O'Neal saw Joanne in New York around this time.
"It was at a party at Wynn Handman's house," O'Neal said. "I
remember Joanne that night. . . . She talked about the stuff
she was doing these days. At that time she was going to do
summer stock. And she's teaching—she really knows how to
use herself. I was envious, if anything, of her ability to stay
alive, active, in positive ways." That ability O'Neal so admired
can, he said, be attributed to a good southern upbringing: "I
mean a sense of responsibility, kind of a spiritual sense, if you
will—a sense of giving it back. And also, she loves to act. Not
everybody does, you know."

That summer Joanne returned to the stage at the invitation

of Nikos Psacharopoulos, artistic director of the theater festival held each summer in Williamstown, Massachusetts. Would she play Amanda in a production of Tennessee Williams's *The Glass Menagerie*? Indeed she would, for a minimum wage and maximum personal satisfaction. James Naughton, Karen Allen, and John Sayles were the other leads. The production opened in August.

Paul was embarking on a new movie, one that had enormous potential. Like so many other film package deals, this one had bounced around from studio to studio before all the elements fell into place. *The Color of Money* had started out as a sequel to *The Hustler*, but according to Martin Scorsese, the man who ultimately directed the film, it became a follow-up, not a sequel.

Newman had originally sent Scorsese a script that was "literally a sequel," incorporating scenes from the original movie. Scorsese did not like the script itself, but he did like some of its ideas, so he met with Newman and talked about rewrites. Scorsese says that he then "came up with a whole new idea" and brought in a screenwriter, Richard Price.

The two men met with Newman. Price told the actor, "Look, it's ridiculous for a sixty-one-year-old man to be playing pool. It's a young man's game." He elaborated on his ideas for the new script. In his version the older man "doesn't play, and not only does he not play but he's become the guy he loathes: George C. Scott. The guy who banned him from pool in *The Hustler*. He's become the stake horse, the cynical gambler."

The men began kicking around other ideas. They finally agreed that the story should be about a guy, Felsen (Newman), who hits bottom and then makes a comeback.

At first the Felsen character was not supposed to play pool in the film. But that of course was changed later. Price recalls that the whole deal came together in Westport as they sat around Newman's pool. Paul looked at Scorsese and said, "Are you good at holding an actor's hands?"

Scorsese replied, "Yes. Yes, I'm very good. I'm excellent at it."

"Okay, let's do it," Newman said.

As the script was being fashioned, a new character was given special prominence: He was the young kid whom Felsen would take under his wing. Scorsese wanted Tom Cruise for the role, having seen and admired his work in *All the Right Moves*. He sent Cruise a copy of the new script. Cruise had met Newman a few years earlier and he had also met Scorsese. He liked them both. So when he received the script (while he was shooting *Top Gun*), he read it and was excited about the project immediately.

Cruise called Scorsese, who asked, "Would you like to do it?"

"Yes sir, I would love to."

During all the negotiations and script rewrites 20th Century-Fox and Columbia had both passed on the project. A financing and distribution deal was finally concluded with Disney's Touchstone Pictures. Paul was not getting a multi-million dollar salary for this project, but when Newman (or Woodward) *want* to do a script, money is never an issue.

While Paul was in pre-production for *The Color of Money*, the Screen Actors Guild gave Newman and Woodward its highest award, the SAG Annual Achievement Award for "their outstanding achievement in fostering the finest ideals of the acting profession." They had the distinction of being the first to receive the honor in tandem. Previous winners included James Stewart, James Cagney, Bob Hope, Rosalind Russell, Charlton Heston, Katharine Hepburn, Pearl Bailey, Frank Sinatra, and Gregory Peck. Of course Newman and Woodward were both also cited for their charitable and humanitarian activities and for their work via the Scott Newman Center.

In recent years one charity the Newmans have been very visibly supporting is the Save the Children Foundation. Paul and Joanne appear in full-page magazine and newspaper ads for Save the Children, posing next to photographs of the seven children they have adopted via the program.

Newman and Hotchner spent a good deal of time giving away the profits from Newman's Own. Philanthropy, on a major scale, takes as much time, effort, and know-how as any big business. Acting and writing are, in effect, simpler tasks.

"It's fun for us to be in the food business," noted Hotchner, "but the giving away of our profits, the charity part of the firm, is the serious business. We take great pride not only in the quality of our products but in the good we are able to achieve through them."

Hotchner explained: "We give to little charities, not to mainstream charities. We give to the very old and the very young. You can pinpoint your giving if you really care about it. You can help a particular group, a particular cause."

But it could be a full-time job. Charity donations from the Newman's Own products were truly diverse: They went to the Aids Medical Foundation, Cystic Fibrosis, and the Alzheimer's Disease Association, Inc., as well as to obvious Newman pets, such as the Actors Studio, Kenyon College, and Yale University. And there were the "little charities," like Hope Rural School and Children's Storefront. The list goes on and on.

Newman's Own products were garnering space in the business magazines. The salad dressing had a three-percent share of a $600 million market, and the popcorn, a ten-percent share of a $30 million market.

One of the hidden assets of the company was that it spent zero dollars on advertising and promotion. While other food companies have to spend millions promoting their products, Paul Newman has merely to pose with his popcorn, salad dressing, or spaghetti sauce and let his public relations agency plant the publicity.

On the back burner for Newman's Own was a granola-type cereal formulated by Joanne, and a lemonade, another of Joanne's ideas, based on an old Woodward family recipe. And they were also now toying with the idea of a Newman's Own toiletry line. The assumption is that if Newman's face is going to sell cologne, he might as well sell it for his own company and give the money away.

Newman has often said that he feels it is "tacky" to market one's self for profit. Newman and Hotchner were determined to keep the food enterprise a fun endeavor. They pricked any pretentiousness with humor. For example, a sign in the office of Newman's Own reads: " 'If we ever have a plan, we're screwed.' Paul Newman to himself at the Stork Club urinal, 1983."

In January 1986 Paul hosted a charity ball benefiting the Scott Newman Foundation. Then he was off to Chicago to begin shooting *The Color of Money*. It was to be a tight, forty-nine-day schedule.

Cruise had come to the project fresh from the set of *Top Gun*. Scorsese, like Alfred Hitchcock, is a director who plans all his shots in advance. He had all his locations chosen. Cruise had to spend a great deal of time with Mike Sigel, who coached him in the art of pool and also helped Paul brush up his pool style.

As frequently happens when films are being made, incidents from real life were incorporated into the script. One day Newman phoned Woodward from the set in Chicago. "I told Joanne I felt scared because there was a real feeling of community and it was so much fun to get up in the morning," he has recalled.

Scorsese and Price worked this into the screenplay, having Newman's character, Eddie, phone his girlfriend from the road to say that things are going so well that he is getting edgy.

Other real-life aspects were worked into the script. Paul had obviously liked Cruise from the beginning, but the respectful young actor called him Mr. Newman until Newman asked Cruise to call him Paul. In the screenplay Cruise's character calls Eddie "Mr. Felsen" until told to call him Eddie.

The cast and crew loved telling jokes. Cruise has recalled, "We had a joke-off every day on the set to see who could tell the worst jokes."

While the film was still in production, the Academy of Motion Picture Arts and Sciences voted Paul Newman an honorary Oscar for his contribution to the film industry. This was the kind of tribute paid to people like Charlie Chaplin, Cary Grant, and Barbara Stanwyck, who, though nominated over the years, had never won an award. This was hardly the type of accolade sought by Paul Newman.

When Warren Cowan called him with the news, Paul was not happy. Newman later diplomatically said he'd had three reactions: "First, I was relieved that I finally had evened the score with my wife.

"Second, I was reminded of an earlier time in my career when the results mattered, when I cared about how a film did at the box office, how a performance was reviewed, whether one was nominated for an Oscar. . . .

"And third, I thought, well, this is very strange, because this award is usually given to someone whose career is ending, and I don't feel that way at all."

Newman's lawyer and friend, Irving Axelrad, who produced *The Color of Money*, said that Paul felt that the Academy had always treated him as second-best. "And now they were acting as if he was old and through."

At first Newman wanted to refuse the award. But naturally, he was too much of a gentleman to do that, and he knew that the advice he was getting—that is, to refuse it would seem like sour grapes—was basically valid.

Reluctantly he agreed to accept, but not in person. It was arranged that Newman would speak via satellite from the set in Chicago.

The Academy, too, was aware of the negative implications of honorary Oscars, so the presenter's speech prepared for Sally Field was carefully worded: This Oscar, Field would say, is usually presented to people who are retired. But this year it goes to someone who is still at the height of his career and in the middle of shooting a picture.

When Newman appeared on the Oscar telecast via satellite, he said, "I'm grateful this award didn't come wrapped as a gift certificate to Forest Lawn." He noted that Spencer Tracy had said that the key to acting was not being caught at it. He acknowledged that he still had a lot to learn; and winning had provided him encouragement: "My best work is down the pike."

Later, Newman said, he was quite bewildered about this honorary Oscar. It was, he said, "for people who are already up to their knees in weeds." He would have preferred getting it for a specific piece of work, and also it did ruin one of his fantasies—that as a wizened man in his late eighties he would be carried on stage on a stretcher to croak "Thank you, finally."

While Newman toiled on the soundstage, Joanne remained involved in and committed to theater. Her interest was not limited to the big time. For years she has been involved with workshops and Off-Broadway groups. Woodward has maintained relationships with people she has worked with through the years, and via one of these actors, Tate Rupert, she was persuaded to try her hand at directing a stage production at his small Off-Off Broadway theater. The play was *Lone Star*, a comedy by James McClure. Also, Joanne was going to star in *The Glass Menagerie* again, this time at the Long Wharf Theater in New Haven.

Newman would not slow down his racing schedule that year. He and Cruise had remained friends after filming ended on *The Color of Money*, and Tom was on hand that season for many of Paul's races. Newman's record for 1986 was mixed. He was involved in three accidents, one in June, one in July, and one in September. But in several of the meets he qualified first and won the races.

Second- and third-generation drivers were now filling the ranks. Eighteen-year-old Scott Sharp, the son of Newman's pal and former partner Bob Sharp, became the youngest SCCA national champion that year, driving the same Datsun 280-Z that both his father and Newman had driven more than a decade earlier. Paul and Jim Fitzgerald had been tutoring the boy for the past two years.

By taking youngsters like Scott Sharp and Tom Cruise under his wing, Paul Newman could not have been unaware that the inevitable presumptions would be made: that he was working out his parental feelings by "adopting" surrogate sons to share his acting and racing careers.

Because of *Top Gun*, Cruise had virtually overnight become the heir apparent to the Newman legacy of sex symbol–movie star. *Top Gun* was the highest-grossing film of the year, and was still racking up record-breaking grosses.

*The Color of Money* suddenly had not only the most widely known sex symbol of his generation but also the hottest young star of the year. *Newman and Cruise.* Furthermore, the blockbuster potential of the package was enhanced by the fact that the picture had even come in $500,000 under budget!

In August there was a sneak preview of *The Color of Money* at a theater in Paramus, New Jersey. Paul, Joanne, and Cruise had driven down from Connecticut, where Tom was staying as their houseguest. Martin Scorsese came over from New York. Audience reaction to the film was good, and Touchstone executives, Scorsese, and the stars decided that perhaps they could move the release date up. The film was scheduled to open in December, but now they would open it in mid-October.

A massive advertising and publicity campaign was launched. The linchpin was a highly unusual photograph of Newman and Cruise for the cover of *Life* magazine. The men were posed side by side, head-to-head, seemingly lying on the top of a billiard table with one man facing north and one, south. It was an attention-getter. Supposedly the editors of *Life* could not decide which actor should be right-side-up, so a compromise was reached. There would be two covers for that issue: the cover with Newman right-side-up would be distributed in the East, and the cover with Cruise right-side-up would be distributed in the west. (Cruise right-side-up outsold Newman in that position.)

The thrust of the publicity, however, centered on Newman and the photographs of Paul holding a billiard cue. After all, this was Newman's vehicle, and, too, it was a follow-up to a Newman classic, *The Hustler*.

Critics who saw the film in advance were impressed with Newman's performance. Although they might argue about the script, all seemed unanimous in praising Newman. *This* time he was bound to get the Oscar.

Perhaps *Newsweek*'s David Ansen touched all bases when he wrote: "At the improbable age of sixty-one, the old bull—arguably America's best-loved male movie star and certainly the most durable—has come down from his ridge in Westport, Conn., to play an aging but still hustling Eddie Felsen in an extraordinary sequel to *The Hustler* called *The Color of Money*. By his side is the hottest young bull in movies today, 24-year-old Tom Cruise, coming down from the skies of megahit *Top Gun* to play a cocky, innocent, hot-dogging pool shooter named Vincent Lauria. The pairing of Newman and Cruise is more than just the casting coup of the year. Guided by the masterful hand

of director Martin *(Taxi Driver)* Scorsese, these icons of two
vastly different generations raise the level of each other's game.
Biting deep into one of the juiciest parts in his 47-movie career,
Newman is mesmerizing, moving and as sharp as a double-
edged-razor—this is as trenchant a performance as he's ever
given. For the relative newcomer Cruise, this image-stretching
role instantly catapults him out of the teen-movie ghetto. Anyone who doubted his seriousness as an actor will have to think
again after seeing this whirlwind display."

Paul Newman, however, had reached a new plateau. As gratifying as praise for his film work was, he said his real satisfaction came from the philanthropic work he could support with
the immense profits from his business activities, and a new
vision had presented itself.

Paul announced that he was donating $4 million to build
what he described as a turn-of-the-century lumber camp on a
three-hundred-acre site in northeastern Connecticut. The site
would be the home of the Hole-in-the-Wall Camp (named after
the famous hideout of Butch Cassidy and the Sundance Kid), a
camp for children with leukemia and other catastrophic blood
diseases. The project would be affiliated with the Yale–New
Haven Medical Center.

The entire project would actually cost about $8 million. The
remaining money was to be raised through individual and cor-
porate donations.

The property, which had a forty-seven-acre lake, was already
purchased, and although the actual building of the camp would
take several years, the group expected to begin the following
summer with several limited two-week sessions.

Dr. Howard A. Pearson, chairman of the pediatric service at
the Yale–New Haven Hospital, noted that there were other
summer camps for children with cancer. But most were small
operations using existing camp facilities and were not designed
for patients who needed specific ongoing medical care. At this
camp doctors and nurses would be in attendance, and the children would not feel out of place because all the children at the
camp would be cancer patients.

It was explained that eventually, when the camp was in full

operation, in the summertime it would be used by the children and in winter it would serve as a place for doctors and patients' families to hold seminars.

Thus far, this camp project is the first that Newman's Own is responsible for founding, not just supporting. Paul made it clear that he was simply the conduit for the money, pointing out the camp was "made possible by salad dressing and by the people who buy the damn stuff."

The opening of *The Color of Money* would be a benefit for another group, the Actors Studio. The premiere was scheduled to take place at the Ziegfeld Theater in New York, to be followed by a party at the Palladium disco and at a pool hall next door to the Palladium. Tickets were selling for $250, and the benefit was expected to raise a quarter of a million dollars.

As part of the publicity buildup Paul gave interviews to certain selected publications. One was *The New York Times*'s Sunday magazine. The cover story was by Maureen Dowd. The *New York Post* obtained an advance copy of the story and began a new feud with the actor a few days later, when Richard Johnson, of the *Post*'s widely-read Page Six gossip page, wrote: "The biggest shock in that gushing profile of Paul Newman in *The New York Times Magazine* on Sunday was the statement: 'Newman is a lean 5-foot-11.' Lean he may be, but anyone who has met Paul face to face says he has never hit 5-foot-11 except in heels. *Page Six* hereby offers $1000 to Newman's favorite charity, or political candidate, for every inch he measures over 5-foot-8—barefoot."

For a week there was no response. But the following Wednesday Paul appeared on NBC-TV's local New York newscast *Live at 5*, with his pal Liz Smith; and he dropped his own bombshell. He challenged the *Post*, saying that if he was only five-eight he'd give them half a million dollars. He dared them to "start playing hardball." The bet would have to be not a hundred dollars or a thousand dollars but one hundred thousand dollars per inch for every inch he measured over five-eight. All to charity, of course. And Newman noted, "For a newspaper that loses ten million dollars a year, it strikes me that losing a thousand bucks on a bet is irrelevant."

For the next few days sanctions on South Africa, the nuclear disarmament talks, and other key news stories seemed to be pushed to second place in the TV and print media as Paul Newman's height was suddenly the hot topic of conversation.

The *Post* consulted the odds makers. Jimmy the Greek said it was a toss-up, but noted that good players didn't bluff when they had no chance of winning. Mike Moore, the vice president of Caesars Palace, was quoted: "We can't lay odds on things like that. But if we could, I'd say it's a hundred to one Paul is over five-eight and five hundred to one he's under five-eleven."

Of course the *Post* hadn't said he wasn't five-eight; they had merely said he wasn't five-eleven. But obviously some verifying had ensued. Newman's Connecticut driver's license said "5'11"." *The New York Daily News*, the *Post*'s rival newspaper, got in on the act, reporting the story and wondering who would wimp out. In fact, headline writers on many newspapers had a field day, with such headlines as "Come on, shorty, measure up!" And "Paul Stands Tall!"

One of the *Post*'s executive editors, Frank Devine, challenged Paul's challenge. "*The Post* stands tall by its September 30 offer. So step forward, Shorty, and be counted." Devine was described in the footnote as being six feet, two inches tall.

By Saturday of that week, however, the *Post* seemed to be backing down. Its famous editorial column devoted space to the feud. A smaller typeface than usual was used, along with a trick headline in which the type grew smaller; it read, "The long and the short of it":

"By the nature of its subject, this is necessarily a short editorial—set in an appropriately small typeface.

"The *Post* will continue its relentless search for the truth about Paul Newman's height. We don't believe he is (as claimed) 5-foot-11. Nor will we be distracted by his relevant assertion, backed by the waving of the green, that he is more than 5-foot-8.

"But no matter what our investigative reporters turn up, let one thing be clear: as the star of *Butch Cassidy and the Sundance Kid, Cool Hand Luke, Harper, Somebody Up There Likes Me, Slap*

*Shot, Hombre, The Sting* and *Hud* he will always, in our estimation, stand ten feet tall."

Obviously the *Post* was unhappy that the situation had escalated. They certainly did not want to be in the position of persecuting an American hero. And obviously Newman, too, was sorry he had gotten himself embroiled in this affair.

He wrote to the gossip columnist Richard Johnson and to the *Post* editor Frank Devine: "Congratulations on your epic and refreshing 'Search for Truth.' Finding truth in *The New York Post* has been as difficult as finding a good hamburger in Albania.

"Sorry you guys turned chicken when it got to the Big Time. I was hoping the *Post* could be insulted strenuously enough to turn this flood of trivial newsprint into something worthwhile; that 'serious' money could be pried loose from y'all and find its way back to the community. Hopeless on both counts.

"I'm sorry I got sucked into operating on the same level that you guys do but give you points on winning that one. Never again.

"Lock the doors, cross your legs, show your teeth, and otherwise behave like people of consequence. . . ."

"P.S. Hey, maybe the whole thing's a hustle. There are some who say I'm barely 5'8" in spikes, but what do they know—or do they?"

And the *Post*'s "Last Word on a Short Subject": The thousand-dollar bet would stand.

Certainly the entire episode underscored once again that when it comes to movie stars, press and public fascination with personal minutiae will always take center stage. Newman's enormously generous gifts to charity generate a single story, whereas a dozen follow-up stories are written regarding the issue of Newman's height.

*The Color of Money* premiere, as expected, received enormous publicity. Photographers were out in force to capture Paul and Joanne, Cruise and Mary Elizabeth Mastrantonio, who also appeared in the film, as well as other stars. Paul and Joanne were dressed conservatively, in a style befitting a dignified couple from Connecticut. Cruise was dressed punk chic.

*Money* was launched to perfection. Most people assume the picture went on to set box office records, but that wasn't quite the case. Despite all the media hosannahs, this movie was not *The Sting* meets *Top Gun*, or *Butch Cassidy*, where people came back to see the film three, four, and five times. Apparently word-of-mouth was not good for *The Color of Money*, and while the film took in $20.7 million in rentals in the U.S. and Canada by the end of the year (a respectable figure), that was basically it for the domestic market. In 1987 the picture would return under $4 million in rentals, a very poor U.S.-Canada showing, indicating that in the movie business, there was no such thing as a *sure* thing no matter who was in the cast. With everyone in the business always shooting for the runaway hit, all ingredients considered, this picture was a disappointment.

Meanwhile, after the initial hoopla accompanying the film's opening had died down, Newman and Cruise headed back to the racetrack circuit. In Brazelton, Georgia, Newman and Fitzgerald were driving in the Valvoline Classic, while Cruise was assisting in the pits. Cruise was also there to take a refresher course from Fitzgerald and contemplate when he, too, would enter the racing circuit.

As usual, Paul was combining two careers. During the fall his time was split between the tracks and the Kaufman-Astoria Studios in New York, where he was directing Joanne in a film version of Tennessee Williams's *The Glass Menagerie*. Karen Allen and James Naughton were recreating the roles they had played in the Williamstown production. John Malkovich would replace John Sayles.

Paul said all were doing the film so they could "put Tennessee on the screen as he was written." All were virtually working for scale so the picture could get made. The budget was $3 million and each actor owned one-sixth of the picture. "Actually, when you come right down to it, it was much easier to get the film made with Paul as director, let's face it!" Joanne later said. "So I suspect that's how it happened, although once we thought of it, it was a wonderful idea because [Paul] knew it very well . . ." (he had once played the part of the gentleman

aller). "We wanted to record the play and yet still make it into
movie but not change it. . . ."

*Menagerie* had been filmed twice before without great success.
ane Wyman and Gertrude Lawrence starred in the first screen
ersion back in 1950, Katharine Hepburn in a television ver-
ion in the seventies. (Back in the 1940s, just after the original
roduction of the play had opened, Hepburn had wanted to
uy the movie rights and film it with Laurette Taylor as
Amanda, Spencer Tracy as the gentleman caller, and herself as
he daughter. George Cukor was to direct. Unfortunately, the
ights were sold before that package could come together.)

*Glass Menagerie* is a theatrical mood piece that does not lend
tself to the film medium. However, it is perhaps one of the
greatest vehicles for an actress ever written, with the central
ole of the mother, Amanda, calling for a multitude of emo-
ions and layers of depth and meaning. On film no character-
zation had yet matched that of the legendary Laurette Taylor,
who had created the role in the original stage production.

The Newmans forged ahead. The goal was to have the pic-
ure ready for preview at the Cannes Film Festival in the
spring.

When, early in 1987, the Oscar nominations were announced, there was little surprise that Newman was in the
running. It was his seventh nomination, and as far as star
power was concerned, no other nominee in the Best Actor category was even remotely in Newman's league. There was no
Henry Fonda, Dustin Hoffman, or Warren Beatty in the running. William Hurt, nominated for *Children of a Lesser God,* was
the only other actor who was an established star. Hurt, however, had just won the Oscar the previous year for *Kiss of the
Spider-Woman,* so it seemed unlikely that he would win two
years in a row. Also nominated that year were Bob Hoskins for
*Mona Lisa,* James Woods for *Salvador,* and Dexter Gordon for
*'Round Midnight.*

Paul made it clear that at this stage of the game he did not
think acting was a competitive sport: "I can understand how
you can be competitive about automobile racing, because you

have to get from one point to another. The first one there is the
winner. . . . But who's to say which performance is better?"

No one can accuse people of campaigning in Newman's behalf in 1987. If he was to win the Oscar it would be because
Academy members wanted to vote for him, not because they
were prodded to. There was talk in the industry that James
Woods was the long shot. *Salvador*, like *Platoon* (which was *the*
favorite in most leading categories), was a film of social significance. *The Color of Money* and *Hannah and Her Sisters*, which had
many nominations, were more traditional in their packaging
and entertainment values.

Paul went to England in early March for the opening there
of *The Color of Money*. He was back in the States in time for the
Academy Awards, and supposedly he even booked a suite at the
Beverly Wilshire in L.A. He did not go to the Coast, however,
and it was said that he was working continuously on the editing of *The Glass Menagerie* in New York City.

In March 1987 Paul Newman was finally awarded the Oscar
for best actor. Ironically, the impact of Newman's win was
inadvertently diffused by presenter Bette Davis. The legendary
Ms. Davis was making the best actor presentation on the Oscar
telecast. Paul and Joanne's friend, Robert Wise, had been set to
accept for Paul if he won.

Things started going wrong when Bette Davis began announcing the nominees and there was confusion as film clips of
the nominated actors didn't correspond to Ms. Davis's narra-
tive. When she finally opened the envelope and announced
Newman had won, Wise came up onstage ready to deliver his
prepared speech. He had just begun when Ms. Davis interrupted him. She wanted to let the nation's viewers know who
Wise was and what his outstanding film achievements had
been. The producer-director looked on helplessly as Ms. Davis
explained that "this man directed *The Sound of Music*! . . . West
Side Story! . . ." She continued rambling on, and it was painfully clear the situation wasn't going to improve. The camera
cut away to hosts Goldie Hawn and Chevy Chase, who were
visibly flustered.

Wise never had an opportunity to finish his speech. Backstage, however, he explained: "I talked to Paul on the phone this morning and he said it would be 'a form of cruel and unusual punishment' to attend again. He's a superstitious fellow. If he came out and didn't get it again, he would have kicked himself. But now the jinx is broken. He's in."

The following morning in New York, Newman was corralled by reporters on his way to the editing room. Just like millions of other ordinary couples, Paul and Joanne had stayed home, fixed dinner, and watched the Oscar show on TV. He said he was thrilled he won. "I'm on a roll now," he joked. "Maybe I can get a job."

Paul was in no hurry to pick up his Oscar. It was several weeks before he got around to claiming the statuette. Warren Cowan and Cowan's former wife, Barbara Rush, were hosting a bash in Hollywood for the writer Danielle Steel. Paul was one of the guests, and Barbara played presenter that night and awarded Newman his Oscar. (Interestingly, Newman's Oscar did not markedly revive box office interest in *The Color of Money*.)

*The Glass Menagerie* was now finished and Paul and Joanne traveled to France to launch it at the Cannes Film Festival. At this point in his career Newman made no pretense about why he and Joanne were there. He was a producer with a film to sell. There were ground rules: Paul would not discuss the Oscar, *The Color of Money*, or any questions about himself as an actor. He was willing to discuss anything pertaining to *The Glass Menagerie*, which he thought the greatest play by the greatest American playwright.

Though Newman did not add it, the implication was certainly clear: This production also starred, if not the greatest American actress, certainly Paul Newman's favorite actress.

As always, Rogers and Cowan were formulating the long-range publicity campaign for the picture. They calculated a late fall release was best; that way *Menagerie* would be fresh in the minds of critics who would be voting for the "year's best" shortly thereafter. In addition, the film was also a natural for preview showings at other selected film festivals, and, of course, as the release date approached, the "public" Newmans would emerge and attend numerous benefits and social functions, with column items and photographs of the couple appearing frequently, sometimes daily.

In addition, Joanne had agreed to do something she had never done before, something which would bring her into the national spotlight just prior to the October release of *The Glass Menagerie:* She would endorse a commercial product. The car maker Audi was looking to establish a new image for its automobile, and Joanne Woodward—mature, refined, classy—appealed perfectly to the kind of audience the company wanted to reach.

It is interesting (as well as slightly incomprehensible) that Joanne chose to associate herself with Audi, since the previous fall there had been enormous negative publicity concerning an alleged defect in the Audi 5000, and the CBS-TV newsmagazine *60 Minutes* had broadcast a dramatic segment about the car and the accidents allegedly caused by this alleged defect. It was a massive public relations problem for the car manufacturer, and apparently people like Joanne Woodward and Dick Rutan, the renowned war hero and aviation expert also featured in the new Audi commercials, were essential to letting the marketplace know that Audi stood for *integrity.* The commercial itself was a kind of beautifully produced and photographed minimovie, extolling Woodward in her various roles as wife, mother, philanthropist, and actress—and showing her, of course, driving the car. The soft-focus photography presented a youthful, vibrant, and active Woodward and all were pleased.

The new Paul Newman food product, "Newman's Old-Fashioned Roadside Virgin Lemonade," premiered in supermarkets that summer. "Joan Collins was restored to virginity after drinking four quarts of it," joked Newman. There were no jokes, however, concerning Newman's involvement with Jacqueline Onassis and other celebrities she had contacted in her drive to stop the erection of a towering building complex at Columbus Circle in New York City. It was argued that the proposed edifice would cast a giant shadow over Central Park, and it was a protest in which Newman participated actively.

Joanne, meanwhile, wasn't twiddling her thumbs waiting for

*Glass Menagerie* to be released. She had directed the Clifford Odets play, *Golden Boy*, in a Massachusetts production.

Away from their causes and their projects, they were definitely not seeking big publicity. If anything, Paul Newman, after more than thirty years on the treadmill, was more aggressive than ever in fending off unwanted attention.

One August evening, freelance photographers, including Judie Burstein and Harry Talesnick, followed the Newmans into the lobby of their Fifth Avenue apartment building as the couple returned from seeing the Broadway play *Fences*. According to Ms. Burstein, when Newman saw her and other cameramen, he said, "The assholes are out tonight." The shutterbugs weren't deterred, however. According to Ms. Burstein, Newman came after *her*, and Joanne "also got into the act. . . . She lunged at the two male photographers with her handbag and spouted a few choice words too," stated Burstein. According to the photographer's account, the actress finally had to "restrain" her husband. Newman's retort to Burstein's accusations that he had cursed and manhandled her: "I couldn't have manhandled that broad with a Mack truck." And as to foul language, he pointed out that it was "no match for the intrusion of the entry into a private building."

At the appropriate place and time, however, the Newmans continued to pose for photographers. Being seen in public was vital to focusing public attention on the upcoming *Glass Menagerie*, and Paul and Joanne were photographed at many events over the next couple of months. He also had not abandoned his racing career and competed in the International Motor Sports Association 150-lap race at Lime Rock in early September.

Newman and Woodward were elated by the public and private response to Newman's "Hole-in-the-Wall" camp. This endeavor had really caught the imagination of everyone, and Newman was surprised—and moved—at the outpouring of funds and support. An unexpected—and staggering—$5 million donation came from the king of Saudi Arabia. A radiant Joanne, busily knitting, was present with Newman when the check was presented to him in Washington, D.C.

Suddenly the couple was everywhere. They attended pre-release screenings of *The Glass Menagerie* at selected film festivals. Joanne attended the opening of the Martha Graham Dance Company in New York; she was co-chairing the upcoming Music for Life AIDS benefit at Carnegie Hall (in addition, the Newmans donated $100,000); and her efforts on behalf of Planned Parenthood et al. continued unabated.

Around the time *Menagerie* premiered in New York, there came from politically right wing circles criticism concerning Joanne's politics and her involvement with another organization, NARAL (National Abortion Rights Action League). Columnist Ray Kerrison, an avid anti-abortionist, angrily asserted that Joanne had done "her bit" very effectively in the ultimately successful campaign to abort ultra-conservative Judge Robert Bork's nomination to the Supreme Court (Gregory Peck and Senators Edward Kennedy and Joe Biden were others singled out by Kerrison for condemnation).

"Woodward stayed behind the scenes, lending her name to a money hustle through the mails to subsidize the attack on Bork," wrote Kerrison. ". . . Back in January, as a member of the National Abortion Rights League, Woodward sent out a mailing asking for money to underwrite the retention of legalized abortion. . . . Woodward passed the hat to train abortion activists, build coalitions, and launch 'an aggressive media strategy'. . . ."

Kerrison stated that after President Reagan had nominated Bork, "Woodward recycled the old pitch for a new mailing, but this time adding an Emergency P.S. . . ." He quoted from her letter, in which Woodward had said that NARAL executive director Kate Michelman considered Bork "the most serious threat to abortion rights in fourteen years. . . ." Joanne went on to note in her letter that over the "next few weeks, NARAL is mobilizing its largest and most critical campaign ever—to stop the nomination of Judge Bork."

At the same time, a controversy involving Newman was developing at the Actors Studio. Newman, once the frightened blue-eyed young man who had auditioned there in the mid-1950s, was now its very assured president. Since Lee Strasberg's death, however, there had been continual problems, and according to one source, Newman and artistic director Ellen Burstyn (who subsequently resigned her post) had different ideas on how things should be run. Insiders claimed a big fight finally took place concerning rock star Madonna, centering on whether or not the aspiring actress should be admitted to the Studio. Burstyn believed that the more stars on board, the better; Newman, however, was against a "star" policy—he believed the studio should encourage unknowns.

Amidst all this, *The Glass Menagerie* opened in New York. Hopes for the picture were high, although expectations, borne of many years experience, were guarded. "I'm convinced it has a great commercial promise, considering what it cost . . ." said Newman. It was, after all, the first Newman-Woodward film collaboration in years and merited and was receiving important attention. The media, however, were not bubbling with excitement as they had when *Rachel, Rachel* was released. There was lots of respect and admiration, but no electricity.

Critical reaction to the film was decidedly mixed. Columnists Liz Smith and Cindy Adams raved about the picture, and there were some highly favorable reviews from Gene Shalit, Siskel and Ebert, and other important critics as well. But there were some highly unfavorable reviews too.

Some said Joanne seemed miscast in the role of Amanda. Others felt Tennessee Williams would have been better served if Newman the director and Woodward the actress had unleashed their wilder sides in their approach to the material.

No matter what the critics said, however, it was apparent the public wasn't interested in a new version of *The Glass Menagerie*. One might conjecture that in this era of self-help, how-to, and having-it-all, *The Glass Menagerie* doesn't seem either timely or relevant. Box office results were below even Paul and Joanne's supposedly modest expectations. Although all concerned with the production emerged with prestige intact, no major awards were in store. When Oscar nominations were announced, Joanne Woodward wasn't in the running. Tennessee Williams's work, however, remains a powerful lure for the actress; reportedly, she will next tackle *Sweet Bird of Youth* onstage.

Woodward loves working in the theater, and says she doesn't enjoy making movies. "Never did," she admits. "It's strange because I think for a long time it probably was the best thing in the world for me. I was not very theatrical and it was marvelous to have a camera up close—but I never really enjoyed doing it because as a kid I started out on the stage and I *loved* working in front of an audience and still do."

Most people don't realize the extent of Joanne's involvement in theater today. She directs workshops and Off-Off Broadway productions and has been instrumental in furthering the careers of young talent. (One protégé is actor Dylan McDermott, who she's directed in four plays. McDermott is beginning to make a name for himself in films.)

Paul's involvement in theater in the eighties thus far has remained behind the scenes. The brouhaha at the Actors Studio was settled in the spring of '88 when Frank Corsaro, the Newmans' old friend, was named artistic director. Corsaro is the first full-time salaried director in the Studio's history. Newman and Ellen Burstyn had apparently settled their differences and Paul lauded her by saying the Studio might have gone under without her efforts. He also vowed to become a more active member of the group and said he was going to direct an original work for them in 1989.

Newman directed himself in a real-life drama in the spring of 1988 when Julius Gold, a millionaire Westport delicatessen owner, sued him, claiming that Newman once promised him a share in the profits of Newman's Own food products. Newman denied the claim and the suit went to trial. The media, of course, had a field day.

Paul, despite decades of experience with the press, failed to handle the unwanted attention with aplomb. He seemed more volatile than ever and he was often hostile and belligerent to reporters, though perhaps not without cause—microphones were shoved into his face and journalists and cameramen followed him to and from the courthouse like a pack of scavengers. Even the fans who showed up weren't polite. But then, they weren't there to see Paul Newman the actor; they wanted to get a glimpse of a real live star, and especially the famous

Newman blue eyes. They had to be disappointed—the actor always wore sunglasses.

Joanne remained off camera and in the background, but she was there as always, offering moral support. The court proceedings came to an unexpected halt when a mistrial was declared because of a technicality. This turn of events was quite a letdown for the litigants and a new trial date was set for the end of the year. Newman was determined to see the matter through to a resolution—his integrity was in question and he was fighting mad.

Newman the actor is finding it more difficult than ever to settle on acceptable screen roles, and it will continue to be difficult for Paul. "I used to do two movies a year," he recently noted. "Now it's lucky if I can find a picture to do every two years—Dustin, Redford have the same problem."

Interestingly, Redford reportedly now views Newman as his best friend and admires him tremendously; he sees him as a man who has it all. Redford says he would love to do another film with Paul. Knowing both men's standards regarding scripts, however, the likelihood of a Newman-Redford teaming in the near future seems remote.

For a while it seemed that Newman would be starring in a film with Jane Fonda, a blockbuster combination in anyone's book. The property was *The Old Gringo*, based on the Carlos Fuentes novel. It was a period piece, with Newman to play a character role, that of Ambrose Bierce, famous American writer who died in Mexico with Pancho Villa's troops. Fonda, whose company owned the property and who would be producing the picture, was to portray spinster Harriet Winslow, a teacher based in Mexico. Luis Puenza, who directed the controversial, critically acclaimed *The Official Story*, was signed to direct. Everything appeared set, when Newman suddenly withdrew, some say because Paul had grown "progressively cooler to the notion of playing second fiddle to Fonda in the picture she's producing." He was replaced by Burt Lancaster, who later also withdrew. Gregory Peck was then signed for the role.

The latest property that has caught Newman's eye (as this

book goes to press) is the Robert Daley novel *Man with a Gun*. It is a police story in which the central character, whom Newman wants to play, is thirty-four years old. Author Daley has expressed serious doubts about a sixty-three-year-old actor in the role, pointing out that as far as his story was concerned, the actions of a thirty-four-year-old man were one thing, but "an older man would know better." However, Daley's pal, Howard Cosell, thought Newman a terrific choice and told Daley not to worry, that Newman wouldn't look his age. Besides, asked Cosell, who the hell wouldn't want to have Paul Newman in their film?

# EPILOGUE

Paul Newman has been so consistently successful in his career because he is a successful *business*man, and he attacked the *business* of show business the way any success-oriented, dedicated, and disciplined *business*man would, by knowing his product and knowing how to sell his product. In his case (as in the case of all actors), his product is himself. And he has marketed himself extraordinarily well while maintaining a self-protecting aloofness.

Joanne Woodward would be an exceptional woman if her only achievement were that she has been married to Paul Newman for almost thirty years. She has said she detests talking about her life with Paul—she has never been one to open her bedroom door for publicity. She claims her life was a disaster until she reached the age of forty-five; it was then that she developed a sense of humor. "I'm the only person I know who enjoys growing old," Woodward has stated.

*He* is the classic movie star in that the public blurs the real and the screen images of Paul Newman. *She* is in a sense more special. She *isn't* the classic movie star *or* the classic movie star wife. She is the only woman in her profession who has her own star identity and the distinction of being successfully married to a superstar.

Newman and Woodward are extraordinary people who have always striven to lead traditional lives. They have, in fact, combined the traditional and the theatrical. Their brand of traditionalism has enabled them to keep their marriage together, to keep their family together, to remain unaffected by Hollywood's values, to make decisions that set them apart from other stars. The Newmans have maintained their equilibrium without sacrificing their success.

Both like to think of themselves as risk takers. (Newman has often described acting as "showing your ass.") Growth is impossible without risk, and both continue to challenge themselves. *The Verdict* was the first film in which many critics and fans saw Newman touch the visceral side of his acting abilities. And Joanne has revealed an incredible depth in recent years—her portrayal of a victim of Alzheimer's disease in *Do You Remember Love?* is almost unbearably poignant and real.

The people who have known and worked with Paul and Joanne over the years are in general agreement on one thing: "Their best work is still to come."

"To me, they've never really touched their full passions," states Paul Zindel. "There's blocks to both of them—a restraint that stops her from finding the Magnani that could blow out from her. There's a stop in Newman that only is beginning to open up."

Joanne, who has successfully returned to the stage, said, "I think what I regret more than anything is that Paul gave up the theater, because he's a wonderful actor onstage. He was a *wonderful* theater actor and I think it was a big mistake. It was a big mistake for me, too, but more so for him because I did finally come back and I do plays a lot now but he never has and I think it was too bad because film is film but for actors the stage is where it's at."

Paul has said he would like to get back on a stage, but thus far he hasn't, and old pals like Jack Garfein strongly agree with Joanne that it's on the stage where Paul Newman the superstar could return to being Paul Newman the actor. Perhaps in the future Newman will go back to live performing—perhaps even in the classics.

The success of the food empire, and the enormous profits that have gone to charity, still amaze him. He summed it up: "Frankly, what I like is when life wiggles its hips and throws me a surprise. All the experts told us that no business in the world could give away one hundred percent of its profits and still survive. Well, we didn't listen to any of 'em, and just look at us. I never thought I'd get into chemistry, but being able to turn salad dressing, spaghetti sauce, and popcorn into a school bus—that's the kind of chemistry that makes this all such a kick."

For years it has seemed that Paul Newman is more interested in auto racing than in anything else. Paul once admitted, "I don't know exactly *why* I do it. Some guys shoot pool, some shoot golf, I race." Regarding his racing, Newman has asserted, "I think the danger of it is *highly* overrated. You have to make a very bad mistake to get in trouble on that track. .... We *do* try not to run into each other. Occasionally, it happens." And he's made light of it. "This sport is a little more dangerous than playing bridge, a little less so than hang gliding."

These sentiments had a hollow ring when, in the late fall of 1987, Newman's close friend, long-time racing buddy and mentor, sixty-five-year-old Jim Fitzgerald, was fatally injured in a crash during the Grand Prix in St. Petersburg, Florida, in which Newman was also competing. The two men were the oldest competitors in the race. "People can't accept that guys in their sixties can do something like this," Fitzgerald had said earlier, "but racing's what keeps us young. . . ."

With Paul's continuing involvement in racing, the once frequent suggestions of his running for political office have subsided.

However: "I'd love to run for office," Woodward has said, "but it requires such knowledge. At my late age, how do I acquire that?"

As one friend observes, "These are two changeable people." So another career switch cannot be dismissed.

One trait Newman exhibits in public has survived unchanged to this day: He appears unapproachable. "I've been accused of being aloof," he says. "I'm not. I'm just wary."

Newman has often compared himself to Thomas Mann's Tonio Kröger, a character who has deeply ambivalent feelings about life and art. He's aware, too, that like Kröger, both he and Joanne are perceived by the bohemians as bourgeois, and by the bourgeoisie as bohemian. Hence, they have one foot in each world and are accepted by neither.

"Being famous means you're not anonymous anymore," noted Newman. "Nobody realizes or can come to respect and love their anonymity until they've lost it." But the Newmans are also realistic about their loss of anonymity. They know what personal comforts fame and money have brought them, and they know what satisfaction can be had from putting their wealth and fame to work for causes they believe in.

Paul and Joanne still zealously refrain from being carried away by their awesome celebrity; both remain keenly aware of the destructive power of an inflated ego. "There is something very corrupting about being an actor. It places a terrible premium on appearance," Newman has said. Paul and Joanne have always known how easy it can be, especially in Hollywood, to start believing one's publicity. A famous person, they have said, has the responsibility for retaining his or her *humanity* . . . and for contributing something of value to society.

Both Paul and Joanne continue to follow this personal credo.

# Index